QUALITY CONTROL SYSTEMS IN ACCOUNTING
A Guide to Implementation

Wayne G. Bremser, Ph.D., C.P.A.

Aspen Systems Corporation
Germantown, Maryland
London, England
1979

Library of Congress Cataloging in Publication Data
Bremser, Wayne G.
Quality control systems in accounting.

Includes bibliographical references and index.

1. Accounting—United States—Quality control.
2. Accountants—United States. I. Title.
HF5616.U5B73   657'.0973   79-18056
ISBN 0-89443-160-9

Library of Congress Catalog Card Number: 79-18056
ISBN: 0-89443-160-9

Printed in the United States of America

1 2 3 4 5

This book is dedicated to
Mary Lou, Wayne, and Jay

Table of Contents

Foreword

Professions are granted a great deal of autonomy in our society, and in return they are expected to govern themselves.[1] Historically, professions have used formal and informal ethical codes, peer review, and other techniques in the process of self-regulation.

Peer review is the review and evaluation of a professional's work by his or her colleagues — a technique used in some professions for a number of years. The concept, however, is fairly new to the accounting profession. Some multioffice CPA firms have been conducting interoffice reviews for a number of years, but for most others, the emphasis on peer review has been stressed only in the last few years. With the establishment of the American Institute of Certified Public Accountant's Division of Firms, the profession is for the first time in a position to regulate CPA firms themselves, and peer review is the principal mechanism of such regulation.

Peer review in accounting is concerned with the quality of the practices used by practitioners. The concern is that the CPA firm use a system of procedures in areas such as independence, acceptance and continuance of clients, hiring, advancement of personnel, professional development, supervision, consultation, assigning personnel to engagements, and inspection, to assure that the work done by the firm is of high quality.

Since peer review is relatively new to the accounting profession, there is not much material in the professional literature to which a practitioner can look when seeking guidance concerning peer reviews. Dr. Bremser has helped to fill this literary gap by writing a readable book for the practitioner seeking knowledge concerning this emerging process.

---

[1]*See* William J. Goode, ''Community Within A Community: The Professions,'' *American Sociological Review,* April 1957, pp. 196-198.

The book explains the pressures and needs of the profession that made peer review inevitable. It also explains how a CPA firm can implement a "quality assurance" system within the firm to meet the requirements of peer reviews. Dr. Bremser systematically discusses the various areas that relate to quality assurance and includes many useful forms that a practitioner might want to use in designing a quality assurance system. Additionally, the book contains detailed references to be used by anyone interested in pursuing or researching this topic further.

Quality Control Systems in Accounting is Aspen Systems Corporation's first venture in the publishing of texts for the accounting practitioner. It is the first of several planned texts that will provide the accounting practitioner with direct "how-to-do-it" knowledge in the expanding and emerging areas of accounting.

Dr. Stephen E. Loeb
University of Maryland
College Park, Maryland

Preface

I first became interested in quality control in certified public accountant (CPA) firms in 1974 when the American Institute of Certified Public Accountants (AICPA) announced its peer review program for multioffice CPA firms. That program ·was a partial response by the accounting profession to the public's demand for greater accountability. (There have been a number of highly publicized audit failures resulting in a decline of the credibility of the audit.) While the multioffice program failed for administrative and political reasons, the peer review concept remained promising. For one reason, Securities and Exchange Commission (SEC) officials supported the peer review concept. In several SEC disputes with CPA firms, the settlement required the firm to have a peer review. However, the main reason why peer review seemed so promising was that it was a monitoring process that required more formalized quality control procedures in CPA firms. It was a significant step for the profession at a reasonable cost.

The accounting profession is committed to improving quality control systems in CPA firms and to peer review. After investigating the accounting profession, key legislators have said they are giving the profession a reasonable opportunity to put its house in order. A major part of the profession's response to this opportunity for continued self-regulation has been the establishment of the AICPA Divisions for CPA Firms. Both the Private Companies Practice Section and the SEC Practice Section require a firm to have a formalized quality control system and peer review. To monitor the accounting profession's progress in keeping this commitment, the SEC has the responsibility of making an annual report to Congress on the profession. This constant monitoring and the threat of regulation are significant reasons why CPA firms must formalize their quality control systems. There are benefits to be derived from improved quality control systems, e.g., more efficient and effective audits, a sounder organization structure for future growth, and reduced legal exposure.

This book explains how to design and implement quality control systems in CPA firms. Important design aspects are examined, and the administrative forms necessary to implement a quality control system are illustrated. References are made to sources of auditing forms that are already used by many CPA firms.

Each of the nine elements of quality control is discussed in a separate chapter (Chapters 6-14). For each element, quality control procedures are analyzed according to their applicability to firms of different sizes. Since there are many factors to be considered in designing a quality control system, alternative procedures are analyzed. Survey data on the views of CPA firm partners regarding the importance and usage of key procedures are presented in each of the element chapters. These survey data show that many procedures have been adopted voluntarily and have proved to be useful. While the nine element chapters are self-contained, the reader should remember that there is some overlap in the elements.

Chapter 15 summarizes the book and gives some advice on how to make the tasks of designing and implementing a quality control system easier. This might be a good starting point for the reader who is already familiar with quality control.

Wayne G. Bremser
October 1979

Acknowledgments

This book would not have been possible without the help and cooperation of many CPAs. I would like to thank the many individuals who took the time to discuss quality control with me or who answered my questionnaire. I want to give special thanks to Harold Sabaroff of Samuel M. Fisher and Company and Dennis Marlo of Main Lafrentz and Company; in the early stages of my research, they helped me obtain a realistic perspective of the problems facing practitioners as a result of the need to establish a formalized system of quality control.

I am also pleased to express my appreciation to Susan Patschak and Karen Parrish who assisted me greatly in the preparation of this book. I would like to take this opportunity to thank Villanova University for supporting my research.

Chapter 1

The Demand For
Public Accountability

Recent years have witnessed accelerating demands for public accountability by society's established institutions. Consumer advocates and environmentalists have made sweeping demands for public accountability, and their efforts have often borne fruit. Beginning with California's "Proposition 13," taxpayers across the nation have demanded accountability from government officials. The demands for public accountability have also affected the professions. For example, medical malpractice suits have cost doctors and insurance companies millions of dollars.

PRESSURES ON THE ACCOUNTING PROFESSION

The accounting profession has not been excluded from this movement. Audit failures have cost public accounting firms millions of dollars, and have greatly increased auditors' liability insurance premiums. These audit failures and disputes over accounting principles have diminished many people's confidence in the accuracy of financial statements. The accounting profession is fighting the accountability battle on two fronts: it is working to establish accounting principles and to stave off the threat of greater government regulation.

Establishing Accounting Principles

The Financial Accounting Standards Board (FASB) is working on the difficult task of establishing accounting principles in our era of chronic inflation. It has spent years on its conceptual framework for financial accounting. The FASB was overruled by the Securities and Exchange Commission (SEC) on oil and gas accounting, and is facing constant pressure to improve financial reporting.

Government Regulation

The other battle front involves attempts by the SEC and Congress to regulate the profession. The SEC has in recent years been more active in establishing accounting regulations than at any other time in its history. Many CPA firms have been disciplined in cases of audit failure. SEC officials have pressured the profession to make changes. New rulings have imposed new responsibilities on CPAs, especially in the area of unaudited statements. Most recently, legislators have taken an interest in the accounting profession. (The late Senator Lee Metcalf and former Representative John E. Moss instigated this campaign.)

The Metcalf Report

In December 1976, a study entitled *The Accounting Establishment* was released by the Subcommittee on Reports, Accounting and Management of the U.S. Senate Committee on Government Operations. This 1,760-page report, which was prepared by the subcommittee's staff, was of such great interest to the profession that almost all copies were purchased immediately by the larger CPA firms. The report contained information on the organization and operation of the accounting profession and accounting firms. A chapter on the "Big Eight" accounting firms included a section on illustrative questionable activities. The "Big Eight" firms were accused of controlling the American Institute of Certified Public Accountants (AICPA) and the FASB. A letter by Senator Metcalf accompanying the report stated:

> In particular, I am disturbed by two of the study's major findings. The first is the extraordinary manner in which the SEC has insisted upon delegating its public authority and responsibilities on accounting matters to private groups with obvious self-interests in the resolution of such matters. The second is the alarming lack of independence and lack of dedication to public protection shown by the large accounting firms which perform the key function of independently certifying the financial information reported by major corporations to the public.[1]

The concentration in the profession and — its domination by the "Big Eight" accounting firms — was severely criticized. The report recommended both increased legal liabilities for auditors and stronger disciplinary mechanisms within the profession. It criticized accounting firms' provision of management advisory services unrelated to accounting and suggested that the federal government might refuse to engage for consulting work all firms that do federal government audits.

The AICPA's Response

The profession answered this criticism in several forms. Most notable was an April 1977 publication, *The Institute Responds,* which was the response of AICPA

Board Chairman Michael N. Chetkovich to Senator Sam Nunn, a member of Metcalf's subcommittee, who requested the response prior to hearings on the accounting profession. Chetkovich's letter to the senator concluded: "An examination of the staff study discloses a significant gap between the purported evidence and the recommendations. Furthermore there is a total lack of evidence that adoption of the recommendations in the staff study would remedy any of the alleged faults."[2] He also emphasized that the profession was taking steps to improve its performance. The Commission on Auditors' Responsibilities was soon to make its recommendations, he wrote, adding that accounting firms had strengthened their quality control systems and their means of avoiding errors.

Proposed Legislation

In June 1978, Representative Moss introduced comprehensive legislation aimed at regulating the CPA firms practicing before the SEC. The bill called for a National Organization of SEC Accountancy. CPA firms with one or more SEC-regulated clients would be required to register. A five-person, SEC-appointed board would be empowered to investigate auditors. The Organization would be empowered to take disciplinary actions against auditors, including economic sanctions, fines, suspension of registration, and expulsion. This bill (which did not become law) was used to pressure CPAs to make their self-regulatory process more effective.

THE EMPHASIS ON QUALITY CONTROL

The accounting profession has responded in several ways to the increased demands for public accountability. One major change has been the development of stronger CPA firm quality control systems — including peer review — in the profession. Peer review includes an examination of a firm's quality control system by outside CPAs. It involves an inspection of sample working papers, financial statements, and auditors' reports for compliance with professional standards. Peer review by outside CPAs is an integral part of a firm's quality control system.

While all CPA firms have quality control systems, they vary in design. However, the profession's new program — based upon AICPA's *Statement on Auditing Standards No. 4* (SAS No. 4) and *Quality Control Policies and Procedures for Participating CPA Firms* issued in 1977 — is causing more standardization among these systems. The AICPA Council approved a voluntary quality control review program for CPA firms in October 1976 after several years of developmental efforts. In September 1977, the AICPA established the Division for CPA Firms, and divided it into two sections — the SEC Practice Section and the Private Companies Practice Section. Each section has its own peer review program, and both are similar to the AICPA voluntary program.

The profession's peer review efforts are not confined to AICPA programs. About twenty associations of CPA firms throughout the country have their own peer review programs. A number of CPA firms have hired other firms to do peer reviews.

CPA REACTIONS

Approximately 2000 firms joined the AICPA Division for CPA Firms in its first year of operation. Statistics circulating around the profession generally estimated this to be about twenty percent of the eligible firms. Member firms are required to have triennial peer reviews. The bulk of the initial reviews were not scheduled until 1980 and 1981, with only approximately two hundred being scheduled for 1979.

During 1978 and 1979 many efforts were made to inform CPAs about quality control. Seminars were held throughout the country. At the AICPA annual meeting in October 1978, a standing-room-only crowd of CPAs attended a panel discussion on the new sections. Walter E. Hanson, chairman of the SEC Practice Section Executive Committee, stated that the clients of the 544 firms in the section accounted for about 80 percent of the SEC-regulated companies, and that the section was aiming at a goal of 95 percent. He portrayed the SEC as being supportive of the section's self-regulation efforts.

At the same meeting Glenn Ingram, Jr., chairman of the Private Companies Practice Section Executive Committee, emphasized the distinct nature of his section. The section is designed to fill the local practitioner's need for a home within the AICPA. The Private Companies Practice Section was still working on its peer review program at the time of the AICPA meeting. However, James P. Luton, Jr., chairman of the section's peer review committee, stated that his section will emphasize the educational nature of reviews and that sanctions will not be a major factor, at least in the early stages of the program.[3]

The SEC is concerned about the profession's self-regulation process. In 1979 officials in the SEC's Chief Accountant's office have estimated that 2500 firms practice before the SEC, meaning that less than twenty-five percent joined the SEC Practice Section in the first year. They were concerned that many CPA firms with only one or two SEC-regulated clients may not join. There was some discussion of a SEC-supervised peer review program as an alternative to the Division for CPA Firms. However, the SEC seemed willing to give the accounting profession a reasonable amount of time to establish its own peer review program.

A GUIDE TO USING THIS BOOK

The basic objectives of this book are to explain the profession's quality control program and to describe the essentials of a quality control system for a CPA firm.

The intended readership includes CPAs, accountants, accounting students, and others interested in the accounting profession.

While the book is practitioner oriented, it should be of interest to accountants who are not in public practice, because they should be aware of their profession's efforts to enhance the quality of audits. Accounting students should read this book because it explains the operations of a CPA firm. Public accountants (non-CPAs) should read this book with the idea that it has implications for their practice in the near future.

This book uses a basic "how to" approach. It explains the various aspects of implementing a quality control system, and refers the reader to additional sources of information that may be needed by a CPA firm. The specific structure of the book is outlined below.

Quality Assurance Systems

The first three chapters of the book provide background on quality control and peer review.

Quality assurance is defined in Chapter 2. The audit process is described as being comprised of four basic stages — client acceptance, audit planning, obtaining evidential matter, and evaluating and reporting. Finally, the historical development of the profession's peer review program is summarized.

Chapter 3 describes the standards development process for quality control, explains the basic need for documentation of quality control systems, and outlines the basic procedures used in a compliance review.

Implementation

Chapter 4 stresses the need for planning. It explains the procedures that a firm should follow in evaluating its quality control system. The AICPA review programs are outlined as being peer review alternatives, but some associations of CPA firms offer similar services. Chapter 4 next describes the potential costs and benefits to a firm from improving its quality assurance system. Five basic strategies for dealing with the profession's standards for quality control policies and procedures are identified as (1) wait and see, (2) improve working papers, (3) gradual implementation, (4) prepare for AICPA Division for CPA Firms membership, and (5) join the AICPA Division for CPA Firms. Each firm is advised to make a commitment to a strategy and to set up a timetable for achieving its objective.

Chapter 5 describes the tasks typically necessary for implementing a quality control system. The process is described by a standard task check list which identifies four basic stages — study, general design, detailed design, and implementation. Many useful procedures and ideas for implementing a system are explained. Guidelines for documentation are provided.

Elements of Quality Control

Each of the nine elements of quality control is discussed in a separate chapter, Chapters 6 through 14. To facilitate the use of these element chapters, they are organized as follows:

- Overview
- Authoritative Policies and Procedures
- General Design
- Tables of Survey Data
- Example Forms
- Reprinted AICPA Quality Control Policies and Procedures
- Example of General Design
- Summary Evaluation of Quality Control Policies and Procedures for Inclusion in a Firm's Quality Control Document
- Summary of Documentation

The overview provides some background as to why the policies and procedures are needed for a particular element.

The authoritative policies and procedures section of each chapter analyzes the AICPA standards in depth. Possible approaches to meeting the standards are examined. References are made to the tables and exhibits at the end of the chapters.

The general design section of the chapter discusses the main features of the general design of the quality control system of a profile CPA firm. The profile CPA firm is described in Appendix A.

Tables of survey data reveal opinions of CPA firm partners on the major quality control policies and procedures. These opinions are taken from a questionnaire that was mailed to 650 CPA firm partners. The methodology of the survey is explained in Appendix C. The survey data shows the estimated importance and usage of the quality control policies and procedures. The data are analyzed in tables according to the size of the responding firms, sample forms, AICPA quality control policies and procedures, a sample general design, and summaries of policies, procedures, and documentation are presented at the end of each chapter for the reader's convenience.

Next, example forms pertaining to the element of quality control are presented. Many of the forms can be used as is by firms. However, some will have to be modified to reflect a firm's standards.

The AICPA quality control policies and procedures are reprinted in each element chapter. The original AICPA booklet contains some additional background material.

An example of a general design for the profile firm is presented next. This demonstrates the use of a systems design technique that I believe will be very helpful to practitioners.

The summary evaluations of quality control policies and procedures for inclusion in a firm's quality control document is presented according to firm size. A sole practitioner has no full-time staff, but part-time or per-diem professionals might be used. A small local firm is visioned as having only one office; it might have as many as 20 to 25 professional personnel. A large local firm is defined as having two or three offices. It might have between 20 and 80 professionals and a few SEC clients. A regional firm has offices in several states and an SEC practice. A national or international firm has many offices, many professionals and an SEC practice. AICPA example procedures are analyzed as to their applicability according to firm size. This analysis was based upon my study of the AICPA materials, my discussions with practitioners, survey data, and other sources. If a procedure is rated as being high in applicability, it should be included in a firm's quality control procedure unless a substitute procedure can be justified. Procedures rated medium generally ought to be used also. Low rated procedures are often optional. These ratings are not absolute guidelines because other characteristics of the firm and its practice can be good reason for substitute procedures or the omission of a procedure.

The element chapters are concluded with a summary of the documentation that is covered in this chapter. The documentation is summarized for the whole book in Chapter 15, Exhibit 15-1.

Practical Advice

Chapter 15 aims to place the strategies and procedures for implementing a quality control system into a realistic perspective. The CPA's professional responsibilities are discussed, and costs and benefits are summarized. The documentation described in the nine element chapters is summarized in Table 15-1. The estimated probable usage according to firm size is given.

The concluding section gives tips aimed at making the design and implementation process less expensive.

NOTES

1. Subcommittee on Reports, Accounting and Management of the U.S. Senate Committee on Government Operations, *The Accounting Establishment* (Washington, D.C.: U.S. Government Printing Office, 1976), p. v.

2. American Institute of Certified Public Accountants, *The Institute Responds* (New York, New York: AICPA, 1977), p. 6.

3. For more details, see: "News Report," *Journal of Accountancy,* December 1978, pp. 14, 20.

BIBLIOGRAPHY

American Institute of Certified Public Accountants.* "News Report." *Journal of Accountancy,* December 1978, pp. 14, 20.

AICPA. *The Institute Responds.* New York, N.Y.: AICPA, 1977.

Subcommittee on Reports, Accounting and Management of the U.S. Senate Committee on Government Operations. *The Accounting Establishment.* Washington, D.C.: U.S. Government Printing Office, 1976.

*All further bibliographic and note references to the American Institute of Certified Public Accountants are to its acronym, "AICPA."

Chapter 2

Quality Assurance and the Audit Process

When people hear the words "quality control," they usually think of a production process such as automobile manufacturing. However, this term has in recent years been discussed frequently in terms of professional services. Most prominent is the discussion of quality control in the medical profession. The public has demanded greater quality control over health care delivery systems. This demand for increased quality assurance has spread to other areas where services are rendered to the public, and it is now an important concern of the accounting profession. Since the demand for public accountability will continue to grow, quality control is of vital concern to all practitioners.

QUALITY ASSURANCE

The term "quality assurance" in this book refers to all efforts a CPA firm makes to assure that (1) financial statements are prepared in accordance with generally accepted accounting principles, and (2) generally accepted auditing standards have been followed. Quality assurance can be viewed at either the firm level or the level of the profession as a whole. The measurement of quality assurance in a firm can be divided into two basic components: practice management and outcome.

Practice Management

Measuring practice management entails an examination of the firm's structure. An accounting firm adopts an organizational structure which it believes will produce high-quality accounting and auditing services in an efficient manner. Quality controls are adopted to assure that organizational goals are met.

Quality controls may be defined as those policies and procedures that an accounting firm uses to assure that its work meets the accounting profession's standards. "Policies" are general guides to action that provide a basis for day-to-day decisions by a firm's operating management. Policies are implemented through "procedures," which are more detailed and vary with circumstances. For example, a firm may have a policy that all engagements must be adequately planned. To implement this policy, it has procedures such as time budgets and work programs. The procedures vary depending on whether the job at hand is an audit or an unaudited engagement.

Outcome

The outcome component relates to financial statements and working papers. Measuring the outcome component involves a review by outside CPAs of an auditing firm's work. Underlying working papers are also examined to see whether sufficient evidential matter has been obtained. This examination of working papers and related financial statements is made on a selective basis to obtain an overall view of a firm's performance. It is the peer review process.

Implementation

To implement a quality control program, a firm must first undertake the process of criteria development or adoption. For a quality control program within a firm, this means that performance standards must be developed for the practice management and outcome components. For the practice management phase, firms establish quality control policies and procedures that are documented to some extent in the firm's manuals and files. These are continually monitored by management to assure compliance. For the outcome phase, criteria for working papers are established, often in the form of accounting and auditing check lists. Criteria for financial statements are established that reflect the profession's standards, and check lists are commonly used to monitor compliance.

Historically, practice management standards have been primarily developed within each firm, while outcome criteria have been developed externally. Now a quality control program is being applied on a profession-wide basis, and standards for both practice management and outcome are externally developed. The practice management standards are somewhat general because there are differences among firms in terms of size, structure, and clientele. The outcome standards for financial statements have not changed. However, the outcome standards for working papers have been made more specific: monitoring now includes external peer reviews by CPAs from other firms (in addition to internal monitoring). Although the element of judgment in performing audits cannot be eliminated, the ultimate result of a profession-wide program should be more uniformity in audit procedures and working papers.

THE AUDIT PROCESS

The stages of the audit process (in their general sequence) are client acceptance, audit planning, obtaining evidential matter, and evaluation and reporting. These stages are briefly described here so that they can be viewed in relation to the elements of quality control.

Client Acceptance

Client acceptance is obviously the first phase of the audit process. The auditor and the client must agree on the scope of services to be performed, and this agreement should be specified in an engagement letter. Note that an investigation into a client is appropriate before an engagement letter is composed. To assess audit risks, an accounting firm should evaluate information on the prospective client's financial situation, business activities, relationships with past auditors, relationships with bankers, reputation, and other factors. Independence from the prospective client is a crucial factor that should be evaluated before investigating audit risk or the firm's capability to do the audit.

Audit Planning

Audit planning begins during the client acceptance stage. During the acceptance stage, a firm decides whether it has sufficient personnel — in terms of both available personnel time and specialized expertise — to perform the audit. The first and second AICPA standards of field work require that (1) the audit be adequately planned, and (2) a proper study and evaluation of the client's internal controls be performed.

The Foreign Corrupt Practices Act of 1977 and related subsequent developments have caused auditors and their publicly-held clients to be more concerned about internal controls than ever before. The Act requires that companies' internal accounting and record-keeping systems be examined. Almost invariably, these systems must be corrected where material weaknesses are found.

Audit planning has both short-run and long-run aspects. Short-run planning involves setting objectives in terms of budgets, development of audit programs, staff assignments, etc., for the current year's engagement. As for long-run planning, a firm must plan to have adequate staff at all levels and adequate expertise. The means for developing these are good personnel management and professional development strategies.

Obtaining Evidential Matter

Obtaining evidential matter as a basis for rendering a report overlaps with audit planning. Documenting the client's system of internal control is a necessary part

11

of the planning phase, and this documentation becomes part of the evidential matter. The third AICPA standard of field work says that evidential matter to support an opinion must be obtained through inspection, observation, inquiries, and confirmations. The auditor must compile this evidence in an efficient but thorough manner if his or her firm is to remain competitive.

Evaluation and Reporting

The evidential matter must be evaluated before an opinion on the financial statements may be rendered. The auditor must be able to judge (1) whether generally accepted accounting principles have been consistently applied, and (2) whether informative disclosures are adequate.

Evaluation of evidential matter is a continuous process throughout the audit. It sometimes requires a revision of audit plans so that more evidence in a particular area can be obtained. Evaluation may even result in a reconsideration of the client acceptance decision.

Elements of Quality Control

Compliance with generally accepted auditing standards is required of every auditing firm. To accomplish this objective, auditing firms establish operating policies and procedures. In 1974, SAS No. 4 categorized these policies and procedures into nine basic elements of quality control. SAS No. 4 explained that these elements applied to all firms to a greater or lesser degree, depending on such factors as the firm's size, philosophy, and organizational structure.

The elements of quality control were stated as:[1]

- *Independence.* Policies and procedures should be established to provide reasonable assurance that persons at all organizational levels maintain independence in fact and in appearance.
- *Assigning Personnel to Engagements.* Policies and procedures for assigning personnel to engagements should be established to provide reasonable assurance that audit work will be performed by persons having the degree of technical training and proficiency required in the circumstances.
- *Consultation.* Policies and procedures for consultation should be established to provide reasonable assurance that auditors will seek assistance on accounting and auditing questions, to the extent required, from persons having appropriate levels of knowledge, competence, judgment, and authority.

- *Supervision.* Policies and procedures for the conduct and supervision of work at all organizational levels should be established to provide reasonable assurance that the work performed meets the firm's standards of quality.
- *Hiring.* Policies and procedures for hiring should be established to provide reasonable assurance that those employed possess the appropriate characteristics to enable them to perform competently.
- *Professional Development.* Policies and procedures for professional development should be established to provide reasonable assurance that personnel will have the knowledge required to enable them to fulfill responsibilities assigned.
- *Advancement.* Policies and procedures for advancing professional personnel should be established to provide reasonable assurance that the people selected will have the qualifications necessary for fulfillment of the responsibilities they will be called on to assume.
- *Acceptance and Continuance of Clients.* Policies and procedures should be established for deciding whether to accept or continue a client in order to minimize the likelihood of association with a client whose management lacks integrity.
- *Inspection.* Policies and procedures for inspection should be established to provide reasonable assurance that the other procedures designed to maintain the quality of the firm's auditing practice are being effectively applied.

The statement gave some brief examples of policies and procedures. Prior to the issuance of SAS No. 4, the Statements on Auditing Standards had been concerned with the audit process. Taking a new direction, SAS No. 4 was directed at the auditing firm itself. This book contains one chapter for each of these quality control elements. At the date of this writing there was a proposal to rescind SAS No. 4 and to include the nine elements of quality control as part of the first "statement on quality control standards system of quality control for a CPA firm" by the AICPA Quality Control Standards Committee.

Relationship to Quality Assurance

The nine elements of quality control in SAS No. 4 are standards for practice management. They are concerned with how the basic functions of management should be applied. The functions of management may be categorized as planning, organizing, staffing, directing, and controlling. Performance of these functions moves an organization towards performance of its goals.

The four stages of the audit process are related to the nine elements of quality control, as outlined in Table 2-1. The basic functions of management are denoted by symbols (P, O, S, D, and C) to indicate the basic nature of each quality control element as it relates to the audit process. For example, independence is primarily a planning function performed during the client acceptance and audit planning stages. It has control aspects, but planning is the primary management function. Independence affects audit planning because it is a factor in assigning personnel to engagements. Inspection, on the other hand, serves as a control function that covers the entire audit process. (The nine elements of quality control also pertain to unaudited engagements, but there are certain differences, especially in the obtaining of evidential matter.)

HISTORICAL DEVELOPMENT

All CPA firms have followed some of the nine quality control elements in their practices. At a minimum, every firm or sole practitioner has standards for client acceptance. However, quality assurance on a profession-wide basis is new because it encompasses some form of external peer review, which features another CPA's review of the outcome or process aspects of the reviewed firm's accounting practice.

Table 2-1 The Audit Process and Elements of Quality Control

Elements of Quality Control	Client Acceptance	Audit Planning	Obtaining Evidential Matter	Evaluating and Reporting
Independence	P	P		
Assigning Personnel		O	S	
Consultation		O	S	C
Supervision		O	D	C
Hiring			S	
Professional Development		S		
Advancement		S		
Acceptance and Continuance of Clients	P			
Inspection	C	C	C	C

Key: Primary Management Functions:

P   = Planning
O = Organizing
S   = Staffing
D = Directing
C = Controlling

External peer review began in 1962, when the AICPA established a Practice Review Program. This program allows firms to submit audit reports and related financial statements to a committee of CPAs for confidential review. Most state CPA societies have adopted practice review programs based on the AICPA format.

Local Firm Program

The next step was the AICPA's establishment of the Local Firm Quality Review Program in 1971. The program began on a pilot basis, and was aimed at providing local CPA firms with an independent review of working papers and reports. Among the program's educational goals was to help practitioners improve the quality of their audit work, work papers, and audit reports. Reviews of selected audit engagements were made using AICPA-prepared check lists. Here again, the review concerned the outcome aspect. More than 200 firms participated in the program during its first five years. The reactions of the reviewed firms were reportedly favorable — and in some cases enthusiastic — because of the educational benefits. In the local firm program, review materials remained with the firm, and no written reports were prepared or made available to others.

The reviews uncovered administrative weaknesses in many cases. This led to the Administrative Practice Review Program, which was aimed at the management of an accounting practice, mainly in terms of profitability and sound business management. While many of the administrative matters reviewed in the program concerned the elements of quality control to some extent, the overall objective was not to test the quality control system. The program became generally available in 1975.

The Need for More

Publicized shortcomings in published financial statements, litigation against auditors, and other pressures made it apparent that the local firm program did not meet the profession's total needs. The most publicized cases of audit failure involved the national and international auditing firms. An important source of pressure was the SEC, which sometimes required external peer reviews as part of its settlements of lawsuits against auditors.

An AICPA plan for multi-office firms was unveiled in April 1974. The program was voluntary, and included these features:

- Firms initiated requests for reviews.
- The review team was to prepare a written report. The only copy of the report was to be given to the reviewed firm.

- The reviewed firm was to prepare a quality control document which described its quality control policies and procedures. The review was to be directed toward whether the policies and procedures were appropriate and being followed.
- The review team was to be guided by nine elements of quality control. These elements became authoritative the following December in SAS No. 4.
- Audit engagements were to be reviewed at a sampling of practice offices.

Thus, this quality control program focused on both practice management and outcome.

The first volunteer under this program was Peat, Marwick, Mitchell & Co. Before the review could be conducted, however, there was a disagreement with the AICPA over whether the results of the report could be publicly disclosed. Peat, Marwick, Mitchell & Co. wanted to inform its clients if the review showed its quality control policies and procedures to be adequate. The firm withdrew its request in early 1975, and hired Arthur Young & Co. in May 1975 to conduct a review based on the multi-office plan. This review was completed in November 1975, and a favorable report was publicly issued.

The AICPA's efforts continued. The Committee on Self-Regulation developed a tentative draft of a plan, and presented it to the AICPA Council in May 1975. The plan called for registration of CPA firms meeting specified quality control standards. The plan featured (1) field tests of firms by a panel of reviewers, and (2) a directory of registered firms was to be issued. A reasonable amount of time would be allowed to correct deficiencies. If a firm could not meet the standards it would be deregistered, and this fact would be publicized in *The CPA Letter* and the *Journal of Accountancy*. This plan received an unfavorable response from both local firms and sole practitioners.

A revised plan was presented to the AICPA Council in October 1975. The means of being reviewed were extended to other forms that met the Quality Control Review Committee's approval. The most notable new forms were firm-on-firm reviews and state society programs. The directory idea was dropped, and it was proposed that a firm not be allowed to indicate its registration on its stationery. Notice of registration and deregistration would appear in the *Journal of Accountancy*. The field test would include an examination of working papers only to the extent necessary to determine whether quality control policies and procedures were operating as represented. No evaluations of specific engagements were to be made.

Recognizing the need for analysis of this program by CPAs from all segments of the profession, the AICPA arranged meetings with its membership throughout the country. The product of this open forum process was the *Proposed Plan for Voluntary Quality Control Review Program for CPA Firms with SEC Practices,* issued in February 1976 by the AICPA Committee on Self-Regulation. The Committee's letter to the AICPA Council expressed an urgency to act:

> The vast majority of Council members attending the regional meetings expressed the belief that we should proceed without undue delay in adopting some form of quality control/peer review program. They recognize that the pressures on our profession are such that we must take positive action to demonstrate our ability to regulate our own profession effectively.[2]

The letter reported that the greatest need for a peer review program was for firms with SEC practices. Thus the program was aimed toward firms with SEC practices and firms preparing for SEC practices. In this program, the firms were to be called "participants" rather than "registrants."

At the time it seemed that the development process was near an end. It wasn't. The focus on SEC practices was seen as too restrictive by many CPAs. In July 1976, the *Voluntary Quality Control Review Program for CPA Firms with SEC Practices or with General Audit Practices* was sent out to all CPA firms. The plan for both types of firms was essentially the same. In October 1976, the AICPA Council adopted the *Voluntary Quality Control Review Program for CPA Firms* which exists today. This program provided for three types of confidential consulting reviews designed to help a firm prepare for compliance reviews, which are the heart of the program. A compliance review must be performed, and a satisfactory short report must be issued, before a firm can be regarded as a participating firm. This program is open to all CPA firms, even those without audit clients. Reviews of quality control procedures include those applicable to unaudited engagements. This program led to the April 1977 issuance of a discussion draft of quality control policies and procedures for participating firms. The final draft of this program was approved by the Auditing Standards Executive Committee in October 1977.

It is expected that few compliance reviews will be performed under this AICPA program. Instead, most will be done under the AICPA Division for CPA Firms. The Division for CPA Firms was established in September 1977, and divided into an SEC Practice Section and a Private Companies Practice Section. Each section has its own peer review program; both are modeled after the AICPA voluntary program. The programs will evolve as experience is gained, but it appears that the basic form, which will be discussed later, has gained acceptance by the profession.

It should be pointed out that peer reviews were being performed during this developmental period. Most of the national CPA firms were reviewed by another firm. Many of the regional firms were also reviewed. Some reviews were conducted by associations of CPA firms which require external peer reviews of their members.

NOTES

1. AICPA, *Statement on Auditing Standards No. 4* (New York, N.Y.: AICPA, 1974), pp. 2-6. Copyright 1974 by the American Institute of Certified Public Accountants, Inc. Reprinted with permission.
2. AICPA Committee on Self-Regulation, *Proposed Plan for Voluntary Quality Control Review Program for CPA Firms with SEC Practices* (New York, N.Y.: AICPA, 1976), p. 1.

BIBLIOGRAPHY

AICPA. *Statement on Auditing Standards No. 4.* New York, N.Y.: AICPA, 1974.

AICPA Committee on Self-Regulation. *Proposed Plan for Voluntary Quality Control Review Program for CPA Firms with SEC Practices.* New York, N.Y.: AICPA, 1976.

Chapter 3

Quality Assurance Systems and Peer Review Procedures

The development of quality assurance systems is a continuing process for firms and for the profession as a whole. Each firm must develop an organizational structure capable of delivering high-quality accounting and auditing services. Modifications to this organizational structure are made as the firm grows and personnel change, so that it can continue to offer a range of services to meet clients' needs.

The developmental phases of quality assurance systems are standards development, documentation, evaluation of performance, and corrective action. This chapter provides an overview of these phases, and summarizes the peer review procedures used in the AICPA's programs. When designing quality assurance systems, the scope of peer review is an important consideration. Documentation must be adequate so that efficient peer reviews can be made.

STANDARDS DEVELOPMENT

Standards development involves adopting criteria for both practice management and outcome. For measurement purposes, both qualitative and quantitative standards may be necessary, depending on the element of quality control. For example, a quantitative measure of 100 percent compliance can be applied for independence policies and procedures, because these should always be followed. For professional development, the quantitative standard might be forty hours of continuing professional education per year, but some qualitative measures are appropriate to judge whether this education is relevant to the individual's needs.

Practice Management Standards

Standards development is a continuing process. Forms, manuals, and memoranda are typical evidence of a firm's standards. Typically, a firm's first serious attempt to formalize standards involves writing a personnel manual. Historically, accounting firms have developed standards for practice management based on their judgment of what was necessary to perform efficient and technically correct engagements. Knowledge of management principles and other firms' standards also affected these judgments. (Outcome standards have been more precise, because the profession has authoritative accounting and auditing standards to serve as guidelines. The profession's quality control programs have required outcome standards to be more precise.)

For practice management, SAS No. 4 defined the nine elements of quality control, but stated that the extent to which policies and procedures apply to a firm depends on such factors as its size, organizational structure, and philosophy. In October 1977, the standards became even more precise when the AICPA Special Committee on Proposed Standards for Quality Control Policies and Procedures issued *"A Guide to Implement the Voluntary Quality Control Review Program for CPA Firms"* (QCR Guide). This QCR Guide contained guidelines for quality control policies and procedures that are to be used for the AICPA quality control compliance reviews. The QCR Guide was also adopted by both sections of the Division for CPA Firms. The QCR Guide is used as the authoritative basis for discussing quality control policies and procedures throughout this book.

Quality Control Document

The QCR Guide states that a firm should document its quality control policies and procedures. This can be done by preparing a detailed quality control document, or by preparing a summary statement that refers to other literature and documents within the firm. Most firms contemplating peer review prepare quality control documents. A quality control document describes a firm's organization by stating how the nine elements of quality control have been implemented. For each element, the firm's policies and procedures are explained in detail. For example, one procedure used to implement acceptance and continuance of clients might be that acceptance of new audit clients requires the approval of the firm's executive partner.

The basic reason many firms have prepared quality control documents is to communicate with external users, primarily clients and external peer reviewers. Besides serving as an interface with external users, the quality control document is an interface between the practice management function and the firm's auditing system. The quality control document can serve as a very important tool of practice management. Preparing it requires firm management to take an objective look at its current procedures, and usually procedures are improved as a result.

Outcome Standards

While outcome standards have traditionally come from external authoritative sources, they have become even more precise in recent years. The standards for financial reporting have become more detailed because of pronouncements by the APB (Accounting Principles Board) and the FASB. Authoritative auditing standards have traditionally been somewhat general with respect to the preparation of working papers.

The Local Firm Quality Review Program was the first step toward more specific standards. In this program, reviewers used an audit engagement check list which covered all phases of the engagement. For example, questions on each balance sheet account asked whether the working papers reflected adequate substantive tests. A check list for unaudited engagements was also used. The check lists have been revised, and they are widely distributed as part of an AICPA publication titled *Technical Practice Aids*. Versions of these check lists are used in the AICPA voluntary peer review program and by the Division for CPA Firms in peer reviews.

Since the check lists (and versions of them) will be widely used in the coming years, all auditing firms must consider them in formulating their outcome standards. The long-term effect of their use will be more uniformity in working paper content and audit procedures among firms.

DOCUMENTATION

If peer reviewers are to measure performance against standards, documentation is required. Documentation of the outcome phase of quality control poses no problem to CPAs, because they routinely prepare working papers and financial statements. However, some firms find that their working papers do not contain all of the items on the working paper review check list. This may be a documentation problem because the audit procedure was performed, or it may be a standards problem because the firm does not generally use the procedure. Obviously certain procedures do not apply to all clients, but the key is to have the working papers show that the audit was adequately planned and adequate compliance and substantive tests were performed.

If an external peer review is planned, a firm must look at its working papers from the reviewer's point of view. A firm doesn't want its reviewer to mark too many "No" answers on his engagement check list.

Recent years have seen a trend toward use of audit check lists, which can be used to document both outcome and practice management. Hundreds are now available from many sources. A firm should consider adopting some check lists, realizing that check lists do not always work out as well as they seem to. Sometimes items are checked even though they have not been done. Some check lists, especially those for financial statements, tend to become outdated very quickly. Some firms are dropping check lists because of these problems.

There are many possible degrees of documentation for the practice management phase of quality control. It is obvious that there is a direct relationship between the required amount of documentation and the size of the firm. Since documentation takes staff time, there is a cost/benefit relationship to be considered. At a minimum, documentation must be adequate to assure managerial control and to meet legal requirements. Some firms preparing for external peer review may need additional documentation. Documentation standards for CPA firms will become clearer as external peer reviews become more widespread.

As a general rule, documentation must be sufficiently extensive to allow reviewers to determine whether a firm's quality control policies and procedures have been followed. Remember that not everything need be in writing, because reviewers can make inquiries of the reviewed firm's personnel. The chapters on the nine quality control elements illustrate the types of documents commonly used in CPA firms.

Since smaller firms have less documentation of their practice management than larger firms, they should realize that reviewers will depend more on outcome measurement, as evidenced by the AICPA programs: the percentage of a firm's engagements (measured by its accounting and auditing hours) to be reviewed is specified as a range, and the percentages are lower for firms with more than 15 offices.

THE EVALUATION OF PERFORMANCE

While all firms have quality assurance standards to some extent, many do not make periodic evaluation, which usually takes the form of a postissuance review of working papers and the related financial statements. The findings of this inspection are then discussed by a committee, and any necessary procedural changes are implemented. This committee typically includes a few partners and managers, depending on the firm's size and personnel. While the internal evaluation process is generally oriented toward examining working papers and financial statements, practice management procedures are also examined.

External Peer Review

While the internal evaluation process is a common form of peer review, external peer review is destined to become the standard for the profession. External peer review can take many forms, some of which were described in the previous chapter. The most comprehensive is the compliance review, which entails both a review of a firm's quality control policies and procedures and a review of working papers.

Compliance reviews may be organized under one of the following mechanisms:

- AICPA Voluntary Control Review Program for CPA Firms
- SEC Practice Section of the AICPA Division for CPA Firms
- Private Companies Practice Section of the AICPA Division for CPA Firms
- Regional or national associations of CPA firms

The reviews are similar under all these mechanisms, because the AICPA Special Committee on Proposed Standards for Quality Control Policies and Procedures has provided guidance for performing reviews. The AICPA publication entitled *Performing and Reporting on Quality Control Compliance Reviews* sets forth the general procedures to be followed in the AICPA program. The Division for CPA Firms peer review manuals contain only a few minor procedural changes.

Peer Review Procedures

The basic procedures of the AICPA's voluntary program and the Division for CPA Firms programs are summarized below. The purpose here is to provide the reader with an overview of the procedures to be followed.

Background

A firm's purpose in considering elements of quality control is to provide reasonable assurance that the firm is conforming to the profession's standards in the conduct of its accounting and auditing practice. To allow for compliance reviews, there must be adequate documentation and other evidential matter. Organizational structure — including factors such as size, degree of operating autonomy allowed personnel in practice offices, the nature of the firm's practice, and administrative controls — must be considered in evaluating quality control policies and procedures. The firm must submit its documented quality control policies and procedures to the review team in the form of (1) a quality control document, or (2) a summary statement of quality control policies and procedures, with references to the firm's supporting publications and files.[1]

Objectives

The objectives of the AICPA compliance reviews are as follows:

Compliance reviews are intended to evaluate whether a reviewed firm's system of quality control for its accounting and auditing practice is appropriately comprehensive and suitably designed for the reviewed firm and whether its quality control policies and procedures are adequately documented, communicated to professional personnel, and are being complied with to provide the firm with reasonable assurance of conforming with the standards of the profession for firms that are participating in the program.

It is intended that this evaluation be accomplished by:

1. Study and evaluation of a reviewed firm's quality control system.

2. Review for compliance with a reviewed firm's quality control policies and procedures by —

   • Review at each organizational or functional level within the firm.

   • Review of selected engagement working paper files and reports.[2]

For Division of Firms reviews there is an inquiry as to whether the firm is in compliance with division membership requirements. A final objective is to report the findings to the reviewed firm.

General Considerations

Confidentiality is assured to reviewed firms:

> The compliance review is to be conducted with due regard for requirements of confidentiality of the rules of conduct of the code of professional ethics of the AICPA. Information obtained as a consequence of the review concerning the reviewed firm or any of its clients is confidential and should not be disclosed by review team members to anyone not associated with the review.[3]

Reviewers must be independent, which prohibits reciprocal reviews by firms, and conflicts of interest with respect to the reviewed firm or its clients are prohibited. Reviewers are screened so that they have knowledge of the type of practice to be reviewed. They must be at the supervisory level in the accounting and auditing function of a CPA firm. In some cases, specialized consultants are used.

Review Team

The review team can be formed on an ad hoc basis for a particular review. This "pickup team" approach can be used under any of the four mechanisms listed above. If a firm-on-firm review of a SEC Practice Section firm is conducted, a quality control review panel is appointed. This panel oversees the review process. This procedure was adopted because there were criticisms — notably from the SEC — that a CPA firm would find it very difficult to give another firm a bad review. On the other hand, some larger CPA firms did not want to abandon the firm-on-firm concept because they doubted that a pickup team could perform an effective review. Reviewers, practitioners and reviewing firms must be members of the organization administering the review.

The Field Review

Field reviews include the following phases.

1. A study and evaluation of the reviewed firm's quality control system.
2. Review for compliance with a reviewed firm's quality control policies and procedures by —
   - Review at each organizational or functional level within the firm.
   - Review of selected engagement working paper files and reports of the firm.
3. Preparation of a written report on the results of the review.[4]

The Divisions for CPA Firms also includes a review to see if there is compliance with membership requirements. Conditions of the engagement may be documented beforehand. For example, in a multi-office firm, the regional and practice offices to be visited may be specified.

Scope of the Review

A firm preparing for a quality control review should realize that the scope of review is limited. It is directed at the firm's accounting and auditing practice, and to phases of the firm's practice related to its accounting and auditing practice. It involves professional standards which must be met. Also, the reviewed firm and review team agree upon a current period of one year to be reviewed. Some flexibility is allowed:

> It is anticipated that quality control policies and procedures may be revised, updated, or amended during the period under review to recognize changing conditions and new professional standards. The scope of the review should encompass the quality control policies and procedures in effect and compliance therewith for the period under review. Client engagements subject to selection for review would be those with years ending during the period under review unless a more recent report has been issued at the time the review team selects engagements.[5]

The business aspects of practice management are excluded from peer reviews. The performance guide excludes the relationship of fees to engagement hours as a review consideration. Compensation of a firm's personnel in relation to their responsibilities is not reviewed. No inquiries are made of clients. Working papers for certain engagements may now be excluded from the review process if legitimate reasons are stated, although this may change.[6]

Study and Evaluation of the Quality Control System

Background information on a firm (to be discussed in Chapter 5) is used as a basis for a study and evaluation of a reviewed firm's quality control system. This study is used to:

> . . . evaluate whether the quality control policies and procedures are appropriately comprehensive and suitably designed for the reviewed firm, are adequately documented, and the procedures for communicating them to professional personnel are appropriate. This evaluation of comprehensiveness and suitability should be considered further by the review team in the course of the review and may be modified by the review team based on the results of its other review and compliance testing procedures.[7]

Quality Control Policies and Procedures for Participating CPA Firms is used as the guide for evaluating whether quality control policies and procedures are adequate for the practice. A quality control policies and procedures questionnaire (quality control document questionnaire) is used. The firm answers whether a particular procedure is followed. Reviewers analyze the adequacy of the procedures and perform compliance tests.

Compliance Tests

A program for compliance tests is based upon the nature of the firm's practice. The aim of these tests is to determine whether the firm's quality control policies and procedures have been communicated to professional personnel and are being followed. Some compliance tests are confined to reviewed practice offices; others are firm-wide. These tests include:

- Inquiries of persons responsible for a function or activity
- Review of selected administrative and personnel files
- Interviews with the firm's professional personnel at various levels
- Review of the results of the firm's inspection function
- Review of selected engagement working paper files and reports
- Review of other evidential matter[8]

Engagement Review

Engagements are selected for review so that a cross section of the reviewed office's accounting and auditing practice is examined. Usually five to ten percent of a firm's total accounting and auditing hours are reviewed. For firms with fifteen or more offices, the standard is from three to six percent.[9] The review of specific engagements is aimed at key areas. Thus the depth of review may vary by engagement, because some engagements are more complicated than others, given the review's objectives:

> The objectives of the review of engagements are to evaluate (1) whether there has been compliance by the reviewed firm with its quality control policies and procedures and (2) whether the quality control policies adopted and procedures established by the reviewed firm are appropriately comprehensive and suitably designed for its accounting and auditing practice. To the extent necessary to achieve these objectives, the review of engagements should include review of financial statements, accountants' reports, working papers, and correspondence and should include discussion with professional personnel of the reviewed firm.[10]

Suspected Failures

The review team's ability to deal with suspected failures of the reviewed firm to reach appropriate auditing and reporting conclusions is limited, because the review team has limited knowledge of clients' businesses and accounting systems. Therefore, the performance guide states:

> In the absence of compelling evidence to the contrary, the review team should presume that representations concerning facts contained in the working papers are correct. The review team should, however, pursue questions about auditing or reporting matters with the reviewed firm when it believes there may be a significant failure to reach appropriate conclusions in the application of professional standards, which include generally accepted auditing standards and generally accepted accounting principles.[11]

The review team must decide whether the significance and pattern of failures indicate that the firm's quality control policies and procedures are inadequate or not being followed. If the reviewed firm is suspected of issuing an inappropriate report, the appropriate authority in the firm is notified. It is the reviewed firm's responsibility to decide on the action to be taken.[12] However, if the review team is not satisfied with the firm's reviewed remedial actions, further steps may be taken.

These actions depend on the reviewing organization. For example, a firm might be expelled from the Division of Firms.

Reporting

Before issuing a report on the review, the review team communicates its conclusions to the firm, typically at a meeting. Recommendations for improvement may be documented. A standard unqualified report is issued unless there are unacceptable scope limitations, deficiencies in quality control policies and procedures, or significant failures by the firm to comply with its quality control policies and procedures. The last paragraph of the standard AICPA report states:

> In our opinion, the system of quality control for the accounting and auditing practice of Jones, Smith & Co. for the (period) ending June 30, 1978, was appropriately comprehensive and suitably designed for the firm, adequately documented, communicated to professional personnel, and was being complied with during the period to provide the firm with reasonable assurance of conforming with the standards of the profession for firms participating in the Voluntary Quality Control Review Program for CPA Firms of the American Institute of Certified Public Accountants.[13]

Unqualified reports on Division for CPA Firms reviews also state whether there is reasonable assurance that the firm conforms with its section's membership requirements. Recommendations for improvements can be made without qualifying the report.

This summary of the evaluation process is intended to give the reader an understanding of the compliance review. The AICPA publication provides more details. A compliance review is generally conducted every three years. Evidence exists that this time interval has considerable support from partners and proprietors of CPA firms.[14]

CORRECTIVE ACTION

Deficiencies in quality control procedures, or significant instances of noncompliance, require corrective action. Corrective actions involve either personnel or organizational change. Deficiencies in abilities, training, or attitude of personnel are possible. A "Letter on Matters that May Require Corrective Action" might be prepared by the review team captain of a Private Companies Practice Section review. The reviewed firm must respond by describing corrective actions taken or planned, or it can describe reasons for disagreement.

Reviews have found the need for more continuing professional education, especially in a smaller firm. Furthermore, reviews have found needed procedural and organizational changes. Reviews frequently result in some recommendations for changes in auditing procedures. For example, the review team might recommend that audit planning by the engagement manager be (1) more formalized, and (2) approved by the engagement partner.

Obviously, it is better to uncover personnel or organizational problems through an internal review rather than through a compliance review. Adequate planning is the key. A firm must continually reevaluate its quality control policies and procedures, and then monitor compliance with them.

NOTES

1. AICPA, *Performing and Reporting on Quality Control Compliance Reviews* (New York, New York: AICPA, 1978), pp. 43, 44.
2. Ibid., pp. 44-45.
3. Ibid., p. 45.
4. Ibid., p. 49.
5. Ibid., p. 50.
6. Ibid., pp. 51-52.
7. Ibid., p. 53.
8. Ibid., p. 54.
9. Ibid., p. 61.
10. Ibid., p. 56.
11. Ibid.
12. Ibid., pp. 56-57.
13. Ibid., p. 63.
14. Wayne G. Bremser, "External Peer Quality Review — A New Direction for the Accounting Profession," *The Virginia Accountant*, June 1976, pp. 12-17.

BIBLIOGRAPHY

AICPA. *Performing and Reporting on Quality Control Compliance Reviews.* New York, N.Y.: AICPA, 1978.

Bremser, Wayne G. "External Peer Quality Review — A New Direction for the Accounting Profession." *The Virginia Accountant*, June 1976, pp. 12-17.

Chapter 4

Planning for Implementation

This chapter explains the planning phase of a firm's efforts to implement a quality control system. It discusses how a firm compares its current system to professional standards to determine where it stands. The potential benefits of peer review and the peer review alternatives are explained. Since the cost of quality assurance is obviously a consideration in the development of a firm's strategy, methods of estimating cost are discussed. Five basic firm strategies are identified. If a firm wants to improve its quality control system, it should make a commitment to a strategy that ultimately leads to an external peer review of some form.

A firm's implementation plan should take a systems approach, aimed at developing a totally integrated quality control system. There must be integration of all subsystems: the nine elements of quality control overlap, and a piecemeal approach results in a greater cost in the long run. A firm should study the information on quality control, and make a commitment to some goal. A firm needing a major revision of its quality control system must assign responsibilities within the firm to study its present system and prepare a general design for a new system. This general design should be converted into a detailed design, including a quality control document, outlines of manuals, forms, and check lists. Finally, the detailed design should be implemented and tested.

A firm may want to postpone preparing a quality control document and making major changes in its quality control system. It may want to wait and observe the evolution of quality control standards and peer reviews. However, it should make a review of its working papers and reports to assure that it keeps pace with developing standards.

SETTING OBJECTIVES

The key to designing and implementing a successful quality control system is to set objectives for the whole firm and follow a systems approach. Using a systems

31

approach, a firm designs an *integrated* quality control system, not one that's designed piecemeal. Under a piecemeal approach, the firm works on the individual elements of quality control separately over an extended period of time: individual subsystems are developed for each element of quality control, and since they are not coordinated from the outset, they may need to be revised later. In contrast, the systems approach entails making an overall plan with integrated subsystems for all elements of quality control.

Under a coordinated systems approach, the cost of installing and running a system is minimized. Unnecessary duplication can be avoided, and possibilities for computerization can be identified and evaluated more effectively. Unnecessary uses of check lists and forms can be avoided. With a systems approach, the benefits of quality control systems should also be maximized, and realized sooner. Since the profession's experience with formalized quality control documents and systems is rather limited, these views are based, in part, on the experience and principles of production management and management information systems specialists. Quality assurance systems are, in effect, managerial control systems, and the success of any managerial control system depends on a firm's information system.

A firm must first get a rough idea about where its quality control system stands with respect to the profession's quality control standards. Alternative strategies for improvement must be examined in light of their associated costs and benefits. Then a commitment to some plan should be made.

Where Do You Stand?

The first step in implementing a new system is to evaluate the current system. Initially, a firm's management should obtain a basic understanding of the profession's quality control programs and standards. Generally, it is best to assign one or more management personnel to the tasks of studying quality control and making recommendations. The terms "project manager" and "system designer" are used in this book to designate the person or persons responsible for investigating and designing a firm's quality control system. The project manager is in charge of the effort to develop a new system. He or she may be aided by other system designers.

Evaluation

The project manager's first step is to evaluate the firm's current quality control system. This involves comparing the firm's current system to authoritative standards. This book is designed to help the systems designer perform this task. The crucial parts of the authoritative literature are summarized or reprinted in the following chapters. At the end of each of the nine chapters (6 through 14) on the elements of quality control, the AICPA quality control policies and procedures are reprinted; and they are also summarized and evaluated for their inclusion in a firm's quality control document. This summary is accompanied by a listing of the suggested documentation for each element. Relevant AICPA publications are listed in Appendix B. References to additional sources that may be needed are contained in the bibliographies at the end of the following chapters.

States of Quality Control

For discussion purposes, Table 4-1 identifies four basic states of a firm's quality control policies and procedures as they relate to selected aspects of the firm's operations. Obviously, many other combinations exist. State IV represents the highest degree of formalization based on the profession's standards. The amount of written policies and procedures and documentation for a firm in State IV depends on firm characteristics such as its size and the type of practice it has.

Table 4-1 Various Formalized States of Quality Control Policies and Procedures

Significant Aspects	States of Formalization			
	I (Low)	II	III	IV (High)
Client policies and procedures	Variable and unwritten	Moderately uniform and unwritten	Standard and documented	Standard and documented
Daily operating procedures	Variable and unwritten	Unwritten	Written	Written and documented
Personnel policies and procedures	Unwritten	Written	Written	Written and documented
Library	Minimal	Minimal	Adequate for practice	Adequate for practice and professional development
Engagement planning; supervision policies and procedures	Variable and unwritten	Moderately uniform and unwritten	Standard	Standard and documented
Engagement review procedures	Variable	Varied	Moderately uniform	Standard and documented
Audit check lists	None	Few	Many used as needed	Usage is programmed
Peer review	None	None	Internal	External and internal

State I represents a firm with an undocumented, relatively informal quality control system. The firm's procedures are variable and unwritten. Its technical library is minimal. The firm makes no use of audit check lists to standardize audit procedures within the firm. Peer review is not used. In contrast, a firm in State IV has a very formalized system. It uses standardized procedures that are documented, including audit check lists. Engagements are reviewed. Its library is adequate. External and internal peer review is used.

Of course, a firm in State I may very well be producing working papers and reports for audited and unaudited engagements that meet professional standards. Certainly the vast majority of firms in State I believe they are doing so.

By identifying the state of the firm's quality control policies and procedures, a practitioner can get a feeling for how much has to be done to meet the profession's standards. The summary charts on quality control policies and procedures and documentation, located at the end of the nine chapters on elements of quality control, should be helpful in such an identification process. Table 15-1 summarizes the documentation described in this book, and indicates the probable usage by firm size.

Formalized Alternatives

After appraising the current state of its quality control policies and procedures, a firm's management must become familiar with the four alternatives available under the profession's quality control programs. For the reader's convenience, the alternatives under the AICPA organizational structure are presented in Exhibits 4-1, 4-2, and 4-3. In Exhibit 4-1, three types of consulting reviews are described. They are intended to help firms get ready for compliance reviews, the fourth type. However, one or more of these consulting reviews might be a reasonable goal for some firms, given their planning horizon. A quality control document review has little value because it is not done at the CPA firm's offices, so the reviewer has little basis for evaluation.

Few firms are likely to choose a compliance review under the AICPA voluntary program, because belonging to the Division for CPA Firms requires a compliance review, and the Division offers more benefits for basically the same cost.

Comparing the SEC Practice Section and the Private Companies Practice Section, we see that many aspects are identical or similar. The SEC Practice Section has a few more requirements. The cost of membership and reviews is higher for the SEC Practice Section. Due to SEC requirements, the reviews under the SEC Practice Section are more stringent.

The Private Companies Practice Section's *Peer Review Manual* allows for a peer review to be suspended without any specified penalty; the SEC Practice Section's *Peer Review Manual* does not contain this provision. Accordingly, SEC Practice Section membership should carry more prestige. The basic steps of a Division for CPA Firms to be taken by a firm participating in a Division for CPA Firms peer review are:

- Arrange for a peer review through Division for CPA Firms.
- Submit quality control document or another detailed description of the firm's quality control policies and procedures to reviewers.
- Answer quality control policies and procedures questionnaire.
- Participate in the review.
- Discuss findings with review team.
- Submit peer review report promptly to the SEC or Private Companies Practice Section.
- If a letter on matters that may require corrective action is received, respond to it.

These steps vary slightly according to whether panel reviews, firm-on-firm reviews, state society, or association reviews are used.

Exhibit 4-1 AICPA Review Programs

1. *Quality Control Document Review.* This is a means of obtaining advice on the adequacy of the quality control document. It could be used by a firm preparing for a compliance review. The cost is a nominal fee ($150 in 1979).

2. *Preliminary Quality Control Procedures Review.* Reviewers come to the firm's offices to evaluate the documented procedures. The reviews are confidential, and might be used as a preparatory step for a compliance review. Cost depends on reviewer hours.

3. *Technical Standards Review.* As in the original local firm review program, confidential reviews of working papers and reports for audited and unaudited engagements are made. Check lists available from the AICPA are used. Cost depends on reviewer hours.

4. *Compliance Review.* Quality control policies and procedures — and compliance with them — are reviewed. Working papers and reports are reviewed. (This review was described in Chapter 3.) Under the AICPA Voluntary Program, a firm can call itself a "participating firm." Compliance reviews are also required for members of the Division for CPA Firms. Cost depends on reviewer hours. Annual membership dues are required.

Exhibit 4-2 SEC Practice Section of the AICPA Division for CPA Firms
Membership

Objectives

1. Improve quality of practice by CPA firms before the SEC
2. Maintain an effective system of self-regulation of member firms through:
   a. Mandatory peer reviews
   b. Required maintenance of quality controls
   c. Imposition of sanctions for failure to meet membership requirements
3. Enhance self-regulation by use of an independent oversight board composed of public members
4. Provide for the development of SEC practice technical information

Eligibility for membership

1. Meet membership requirements
2. Membership application

Requirements

1. All partners, shareholders, or proprietors of the firm resident in the U.S.A. are eligible for AICPA membership
2. Adherence to quality control standards set by the AICPA Quality Control Standards Committee
3. Peer reviews at least every three years, and more often if needed
4. All professionals in the firm, who reside in the U.S.A., participate in at least 120 hours of continuing professional education over three years, and a minimum of 20 hours per year
5. Audit partners of SEC engagements must be rotated at least every five years
6. Concurring review of the audit report of a SEC engagement is required before issuance
7. File an annual report which is open for public inspection
8. Minimum amounts of liability insurance
9. Limit management advisory services to accounting and financial areas; annually report on these services
10. Report on certain disagreements with client management
11. Pay dues[1]

Cost

1. Annual dues are nominal
2. Team reviews at average standard billing rates according to size of firm
3. Liability insurance depends on firm's practice

Exhibit 4-3 Private Companies Practice Section of the AICPA Division for CPA Firms Membership

Objectives

1. Improve quality of services of member CPA firms
2. Maintain an effective system of self-regulation of member firms by:
   a. Mandatory peer reviews
   b. Required maintenance of quality controls
   c. Imposition of sanctions for failure to meet requirements
3. Provide a means for members to make known their views on professional and technical matters

Eligibility for membership

1. All partners, shareholders, or proprietors of the CPA firm must be AICPA members
2. Membership application with nonfinancial data must be completed

Requirements

1. AICPA memberships maintained
2. Adherence to quality control standards set by the AICPA Quality Control Standards Committee
3. Peer reviews at least every three years, and more often if needed
4. All of a firm's professionals in U.S.A. must have at least 40 hours of continuing education annually
5. Minimum amounts of liability insurance
6. Pay dues
7. Comply with the section's rules and regulations[2]

Cost

1. Annual dues are nominal
2. Team peer reviews billed at standard hourly rates (determined annually) for reviewers, plus expenses
3. Liability insurance depends on firm's practice

Any firm believing it has a high-quality practice will eventually want to join one of these sections, unless there are some unforeseen implementation problems for the sections.

Joining an association of CPA firms is another possible course of action. These associations are increasing in number, indicating the benefits of firms pooling their resources. The associations typically provide forms, check lists, manuals, reviews, and other services. Costs vary, and in some cases are based on a percentage of each member firm's billings. Many of these associations require membership in the AICPA Division for CPA Firms. The bibliography refers you to sources of information on associations.

Potential Benefits

In selecting a strategy, a firm must weigh costs and benefits. The ease of doing this depends on the firm and its management. A firm management which has established long-term goals, periodically reviewed in a systematic planning process, will find this much easier than a firm that does little formalized planning.

Exhibit 4-4 lists ten potential benefits to a firm from improving its quality assurance system. The magnitude of a benefit to a particular firm varies, depending on both the amount of improvement to be done and the firm's practice.

The first and second benefits are general in nature, and are the most interesting. Some firms will be able to increase profits in the long run, and possibly sooner. This could result from the firm's being better organized and having better managerial control. I am convinced that this can happen because I have talked to practitioners who were pleased with peer reviews and the effect they have had on improving management. Some have learned new auditing techniques that allow more efficient auditing (the third benefit listed). The review process caused them to consider all aspects of their practice, and they found many opportunities for improvement. This can facilitate firm expansion because there can be more teamwork within the firm. Growth is facilitated by a documented organizational system.

The fourth and fifth benefits are also related. More effective auditing can result in a smaller chance of audit failure. If a firm having adequate quality control policies and procedures does become involved in litigation, it has a better courtroom defense. Being a member of the AICPA Division for CPA Firms diminishes

---

Exhibit 4-4 Potential Benefits to a Firm from Improving Its Quality Assurance System

1. Increase profits.
2. Facilitate firm expansion.
3. Provide for more efficient auditing.
4. Provide for more effective auditing; i.e., less chance of audit failure.
5. Reduce the firm's legal exposure by having a better defense in the case of threatened litigation.
6. Maintain the firm's ability to obtain professional liability insurance.
7. Enhance the firm's ability to attract and retain high-quality personnel.
8. Develop professional personnel more quickly.
9. Enhance the firm's image.
10. Enhance the profession's image.

the chance of a lawsuit getting to the courtroom, because the plaintiff is aware of the firm's defense. A firm can show that it took reasonable steps to prevent audit failure. This is not to say, however, that a member firm is immune from litigation.

My own experience with courtroom strategy is instructive. The moral of one case was that litigation against accountants is not settled solely on the basis of the facts, and impressions can be important.

In 1975, I was contacted by a CPA from a large firm. His firm was working with a prestigious law firm on the accountant's side of a lawsuit. By the time I was asked to become involved, many pages of depositions had been taken, with a long list of charges against the CPA. I was curious as to why the lawyers wanted me to be an expert witness when they already had a prestigious CPA firm on their side. After all, they already had expert practitioners who would testify to the competence of the audit. The answer to my curiosity was very revealing. It was to be a jury trial, and it had become clear that the other side was not going to settle out of court. The threatening event causing them to seek my services was the plaintiff's strategic move to hire a Ph.D. to testify as an expert witness. Apparently, the CPA's lawyers feared the plaintiff's lawyers' efforts to impress the jury with this man's credentials by calling him "Doctor" during his testimony. The CPA's attorneys wanted to counter with the same weapon.

Getting to the specifics of quality control, I examined the working papers to assess the adequacy of the auditor's examination. The financial statements were prepared by the auditor because the case involved a relatively small company and a small auditing firm. Using the AICPA check lists seemed to be a logical approach.

A lawyer's strategy in defending any case like this is to be prepared for any question with a reasonable answer. Before using an expert witness, a lawyer determines what the expert is likely to say and whether this is likely to help the client's case. Therefore, I had a conference with a lawyer to discuss the possible deficiencies and questions. There were many "No" answers to the AICPA check list questions. The lawyer was very concerned when I explained the check list and the result. He asked whether the accountant had access to the check list, and of course the answer was "Yes." The check list immediately became a part of the defense file because it was a possible weapon for the other side. The obvious defense against this possible weapon was that the check list was new, and that an examination of most CPA firms' working papers would produce a great number of "No" answers.

The audit in question was performed in 1974. For an audit performed in the coming years, will that defense hold water? As more firms adopt quality control programs, working papers will become more standardized throughout the profession. If a defendant practitioner does not have a formalized program, his case will be weakened. There will be no persuasive response to such questions as "Why doesn't your firm have a quality control document?" or "Why didn't your firm have peer reviews to assure that your audit techniques and working papers meet professional standards?'' For this reason, the sixth benefit is listed: satisfactory peer review may soon be necessary to obtain liability insurance.

The seventh benefit in Exhibit 4-4 is based on the view that high-quality professionals work for what they perceive to be high-quality firms. Therefore, having good control systems could be a factor in recruiting staff at the entry level. My experience with accounting students and young accountants supports this idea. When these entry-level people are looking for jobs, they are seeking concrete evidence about the firm and its personnel. They want to join a high-quality firm. Documenting personnel policies and procedures on hiring, advancement, and assigning personnel can also help retain personnel. They know the system. It is easier for them to form expectations about their future. A system of periodic evaluations lets them know where they stand. The presence of organized professional development can help attract them to the firm initially, and can help to develop them more quickly.

The ninth and tenth benefits are related to image enhancement.

The firm's image may be enhanced by joining the Division for CPA Firms. This may be satisfying to the firm's owners. A high proportion of membership in the Division for CPA Firms will enhance the profession's image. Each firm can help by joining.

Commencing in 1980, a directory of all members of the Division for CPA Firms will be published annually. No distinction as to section is made. Thus, recognition to participating firms is given.

Estimated Costs

The costs of quality assurance must be evaluated in determining whether and when to implement a system. The following cost elements are relevant:

- Designing and implementing the system
- Operating and maintaining the system
- Annual participation fees and liability insurance
- Compliance reviews
- Professional development

The cost of establishing a system may be difficult to estimate. Since this endeavor is unique for each firm, the required time commitment is difficult to estimate. Chapter 5 contains an outline of typical implementation tasks, which may provide some help in estimating time. This estimate could be converted into dollars by preparing a budget. In the final analysis, the cost estimate must be based on the relevant cost to the firm. The out-of-pocket cost may be small if most of the effort is made during slack periods. Then again, it might cost overtime pay or the leisure time of a partner. Hiring a consultant might be an effective method of reducing the costs of designing and installing an adequate system.

The costs of operation and maintenance become clearer as the system's design becomes more precise. I interviewed many CPAs about quality control when researching this book. Only one or two complained about this cost. In selecting among alternative system designs, however, these costs are an important consideration. The summary charts on quality control policies and procedures and documentation, located in each of the nine element chapters, provide an idea of the impact on the firm in terms of additional operating procedures and documentation. A review of the AICPA working paper check lists provides an indication of additional effort required on engagements, but in the long run these costs may not be avoidable because of the trend toward standardization of working paper format.

Annual participation fees in the Division for CPA Firms are nominal. Liability insurance is expensive. This may not be a relevant cost, because many firms already have insurance. In the long run, the liability insurance rates for Division for CPA Firms members may be lower than for nonmembers. Discounts are already available to reviewed firms in some states.

The cost of compliance reviews can be large. Fees vary over time, and depend on the type of review team. If a firm-on-firm review is conducted, the fees are negotiated. If a team is used, the average hourly rate for the SEC Practice Section committee appointed review is higher than for the Private Companies Practice Section. The net cost of reviewing could be offset, in a sense, by fees received by the firm if its personnel serve as reviewers on a pickup team.

Estimated costs of compliance reviews are presented in Table 4-2. Firm size is measured in terms of professional personnel. A primary determinant of required review hours is the percentage of the firm's billable hours charged to clients for accounting and auditing services. Based on AICPA programs, five to ten percent of the reviewed firm's total accounting and auditing hours are typically reviewed, if there are less than fifteen practice offices.[3] The review team requires one to three percent of these hours to make the review. In constructing Table 4-2 costs for reviewing both five and ten percent of the firm's accounting and auditing hours were calculated using a two-percent review time. The time required to study documents and test compliance varies by type of firm, but generally increases with firm size. Other assumptions appear in the table. The costs are based on a Private Companies Practice Section review rates for 1979. These will probably increase with inflation. Current rates are available from the AICPA.

Initially, you can expect the costs to be toward the higher end of the range presented. Reviewers have some learning to do, and tend to examine a higher percentage of engagement hours the first time a firm is reviewed. Remember, these reviews occur only once every three years. Therefore, a firm of twelve professional personnel is looking at an average cost of only $700-$800 per year.

Table 4-2 Estimated Costs of Compliance Reviews

(1) Number of Professional Personnel in Firm	(2) Percentage of Accounting and Auditing Hours	Reviewer Hours			Total Cost**	
		(3) Study Documents	(4) Test Compliance	(5) Review 5% of Reports and Work Papers*	(6) 5%	(7) 10%
3	40%	3	2	3	$ 530	$ 710
3	60%	3	2	4	$ 570	$ 790
6	40%	5	8	4	$1,100	$1,260
6	60%	5	8	6	$1,340	$1,480
12	50%	6	12	10	$1,660	$2,120
12	70%	6	12	14	$1,820	$2,650
24	60%	8	16	25	$2,770	$4,040
50	60%	8	20	51	$4,510	$7,360

Key:

* Computed by taking column (1)×(2)×1715×0.02×0.05
  — 1715 hours of chargeable time per person is assumed.
  — an average of 2% review time per engagement-hour is assumed.
  — 5% is the minimum expected number of engagement hours to be reviewed; a minimum of 3 hours is assumed.

** 5% and 10% refer to the number of accounting and auditing engagement hours reviewed. Expenses are assumed to be $150 per reviewer plus $60 per day. An average hourly rate of $40 is assumed, based on 1979 rates. A two-day review is assumed.

Finally, a firm's professional development costs might increase. All professional staff of Division for CPA Firms members are required to have 120 hours of continuing professional education over a three-year period.

FIRM STRATEGIES

Five basic strategies for dealing with the standards for quality control policies and procedures are described below. These basic strategies were identified from interviews with practitioners and from a survey on the topic (see Appendix C). These strategies are:

- Wait and see
- Improve working papers
- Gradual implementation
- Prepare for membership in Division for CPA Firms
- Join the Division for CPA Firms or an association of firms

There are, of course, variations on each of these.

Many firms, especially smaller ones, are going to wait and see what happens with peer reviews. They want more information on the requirements and procedures of the review process. They want more information on costs and benefits. Some sole practitioners and very small firms do not even believe that peer review is intended for their practices.

Some firms have seen the need to improve their working papers with a minimum effect on procedures. They have examined the AICPA check lists and found that their working papers appear in need of improvement. Underlying this strategy is a desire to improve working papers first, because they are most crucial, and to worry about documented policies and procedures later.

Gradual implementation of quality control policies and procedures over several years is another possible objective. This might be done with the idea of achieving an acceptable system, and then possibly joining the Division for CPA Firms or an association of CPA firms. This strategy minimizes the impact on a firm's personnel, and allows the firm to avoid the costs of being a leader rather than a follower. This strategy calls for the firm to focus on a few quality control elements at a time. For example, the first step might be to write a personnel manual. This approach can cost more in the long run because systems planning is not integrated, and systems developed early in this process may have to be reworked later. In addition, the benefits of a complete quality control system are postponed.

Some firms are preparing for AICPA Division for CPA Firms membership. They do not want to join until they feel their system could pass a peer review.

The final alternative is to join the Division for CPA Firms. Many firms have joined. Most of these seem to view their quality control systems as good, but believe that some revisions must be made. Some firms joined before preparing a quality control document. An advantage of joining one of the Divisions for CPA Firms in the earlier years is that reviewers will be more flexible because procedures are new. As time passes they will be more rigid. A similar strategy is to join an association of CPA firms that requires compliance reviews.

MAKE A COMMITMENT

A firm's commitment to a strategy is a necessary prerequisite to significant improvement of quality controls. Goals — and a plan for achieving them — should be established. Assuming the objective is to have a compliance review, a deadline — and a timetable for achieving it — should be set. Target dates for completing the following phases of the system project are generally appropriate:

1. study of the current system
2. development of a general design of a new system
3. development of a detailed design of a new system
4. cutover to a new system
5. compliance review

A more detailed timetable might be appropriate, depending on the number of people involved and the significance of the system change.

Participation and Control

Responsibilities within the management group must be assigned. Typically, one partner should be appointed project manager. Other partners and managers might assume supporting responsibilities. Periodic reporting on progress is essential to monitor progress and to involve a maximum number of firm personnel. If management personnel are allowed an opportunity to evaluate and comment on the system during the design phase, they are more likely to accept, support, and comply with it after cutover.

His Firm/My Firm

This is an appropriate place to discuss what Robert K. Whipple has termed a "his firm/my firm" accounting entity. After many years on the AICPA's Management of an Accounting Practice Committee, Whipple has described this typical firm in this way:

Each of the partners really has his own practice. Collectively they share space and certain expenses. There are "my clients" or "his clients." It is "my way" of doing things or "his way." This staff person reports to "me" or that staff person reports to "him." There are few, if any, common procedures, policies or goals.[4]

He describes the shortcomings of a "his firm/my firm" approach, as compared to the benefits of "our" firm. In "our" firms, "Everything is ours — our clients, our procedures, our philosophy, our people, etc."[5] "Our" firms are well-managed, and work is subject to review and dictated by firm-wide policies, procedures, and standards.

Whipple's article in the *Journal of Accountancy* is appropriate reading for firm managers contemplating a change in their quality control systems: an effective system will require firms to shift, to some extent, away from the "his firm/my firm" mold. Firm management must be aware of this and be willing to make some change. The benefits listed in Exhibit 4-4 are more likely to occur for an "our" firm.

NOTES

1. AICPA, *Organizational Structure and Functioning of the SEC Practice Section of the AICPA Division for CPA Firms* (New York, N.Y.: AICPA, 1978).
2. AICPA, *Organizational Structure and Functions of the Private Companies Practice Section of the AICPA Division of CPA Firms* (New York, N.Y.: AICPA, 1978).
3. SEC Practice Section Peer Review Committee, "Standards for Performing and Reporting on Quality Control Compliance Reviews," *Division for CPA Firms SEC Practice Section Peer Review Manual* (New York, N.Y.: AICPA, 1978), pp. 2-25, 2-26.
4. Robert K. Whipple, "Firm Entity-Foundation for Success," *Journal of Accountancy*, September 1978, p. 48.
5. *Ibid.*, p. 48.

Chapter 5

Implementation of a Quality Control System

Common tasks for implementing a quality control system are described in this chapter. A standard task list is used as the basis for discussion. The four stages are the study phase, general design phase, detailed design phase, and implementation phase. The general design is a broad description of the system in a concise form. In this form, the quality control system can be discussed and approved by the partners. After approval, it can be converted into a detailed design, which includes drafting the quality control document.

IMPLEMENTATION TASKS

The extent and documentation of planning for a new quality control system depend on the size of the project and the organization. By assigning responsibility for the entire project to a single manager, the chance of success is enhanced. This project manager should be given sufficient control over financial and personnel resources to complete the project. By breaking down the project into four phases — study, general design, detailed design, and implementation — the project manager can methodically work towards the goal of implementing a system at the lowest possible cost to the firm. Using this approach also allows the management group to monitor progress and participate in the system's development.

The four phases are presented in Exhibit 5-1, and the standard tasks associated with each phase are listed. The letters under each task represent associated subtasks. The steps in Exhibit 5-1 are being presented as standard tasks and subtasks; as such, the importance of each to a particular project varies according to the extent of the project. This standard task list can be useful to the project manager because it breaks the project down into manageable packages. Even though some of the tasks may seem trivial, they should all be considered.

Exhibit 5-1 Standard Task List for Implementing a Quality Control System

I. Study Phase

Task 1 Make a commitment.
   a. Meet to set objectives.
   b. Assign project responsibilities.
   c. Establish a timetable for documenting quality control policies and procedures.

Task 2 Study the firm's quality control policies and procedures.
   a. Evaluate the firm's organization.
   b. Describe the firm's philosophy and history.
   c. Inventory the firm's personnel resources.
   d. Analyze the firm's operations by type of service.

Task 3 Evaluate literature on quality control.

Task 4 Compile the firm's data, sorted by element of quality control.

Task 5 Appraise adequacy of the firm's working papers.

Task 6 Prepare and submit a proposed course of action.

II. General Design Phase

Task 1 Establish peer review objective (consulting or compliance).

Task 2 Identify required subsystem modifications.
   a. Develop lists of alternative subsystems.
   b. Develop scope of the work to be undertaken.

Task 3 Prepare a general design showing key aspects of the new system.
   a. Describe responsibility and accountability.
   b. Estimate costs.

Task 4 Approve general design.

III. Detailed Design Phase

Task 1 Disseminate to personnel the nature of the quality control system effort.

Task 2 Develop dominant trade-off criteria.

Task 3 Draft quality control document.
   a. Firm philosophy
   b. Organization charts by element or subsystem
   c. Policies and procedures

Task 4 Determine the degree of automation possible for each activity.

Task 5 Design data base or master files.
   a. Client
   b. Personnel
   c. Engagement
   d. Library

Task 6 Develop computer support if required.

Task 7 Develop input and output formats.
   a. Design forms and check lists.
   b. Design reports.

Task 8 Outline manuals.
   a. Personnel
   b. Accounting and auditing

Task 9 Document detailed design.

Task 10 Approve detailed design.

IV. Implementation Phase

Task 1 Plan the implementation.
   a. Identify tasks.
   b. Establish interrelationships among tasks, and schedule them.

Task 2 Organize for implementation.

Task 3 Write manuals.

Task 4 Train personnel.

Task 5 Obtain hardware.

Task 6 Develop software.

Task 7 Obtain forms and check lists and develop new ones as needed.

Task 8 Obtain data and construct necessary master files.

Task 9 Acquire library resources.

Task 10 Test the system's parts.

Task 11 Test the complete system.

Task 12 Cutover and debug the system.

Task 13 Evaluate the system in operation.

While the standard task list presents the tasks for each phase, the project manager must do some sequence planning for the major tasks. Many of the tasks can be done simultaneously. Others cannot be started until another is complete. A project sequence chart, listing the major tasks with their starting and completion dates, could be helpful in planning and controlling the project. An example of a project sequence chart is presented in Table 5-1. Only the most important tasks are included, and some tasks are combined.

The sample project sequence chart in Table 5-1 depicts the study phase for a hypothetical firm as starting on 11/1/79 and ending on 12/15/79. While the general design phase covers the period 12/16/79 to 1/31/80, some of the major tasks are started after 12/16/79 and are completed before 1/31/80. If the actual starting date were later than estimated, the project manager might revise the estimated completion date. Alternatively, the intensity of the effort could be increased so that the target date could be met. In summary, the advantage of a project sequence chart is that it shows a coordinated time plan. It can be used for monitoring progress, and for changing plans as needed.

STUDY PHASE

The study phase really begins during the initial consideration of the profession's quality control programs. However, it formally begins when the firm makes a commitment to take action. Responsibilities are assigned and a timetable is established, as discussed above.

Table 5-1 Project Sequence Chart

Task	Start		Complete	
	Estimated	Actual	Estimated	Actual
1. Study firm's quality control system.	11/ 1/79		12/15/79	
2. Prepare and submit a proposed course of action.	12/ 1/79		12/15/79	
3. Develop the general design.				
a. Key elements of system, communication, and monitoring	12/16/79		1/31/80	
b. List of files needed	1/ 2/80		1/ 5/80	
c. List of manuals needed	1/ 2/80		1/ 5/80	
d. Checklists needed	1/ 2/80		1/15/80	
e. Computer hardware and software	1/ 2/80		1/31/80	
4. Develop the detailed design.				
a. Quality control document	2/ 5/80		3/ 8/80	
b. Data base	2/ 5/80		3/ 8/80	
c. Computer equipment and software	2/28/80		3/ 8/80	
d. Manuals	2/ 5/80		3/ 8/80	
e. Reports	2/ 5/80		3/ 8/80	
5. Implement and install the system.				
a. Write manual	3/15/80		4/15/80	
b. Train personnel	4/15/80		5/15/80	
c. Cutover	7/ 1/80		7/ 5/80	
d. Peer review	10/15/80		10/18/80	

Firm Organization

At first, studying the firm's organization might seem a trivial task to the project manager. After all, the project manager has probably worked with the firm for many years, and "knows how things are." However, documenting the firm's organization might be helpful to the project, and it is required information for reviewers, who use this information in planning their reviews. Statistical information is acceptable, even if only estimates are provided. Examples of information obtained by reviewers include:

1. Description of the firm's organization (an organization chart may be useful).
2. Firm philosophy, including matters such as —
   a. Firm goals or objectives.
   b. Operating practices regarding service to clients and development of personnel.
   c. Policies relating to industry specialization or practice specialists.
   d. Operating autonomy of practice offices (the extent of decentralization of authority).
3. Firm profile. (If the reviewed firm is a multi-office firm, the information should be broken out by individual practice office. Offices that are a part of a larger practice unit may be grouped together.)
   a. Size — accounting and auditing hours. (If such an analysis is not available, the reviewed firm may analyze total billings by function, or make an estimate of the percentage of accounting and auditing work.)
   b. Number of professional accounting and auditing personnel, analyzed by level.
   c. Number of accounting and auditing clients, classified as "audited" or "unaudited" and by type—publicly-held, privately-held, or nonprofit.
   d. Firm management-level personnel, analyzed in terms of years with the firm and areas of expertise.
   e. The firm's industry specialties and specialty practice areas, such as SEC or regulated industries.
   f. Extent of use of correspondent firms on engagements.
   g. Extent of international practice.
   h. Description of recent mergers.
   i. Newly opened offices.[1]

Describing firm philosophy might be difficult for a "his firm/my firm" organization. Since the best quality control systems are possible in "our" firms, developing a realistic firm philosophy might be a crucial task. "His firm/my firm" partners should generally find it worthwhile to discuss goals and objectives for the practice, and policies for clients and personnel. The personalities of the partners and the business relationship between them should be considered in determining whether a firm philosophy is documented. Some of the references in the bibliography refer to articles on how partners' meetings might be conducted to accomplish this.

Compile Firm Data

Firm data should be sorted by element of quality control. This data would include:

- Check lists
- Manuals
- Memos
- Office forms
- Personnel forms
- Library statistics
- Descriptions of procedures

The descriptions of procedures could be in the form of an outline, flow chart, organization chart, or narrative.

The appropriate point of reference for describing policies and procedures is the AICPA standards. Procedures should be described in those terms. The summary charts in the element chapters (6 through 14) should be helpful guides. One possible way is to photocopy these summaries on legal-sized paper. The blank space next to summarized policies and procedures can be used to describe the firm's policies and procedures.

Organization Chart

An organization chart can be a useful device. Since personnel typically perform different managerial roles in a firm's various functions, a separate organization chart is appropriate for each element of quality control. For each function, one individual should be responsible and accountable to someone else, who might be a partner or the partnership group.

A linear organization chart is an effective way of depicting interfunctional relationships within a CPA firm. An example of a linear organization chart for the hiring element of a firm is presented in Table 5-2. The three AICPA policies are at the top of the chart. For maintaining the hiring program, the administrative partner has the responsibility to operate the system. The administrative partner and the executive partner plan for hiring, and answer to the partnership group. The administrative partner also has responsibility to establish qualifications, but must seek the executive partner's approval for some hiring offers. In the orientation function, the administrative partner has overall responsibility, and other personnel execute the system by interviewing applicants. (The legend includes symbols that are not used for hiring but would be appropriate for other elements.)

A linear organization chart offers the potential advantages of (1) identifying the degree of responsibility of each decision-maker, (2) providing a graphical representation of the firm by function, (3) showing redundancies, (4) pointing out a lack of responsibility, and (5) showing potential bottlenecks. In summary, a linear chart shows the role of each manager in a firm's operational functions.

File Folder System

In the study phase, a file folder system is usually helpful. The following folders are recommended:

- Authoritative standards
- Related literature
- Firm background
- One folder for each element of quality control
- Working papers
- Ideas for the new system
- Planning

Table 5-2 Example Linear Organization Chart for Hiring

	Maintain a Program	Establish Qualifications for Hirees	Conduct Orientation for Applicants and New Personnel
Executive Partner	PQ	A	E
Partner — Audit and Administration	PQ, O	O	O
Partner — Audit and Other			E
Partner — Tax and Other			E
Manager			E
Staff			E

Key:

A - Approval
M - Monitor process
PQ - Planning quality control element
PE - Planning engagement
O - Operate system (administer)
R - Review
D - Document quality control procedure
E - Execute quality control procedure

While the use of the folders is self-explanatory, the possible exception is the working papers folder, which relates to the fifth task. A firm's working papers should be analyzed on a selected basis using the AICPA working paper check lists. These are included in the AICPA's *Technical Practice Aids*, which should be in every CPA firm's library. Possible deficiencies should be analyzed and summarized.

GENERAL DESIGN PHASE

The study should lead to a peer review objective, which may simply be a reconfirmation of the objective set at the outset of the study phase.

Preparing a general design of the new quality control system on an element-by-element basis is a useful step. It helps the project manager focus his or her attention on the major aspects of the subsystems. It also facilitates the integration of subsystems. Table 5-3 identifies four major subsystems of a CPA firm. Each of the nine elements of quality control is classified under a practice management subsystem, according to its primary impact. Of course, the elements are interrelated and affect all subsystems. Business management — office layout, compensation, financial records, etc. — has no primary element assigned to it, and peer reviews do not cover this subsystem. A general design, showing the key aspects of the system, provides a vision of the total system to the project manager. This proves invaluable during the detailed design phase.

Table 5-3 Integrated Subsystems of a CPA Firm

Subsystem	Primary Quality Control Elements
Practice Management	
Firm Staffing	Hiring
	Professional Development
	Advancement
Client Management	Acceptance and Continuance of Clients
	Independence
Engagement Management	Supervision
	Consultation
	Assigning Personnel to Engagements
	Inspection
Business Management	None

Another important reason for developing a general design is to have a means of informing the partnership group of the proposed system's major aspects. In this form, it can be discussed, modified, and approved at a partners' meeting. Since a general design is stated in broad terms, it is easy for partners to comprehend and discuss. If the general design phase were omitted, discussion would be postponed until the quality control document was prepared. Since the quality control document is very wordy, partners might find it hard to get a total picture of the system from that document.

A general design should be as concise as possible.

Exhibit 5-2 shows an example of a general design for hiring. The procedures are categorized under operational responsibilities, communication, monitoring, and documentation to reflect the nature of quality control systems. These characteristics were first outlined by the AICPA's Quality Control Standards Committee in its *"Proposed Statement on Quality Control Standards: System of Quality Control for a CPA Firm."* This example uses names of personnel, which is best for smaller firms. The alternative is to use titles such as administrative partner and personnel manager. Titles work best for larger firms.

DETAILED DESIGN PHASE

During the detailed design phase, all personnel should be alerted to the nature of the firm's quality control system effort. This will promote acceptance during implementation. Trade-off criteria should be developed to guide this effort. For example, an objective might be to give new staff the most diversified experience possible. Again, I shall comment on the major tasks in Table 5-3.

Draft Quality Control Document

In drafting the quality control document, the general design is converted into detailed policies and procedures. The AICPA's *"Quality Control Policies and Procedures for Participating CPA Firms"* is the basic guide. The sample policies and procedures in this document are reprinted and a summary evaluation for their inclusion in a firm's quality control document is presented in the nine element chapters. Use these summaries. Sample quality control documents from the AICPA and other firms may also be helpful.

Attitudes of practitioners toward major policies and procedures are presented in the element chapters. These could be helpful to you, as a practitioner, for several reasons. First, they will give you an idea of what others are doing and what they are going to do. They also point out the differences in firms according to size. They can be of psychological help, too. They will show you that many other CPA firms are in a position similar to yours. You are not alone in having to make changes.

Exhibit 5-2 Example of General Design for Hiring

1. Operational Responsibilities: Mr. B. and Mr. H. plan for personnel needs and establish qualifications and guidelines for potential hirees. Mr. H. has the responsibility for all recruiting and orientation. Mr. H. has the authority to hire at all levels, except that Mr. B. must approve offers made at the manager level and above.

2. Communication: Qualifications and guidelines for hirees and hiring procedures are included in the personnel handbook.

3. Monitoring: Mr. B., Mr. H., and Ms. P. make an annual evaluation of hiring.

4. Documentation:
   a. Staff evaluation form
   b. Staff application form
   c. Personnel manual
   d. Orientation check list

Reviewer Point of View

A general rule in drafting the document is to keep the reviewer's point of view in mind at all times. A copy of the reviewer's compliance review program guidelines should be used. The *Division for CPA Firms Private Companies Practice Section Peer Review Manual* contains these guidelines according to firm size — sole practitioner, 2 to 20 professionals, 20 to 50 professionals, and 50 or more professionals. This program basically restates the sample AICPA policies and procedures in question form. A "No" answer to a policy question means that the firm does not have a comparable policy or substitute procedures. Example procedures are checked if the firm uses them. Although the firm can explain the reason for a "No" answer or an unchecked procedure, it would seem logical to avoid these answers, which cause the reviewer to make a special judgment as to whether substitute procedures are adequate.

Preparing the quality control document in book form generally works best. Use an index and start each element on a new page. This format makes a good impression on reviewers, and amending the document is easy.

Another general rule is to avoid too much detail in preparing a quality control document. Practice management does require judgment in day-to-day operations, and this must be recognized. For example, in the assignment of personnel to engagements, objectives might be continuity, opportunities for on-the-job training, and rotation of personnel. However, there is no need to give details of the decision process when there is a conflict among the objectives. Detail can also be avoided in the quality control document by referring to documented procedures in firm manuals, check lists, and forms.

Documentation

Since documentation is a key element of quality control systems, forms and manuals must be designed. Their content will depend on the data bases to be used. Master files for clients, personnel, and engagement processing will need both record formats and input/output formats. This might be a good time to think of computerization: costs of minicomputers are falling. The firm might see a payoff if these files and its business management files (accounts receivable, accounts payable, and general ledger) can be computerized simultaneously.

Exhibit 5-3 contains a forms use and design check list. Forms should be easy to use and be kept to a minimum. Item 10 under "Design" is an idea to keep in mind. If instructions are contained on the form, front or back, the need for instructions in the firm's personnel, accounting, and audit manual can possibly be avoided. This can be important for forms to be used by audit personnel in the field.

Manual or Memos

Documentation of a firm's personnel policies and procedures and its auditing and accounting procedures is required. A firm has a choice, for certain items, of documenting its procedures either in its quality control document or in a manual. Instead of a manual, memos can be prepared and filed. For example, qualifications for hirees could be stated in the quality control document, or the quality control document could refer to a manual or a memo.

Whether a manual or a memo system should be used is a matter of the firm's preference. If all of the personnel-related memos are kept in a file, you in a sense have a manual. A manual has an appearance of being more formal, and it gives a more authoritative impression. Therefore, staff members might take its contents more seriously. The need for manuals generally increases as the firm grows. The main disadvantage of manuals is that they are more costly to prepare and maintain. A more detailed discussion of a personnel manual is contained in the chapter on hiring. The chapter on supervision gives further consideration to an accounting and auditing manual.

The quality control document, forms, report formats, check lists, master files, record formats, manual outlines, etc., can be assembled into the detailed design. When the detailed design is approved, implementation can begin.

Exhibit 5-3 Forms Use and Design Check List

Use

1. What is the form's purpose?

acknowledge	identify
authorize	route
verify	control
budget	order
schedule	record
warn	plan
request	

2. Who fills out the form?
3. Who reads the form?
4. Is the form really necessary?
5. Can the form be integrated with another form?
6. Is it clear when the form will be used?
7. Is the retention period appropriate?

Design

1. Is there a title?
2. Does the form number incorporate the date?
3. Is the size practical?
4. Does the number of copies meet intended distribution needs?
5. Is there enough space to write in required information?
6. Are appropriate authorizations on the form?
7. Does the form allow for easy filing?
8. Can time-consuming writing be eliminated by using a check list format?
9. Is the form easy to understand so that instructions do not have to be reviewed before it is completed?
10. Should some instructions be included on the form so that firm manuals do not have to contain instructions?
11. Can colored paper or print be used to enhance the functioning of the form?

IMPLEMENTATION

The complexity of implementation varies directly with firm size. Larger firms have more personnel to train, more documents, and more detail in manuals. An implementation schedule is generally helpful.

Three basic implementation methods may be used for the quality control system. A direct cutover could be used, whereby the old system is cut off on a particular date and a new system is adopted. This is practical where the amount of change is small.

Phasing in the new system is appropriate for most firms. Subsystems are converted to the new system as they are ready. For example, the staffing subsystem might be ready first.

A piecemeal approach might be appropriate, especially in smaller firms. Parts of the system are tested, and redesigned if necessary. For example, a review check list for working papers might be used for a month, then revised.

Many of the tasks in Exhibit 5-1 can be performed simultaneously. Tasks 1 through 11 must be complete before 12 is completed. Debugging might involve some changes to manuals, or to the quality control document itself.

A REALISTIC PERSPECTIVE FOR PRACTITIONERS

The systems approach presented in this chapter is generalized. Some firms can take short-cuts and omit procedures, depending on their current system and management structure. Do not let the lengthy discussion of the planning and implementation tasks convince you that the project is bigger than it actually is.

Talk to other practitioners about what they are doing. Have confidence in your practice. Use the resources available from AICPA — quality control standards, sample quality control documents, MAP Handbook, and Technical Practice Aids.

In developing the quality control document, avoid too much detail. Ask yourself: "What is the reviewer's point of view?" Remember, the review of engagement outcome is important. Five to ten percent of the accounting and auditing hours are reviewed. An excellent-looking quality control system cannot compensate for a poor score on the outcome review.

NOTES

1. AICPA, *Performing and Reporting on Quality Control Compliance Reviews* (New York, N.Y.: AICPA, 1978), pp. 52, 53.

BIBLIOGRAPHY

AICPA. *Division for CPA Firms Private Companies Practice Section Peer Review Manual.* New York, N.Y.: AICPA, 1979.

AICPA. *Division for CPA Firms SEC Practice Section Peer Review Manual.* New York, N.Y.: AICPA, 1978.

AICPA. *MAP Handbook.* New York, New York: AICPA, 1978.

AICPA. *Organizational Structure and Functions of the Private Companies Practice Section of the AICPA Division of CPA Firms.* New York, N.Y.: AICPA, 1978.

AICPA. *Organizational Structure and Functions of the SEC Practice Section of the AICPA Division of CPA Firms.* New York, N.Y.: AICPA, 1978.

AICPA. *Performing and Reporting on Quality Control Compliance Review.* New York, N.Y.: AICPA, 1978.

AICPA. *Voluntary Quality Control Review Program for CPA Firms.* New York, N.Y.: AICPA, 1978.

AICPA. *Sample Quality Control Documents for Local CPA Firms.* New York, N.Y.: AICPA, 1978.

AICPA. *Technical Practice Aids.* New York, N.Y.: AICPA, 1978.

AICPA. *Voluntary Quality Control Review Program for CPA Firms.* New York, N.Y.: AICPA, 1978.

Bickle, John W. "Structure of CPA Firms — Time for a Change?" *Journal of Accountancy,* June 1975, pp. 102-104.

Bremser, Wayne G. and Dascher, Paul E. "Accounting Careers in Perspective." *CPA Journal,* January 1975, pp. 46-48.

California Certified Public Accountants Foundation. *Quality Control Documentation In the Local CPA Firm.* Palo Alto, Calif.: California Certified Public Accountants Foundation, 1978.

Cerullo, Michael J. "In-Home Computers for CPA Firms." *The CPA Journal,* June 1976, pp. 9-13.

Chilton, Carl. "The Partner's Annual Meeting." *Journal of Accountancy,* May 1975, pp. 91-92.

De Mas, J.N. "How to Develop Manuals of Forms and Procedures." *Practical Lawyer,* December 1972, pp. 33-40.

Jackson, Clyde W. "How to Write a Manual." *Journal of Systems Management,* December 1973, pp. 38-39.

Jeffries, David and Mecimore, Charles. "The 1976 Survey of Practices on Policies of Ohio CPAs." *The Ohio CPA,* Autumn 1977, pp. 83-86.

Larson, Charles B. "Partners' Retreats." *Journal of Accountancy,* December 1977, p. 34.

Laveral, Frank. "How Good Is Your Firm's Quality Control?" *The Practical Accountant,* March/April 1977, p. 48.

Miller, Richard L., Jr. "Ten Rules for Safe Accounting Practice." *The Practical Accountant,* March/April 1977, pp. 62-67.

Muench, William F., Jr. "Computer Time-Sharing for CPAs." *Journal of Accountancy,* January 1979, pp. 65-69.

Myers, Gibbs. "Forms Management, Part 1: Why Forms Management?" *Journal of Systems Management,* September 1976, pp. 20-23.

Myers, Gibbs. "Forms Management, Part 2: How to Design Business Forms." *Journal of Systems Management,* October 1976, pp. 21-24.

Parson, John W. "What Makes a Managing Partner." *Journal of Accountancy,* September 1977, p. 64.

Prentice-Hall, Inc. *SEC Compliance Financial Reporting and Forms.* Englewood Cliffs, N.J.: Prentice Hall, updated monthly.

Rea, Robert C. "Association of CPA Firms." *Journal of Accountancy,* September 1978, pp. 42-48.

Rea, Robert C. "More on Associations of CPA Firms." *Journal of Accountancy,* December 1978, p. 48.

Rea, Robert C. "Strategies for Healthy Growth." *Journal of Accountancy,* February 1977, p. 41.

Shine, J. Robert. "Revolving Door for Partners." *Journal of Accountancy,* July 1977, p. 37.

Telling, Raymond. "Long-range Planning for a Local Firm." *Journal of Accountancy,* August 1977, p. 40.

Wallace, Melvin. "How to Organize and Conduct an Annual Audit." *The Practical Accountant,* January/February 1978, pp. 73-75.

Ward, Geoffrey H. "One Way to Manage an Accounting Firm." *Journal of Accountancy,* February 1976, pp. 82-84.

Whipple, Robert K. "Firm Entity — Foundation for Success." *Journal of Accountancy,* September 1978, pp. 48-54.

Zitmann, Albert. "The Local Firm Quality Review Program: A Chance to Check your Firm's Performance." *The Practical Accountant,* May/June 1975, pp. 70-74.

Chapter 6

Independence

The four AICPA objectives and related procedures for independence are explained and analyzed in this chapter. The AICPA quality control policies and procedures containing the objectives and example procedures are reprinted in Exhibit 6-3 and summarized with comments in Table 6-3. An example of an independence check list and an independence compliance letter are presented because some firms will want to adopt versions of these forms. Independence documentation is summarized in Table 6-4. Client lists are optional for smaller firms.

The opinions of CPA firm partners on selected quality control procedures are presented in Tables 6-1 and 6-2. These opinions on the importance and usage of quality control procedures should provide perspective to practitioners on what other CPAs are thinking and doing. For the reader's convenience, all tables and exhibits are presented at the end of the chapter.

OVERVIEW

The CPA's ability to be truly independent is seriously questioned by many. SEC officials, legislators, and financial writers have asked whether a CPA firm is truly independent if it is hired by management. When a controversy over the accounting or disclosure of a particular item arises, can the CPA truly stand up to management to defend his opinion of what is proper? Does the threat of losing a desirable audit fee place the CPA in a compromising position?

There is increased pressure on CPAs to convince the public of the profession's ability to conduct audits in accordance with the second of the generally accepted auditing standards; that is, while maintaining an independence in mental attitude. Serious doubts about the auditor's independence arose in the 1960's. The business and financial press was on the lookout for cases where an auditor who disagreed with a firm's accounting policies was replaced by a more receptive auditor. While accountants understand that differences in judgments are possible when precise accounting standards do not exist, others may not. The profession's main response to these accusations has been to recommend the use of outside audit committees.

Another problem with independence has arisen from the provision of management services by CPAs. Some believe that management services should be prohibited because they involve the CPA in the management process of the firm he is auditing, and because the CPA firm stands to lose fees if a client is lost. Since the management services personnel are not the same as the audit personnel, and since CPAs limit management services to accounting-related areas, CPAs reject this criticism. The SEC Practice Section has specific guidelines in this area.

For the element of independence, a firm's objective is to establish policies and procedures reflecting the AICPA professional ethics on independence. The major procedures are (1) to make client lists available, and (2) to have personnel sign an annual statement that they comply with the firm's policies and procedures. Responsibility is assigned for administration of the procedures and for resolving exceptions.

AUTHORITATIVE POLICIES AND PROCEDURES

The AICPA quality control policies and procedures are presented in Exhibit 6-3. Four objectives are numbered, and firms should establish policies and procedures to meet them. Examples of procedures are identified in Exhibit 6-3 by letters. Procedures are identified in the text by using the objective number, the letter, and possibly small roman numerals (2b(ii), for example). Common procedures and the peer reviewer's approach are discussed below for each objective.

Adhere to Authoritative Independence Rules

Objective 1: REQUIRE THAT PERSONNEL AT ALL ORGANIZATIONAL LEVELS ADHERE TO THE INDEPENDENCE RULES, REGULATIONS, INTERPRETATIONS, AND RULINGS OF THE AICPA, STATE CPA SOCIETY, STATE BOARD OF ACCOUNTANCY, STATE STATUTE, AND, IF APPLICABLE, THE SEC AND OTHER REGULATORY AGENCIES.

The quality control document should require firm personnel to adhere to relevant authoritative rules on independence. A partner or committee should be assigned the responsibility to provide guidance on independence matters. The AICPA technical information service or a state society's similar service can be appropriately listed as a source of information when questions cannot be resolved within the firm.

My research did not uncover any clever ways of identifying or resolving nonroutine questions. A check list might help to identify nonroutine questions. Their resolution would generally involve a very experienced CPA.

Documentation

A memo documenting the resolution of important independence questions is typically prepared for the files. Personnel involved in the question review and either initial or sign the memo. Table 6-1, part 1 shows that the CPA respondents in the survey described in Appendix C believe documentation of important questions to be an "important" procedure. The estimated usage generally ranged from "occasional" to "common."

A possible drawback of requiring the documentation of unusual independence questions is that open discussion of these questions may be inhibited within the firm. Table 6-2 reports little agreement with this notion among the CPAs surveyed.

Peer Reviewers

Reviewers examine a firm's independence policies and procedures to see that AICPA standards are met. They check to see whether someone with adequate authority has been assigned the responsibility to provide guidance and resolve questions. They review the documented resolutions of independence questions, if any.

Communicate Policies and Procedures

Objective 2: COMMUNICATE POLICIES AND PROCEDURES RELATING TO INDEPENDENCE TO PERSONNEL AT ALL ORGANIZATIONAL LEVELS.

The quality control document should indicate the means for communicating independence policies and procedures. In accordance with procedures 2a and 2d, the document might simply refer to authoritative sources kept in the firm's library. The basic source is AICPA's *Professional Standards, Volume 2* and rulings and interpretations by state CPA societies and other state authorities. For firms with SEC practices, Regulation S-X and Accounting Series Releases of the SEC are additional sources. To supplement these basic sources, a firm's personnel manual or a file memo might contain an independence check list to help personnel interpret the independence standards. Exhibit 6-1 contains a sample check list. The items in the list paraphrase Rule of Conduct 101 of the AICPA Code of Professional Ethics.

Emphasizing Independence

Procedures for emphasizing independence (2b) should be stated in the quality control document. Methods of implementing vary, depending on the individual accountant and the firm. Objective 4 is accompanied by some procedures for doing this. Emphasizing independence of mental attitude during engagements received a high importance and usage score from the CPAs surveyed, with only minor differences due to firm size.

Emphasizing independence during training sessions generally seems to be confined to audit training sessions for junior accountants. Table 6-1, part 4 shows that the CPAs did not view this procedure to be as important as emphasizing independence during engagements. Importance scores increased with firm size. Estimated usage averaged out to be less than "occasional," except for the firms having more than 80 professional personnel.

Client Lists

Since independence rules vary according to the type of engagement, a logical procedure is to have a means of identifying clients accordingly. Procedure 2c recommends the use of client lists and a procedure for communicating changes in the list to personnel. The use of client lists is optional for smaller firms.

Client lists generally contain the following headings:

- Client number
- Client name
- Industry
- Type of engagement
- Responsible partner or manager

Some firms use a client number code that reflects the type of engagement and/or the responsible partner. Listing by industry is optional; some firms use the Standard Industrial Classification (SIC) Code numbers. To update the list, memos containing the above data are issued to personnel periodically, usually monthly, with additions and deletions. The list is revised periodically. Procedure 2c applies to accounting and auditing clients only: other types of engagements do not require this control. In Table 6-1, part 3, the perceived importance of client lists increases with the size of the CPA's firm. Estimated usage averaged out to be in the "occasional" range, except for the "more than" 80 group, where it was in the "common" range.

Substitute procedures for client lists might be acceptable for communicating this client information to staff members. For example, a small firm might feel that typing a long list of clients each year is a waste of time. The procedure might be to type a client list at the outset. Deletions would then be crossed off, and additions typed onto the end. Rather than use memos to update the list, additions and deletions would be posted on a bulletin board for a period of two months. There are many possibilities.

Peer Reviewers

Reviewers examine how independence policies are communicated and emphasized, including a check of the firm's library to see that it contains the profession's independence standards. In doing this, selected staff may be interviewed. The firm's training programs may be reviewed. For identifying pertinent clients, the reviewer's test is whether client information is communicated effectively.

Confirm Independence of Other Auditors

Objective 3: CONFIRM, WHEN ACTING AS PRINCIPAL AUDITOR, THE INDEPENDENCE OF ANOTHER FIRM ENGAGED TO PERFORM SEGMENTS OF AN ENGAGEMENT.

To assure complete independence, the principal auditor confirms the independence of other firms. This objective has no operational relevance if other firms are not hired to perform segments of engagements, but it should be covered by the quality control document because the situation may arise in the future. If a firm does use other auditing firms, the form and content of independence — as it relates to presentations — should be in its accounting and audit manual. It could be documented elsewhere. For example, the quality control document might refer to a file.

Peer Reviewers

Reviewers check for form, content, and frequency of representation.

Monitor Compliance

Objective 4: MONITOR COMPLIANCE WITH POLICIES AND PROCEDURES RELATING TO INDEPENDENCE.

Responsibility must be assigned for monitoring independence policies and procedures. In accordance with procedure 4a, written representations should be obtained from firm personnel.

Exhibit 6-2 illustrates an independence compliance letter. To avoid conveying a feeling of distrust, a careful orientation of firm personnel to this procedure should emphasize that this is becoming a profession-wide procedure. To supplement this, the signed weekly time reports of some firms contain a statement that the person's status has not changed.

Referring to Table 6-1, part 5, the estimated usage of written representation was between "rare" and "occasional" for all but the "more than 80" group, where it was in the "almost always" range. Similarly, the "more than 80" group viewed this procedure as "essential," and the scores dropped with firm size to the "some importance" or "little importance" ranges. While the perceived benefit is not great, there is no reason for omitting written representations from the quality control document because they are easy to do.

Some firms exempt partners from the written representation procedure. One justification for this is that signing the firm name on behalf of the partnership is a written representation that the partner is independent of the client. Many partnership agreements contain a clause explaining the partners' responsibility to be independent.

Monitoring responsibility must be assigned for the obtaining of representations and the resolving of exceptions. Also, outstanding accounts receivable must be reviewed periodically to guard against the possibility that long-term loans will be made to clients. Prior years' fees should be received before starting an engagement for a SEC-regulated client, and before issuing the report of a non-SEC-regulated client.

Peer Reviewers

To check compliance, peer reviewers examine the files for written independence representations when they are required by firm procedures. Monitoring procedures are evaluated for adequacy. Reviewers determine whether monitoring responsibilities are assigned to someone with adequate authority. Accounts receivable subsidiary ledgers might be reviewed to search for long-term loans.

GENERAL DESIGN

A sample general design for independence is presented in Exhibit 6-4. It shows that responsibilities for operating, communicating, and monitoring might be split up among several management personnel. To repeat, the purpose of the general design is to serve as a means for easy discussion within the management group. It shows the responsibilities and the overall system. After being approved, these can be merged into the quality control document. Alternate formats could be used to accomplish the same purpose.

A summary of AICPA objectives and sample procedures to implement them is presented in Table 6-3. A procedure's applicability according to firm size is a generalization based upon current standards. Several characteristics of firms are recognized in the accounting profession's quality control programs as determinants of the appropriate quality control policies and procedures for CPA firms. Therefore, a firm must consider all of its characteristics in designing procedures and assigning responsibilities. Similarly, forms, check lists, and other documentation shown in this book and elsewhere must be modified to fit the individual firm's needs. Table 6-4 summarizes independence documentation.

Exhibit 6-1 Independence Check List

1. Do you have a direct or indirect material financial interest in an *audit* client or its subsidiaries and affiliates?
2. Do you have a financial interest in any major competitors, investees, or affiliates of an *audit* client?
3. Do you have any outside business relationship with an *audit* client or an officer, director, or principal stockholder thereof, having the objective of financial gain?
4. Do you owe any client an amount, except a normal consumer note payable or home mortgage made by a financial institution under normal lending procedures, terms, and requirements?
5. Do you have a note or account receivable from a client, except for a deposit in a financial institution?
6. Do you have the authority to sign checks for a client?
7. Are you connected with a client as a promoter, underwriter or voting trustee, director, officer, or in any capacity equivalent to a member of management or an employee?
8. Do you serve as a director, trustee, officer, or employee of a nonprofit organization that is a present *audit* client?
9. Has your spouse or minor child been employed by a client?
10. Has anyone in your legal family, or any blood relative, been employed in any type of managerial position by a client?
11. Are any billings delinquent for *audit* clients that are your responsibility?

NOTE: An explanation is required for each "No" answer.

Exhibit 6-2 Independence Compliance Letter Form

OFFICE_____

NAME_____

I have read the Firm Independence Policy and AICPA standards. I believe I understand the independence policy and standards. I am in compliance except for the exceptions listed below.

EXCEPTIONS TO POLICIES: (A "No" answer to an independence check list item in the firm personnel manual is an exception. Give details as to names, addresses, amounts (relationships of amounts to your net worth is relevant), etc. Leaving the spaces blank indicates you have no exceptions.)

ARRANGEMENTS MADE TO DISPOSE OF ABOVE EXCEPTIONS TO COMPLY WITH POLICIES:

_____   _____
Signature   Date

_____   _____
Exceptions Approved By   Location

Instructions: Sign and return to_____
within one week after starting to work. Annually, a new form must be completed during the first week of December.

Exhibit 6-3 AICPA Quality Control Policies and Procedures for Independence

1. **Require that personnel at all organizational levels adhere to the independence rules, regulations, interpretations, and rulings of the AICPA, state CPA society, state board of accountancy, state statute, and, if applicable, the Securities and Exchange Commission and other regulatory agencies.**
   a. Designate an individual or group to provide guidance and to resolve questions on independence matters.
      (i) Identify circumstances where documentation as to the resolution of questions would be appropriate.
      (ii) Require consultation with authoritative sources when considered necessary.

2. **Communicate policies and procedures relating to independence to personnel at all organizational levels.**
   a. Inform personnel of the firm's independence policies and procedures and advise them that they are expected to be familiar with these policies and procedures.
   b. Emphasize independence of mental attitude in training programs and in supervision and review of engagements.
   c. Apprise personnel on a timely basis of those entities to which independence policies apply.
      (i) Prepare and maintain for independence purposes a list of the firm's clients and of other entities (client's affiliates, parents, associates, and so forth) to which independence policies apply.
      (ii) Make the list available to personnel (including personnel new to the firm or to an office) who need it to determine their independence.
      (iii) Establish procedures to notify personnel of changes in the list.
   d. Maintain a library or other facility containing professional, regulatory, and firm literature relating to independence matters.

3. **Confirm, when acting as principal auditor, the independence of another firm engaged to perform segments of an engagement.**
   a. Inform personnel as to the form and content of an independence representation that is to be obtained from a firm that has been engaged to perform segments of an engagement.
   b. Advise personnel as to the frequency with which a representation should be obtained from an affiliate or associate firm for a repeat engagement.

Exhibit 6-3 continued

4. **Monitor compliance with policies and procedures relating to independence.**

   a. Obtain from personnel periodic, written representations, normally on an annual basis, stating that —
      (i) They are familiar with the firm's independence policies and procedures.
      (ii) Prohibited investments are not held and were not held during the period. As an alternative or additional procedure, a firm may obtain listings of investments and securities transactions (numbers of shares or dollar amounts need not be included) from personnel to determine that there are no prohibited holdings.
      (iii) Prohibited relationships do not exist, and transactions prohibited by firm policy have not occurred.

   b. Assign responsibility for resolving exceptions to a person or group with appropriate authority.

   c. Assign responsibility for obtaining representations and reviewing independence compliance files for completeness to a person or group with appropriate authority.

   d. Review periodically accounts receivable from clients to ascertain whether any outstanding amounts take on some of the characteristics of loans and may, therefore, impair the firm's independence.

Exhibit 6-4 Example of General Design for Independence

Operational Responsibilities

Partner A is responsible for providing guidance, resolving questions on all independence matters, and updating the firm's policies as professional standards change. Engagement partners are responsible for confirming the independence of associated firms.

Communication

Partner B is responsible for maintaining and distributing client lists and updates. Partner A is responsible for the independence section of the personnel manual. Managers emphasize independence during engagements.

Monitoring

Partner A is responsible for obtaining written independence representations from staff personnel. Partner B periodically reviews accounts receivable. All partners report their investments annually.

Documentation

1. AICPA *Professional Standards, Volume 2:* Concepts of Professional Ethics, Rule of Conduct 101, and related interpretations
2. Personnel manual, independence check list
3. Annual independence certificate
4. Client lists, update memo

NOTE: The profile firm is described in Appendix A.

Table 6-1 Opinions on Independence Policies and Procedures

| Quality Control | Number of Professional Personnel in Firm | | | | | | | |
| | 1 to 5 | | 6 to 20 | | 20 to 80 | | More than 80 | |
Policy or Procedure	Mean	CV	Mean	CV	Mean	CV	Mean	CV
(1) The resolution of important independence questions should be documented.								
Importance	4.13	41%	4.24	13%	4.08	26%	4.91	6%
Usage	3.25	56%	3.01	44%	2.91	56%	4.73	11%
(2) Independence of mental attitude is emphasized during engagements.								
Importance	4.53	14%	4.52	18%	4.50	15%	4.68	15%
Usage	4.30	21%	4.15	25%	4.25	35%	4.38	19%
(3) Client lists are distributed to the staff and updated.								
Importance	2.67	70%	3.05	43%	3.75	23%	4.09	25%
Usage	2.98	55%	2.79	63%	2.40	52%	3.90	33%
(4) The firm has training sessions that periodically emphasize independence.								
Importance	3.13	48%	3.24	29%	3.83	19%	4.23	22%
Usage	2.43	55%	2.14	50%	2.29	51%	3.96	32%
(5) The firm periodically obtains written representations of compliance with independence policies and procedures from staff personnel.								
Importance	2.27	63%	2.95	39%	3.33	39%	4.73	15%
Usage	1.88	65%	1.70	58%	1.78	56%	4.69	23%
Number of respondents	9		21		13		16	

NOTE: The mean responses are based on a five-point scale. They can be interpreted according to where they fall within the following ranges:

Importance	Range	Usage	Range
Unimportant	1.00-1.5	Rare	1.25-1.88
Little importance	1.51-2.5	Occasional	1.89-3.13
Some importance	2.51-3.5	Common	3.14-4.38
Important	3.51-4.5	Almost always	4.39-5.00
Essential	4.51-5.0		

For example, an importance score of 1.81 indicates that the respondents viewed the procedure as being of little importance. CV represents coefficient of variation. The higher the coefficient of variation, the greater the variability in the responses of the CPA firm partners in a particular group. See Appendix C for a description of the study.

Table 6-2 Opinions on Independence Documentation

Statement	Number of Professional Personnel in Firm				
	1 to 5	6 to 20	20 to 80	More than 80	Total
Requiring firms to document unusual independence questions will inhibit their open discussion within the firm.					
Strongly agree	3.7	4.4	7.1	2.6	4.0
Agree	14.8	8.9	0.0	0.0	6.4
No opinion	22.2	15.6	28.6	5.1	15.2
Disagree	33.3	42.2	50.0	15.4	32.8
Strongly disagree	25.9	28.9	14.3	76.9	41.6
Mean	2.37	2.18	2.36	1.36	1.98
Number of CPAs responding	28	45	15	40	128

NOTE: All numbers, except means, are stated as a percentage of the column total responding. The means are based on a scale of 1 to 5, where "strongly disagree" is 1 and "strongly agree" is 5. See Appendix C for a description of the study.

Table 6-3 Independence. Summary Evaluation of Quality Control Policies and Procedures (for inclusion in a firm's quality control document).

Summarized AICPA Objective/Procedures to Implement	Procedure's Applicability to Firm					Comments
	N	R	LL	SL	SP	
1. Firm personnel must adhere to authoritative rules on independence.						
a. An individual or committee (state who) is responsible to:						
(i) Provide guidance and resolve questions.	H	H	H	H	H	
(ii) Seek advice from authoritative sources when necessary.	H	H	H	H	H	Sources are AICPA, SEC, state societies
2. Communicate independence policies and procedures to all personnel.						
a. Advise personnel of firm's policies and procedures.	H	H	H	H	H	Personnel manual and library are references
b. Independence of mental attitude is emphasized during engagements and training sessions.	H	H	H	H	H	Effective during engagements
c. Apprise personnel of pertinent clients, affiliates, etc.	H	H	H	H	H	In some firms, partners report their investments annually
d. Prepare client lists	H	H	H	M	L	
e. Maintain authoritative literature.	H	H	H	H	H	

	N	R	LL	SL	SP	
3. The principal auditor confirms the independence of another firm performing segments of the engagement.						
a. Inform personnel as to the content of independence representations that are to be obtained.	H	H	M	M	L	
b. Periodically obtain representations from affiliate or associate firms that are used in repeat engagements (state frequency and responsibility).	H	H	H	H	H	One year is the normal interval
4. Monitor compliance with policies and procedures.						
a. Periodically obtain written representations of compliance from firm personnel.	H	H	H	H	L	One year is the normal interval; Unnecessary for partners
b. Assign responsibility for resolving exceptions.	H	H	H	H	H	
c. Assign responsibility for obtaining independence representations.	H	H	H	H	H	If partners periodically report their investments, these are analyzed
d. Periodically review accounts receivable.	H	H	H	H	H	

Key:

H - High
M - Medium
L - Low

N - National or international firm
R - Regional firm
LL - Large Local firm (possibly two or three offices)
SL - Small Local firm (one office)
SP - Sole Practitioner (possibly one part-time staff member)

Table 6-4 Summary of Independence Documentation

Documentation — Purpose	AICPA Procedures
Quality control document — informs staff of policies and procedures	all
Authoritative standards and interpretations — reference source for personnel	2a
Personnel manual — communicates firm's independence policies and procedures; a check list might be used	2a
Accounting and auditing manual — contains procedures for when another firm is hired to do part of an audit	3a
Independence compliance letter — written representation from staff	4a
Client lists and update memo — apprise personnel of pertinent clients	2c

BIBLIOGRAPHY

Journal of Accountancy. "Special Report — POB Scope of Service Hearing." *Journal of Accountancy,* October 1978, pp. 20-28.

New York Society of CPAs. "Professional Conduct — Independence." *The CPA Journal,* March 1977, pp. 72-76.

Chapter 7

Acceptance and Continuance of Clients

This chapter analyzes the two AICPA objectives for client acceptance and continuance. The AICPA quality control policies and procedures stating the objectives and sample procedures are reprinted in Exhibit 7-5 and summarized with comments in Table 7-4. An example of a check list for assessing client risk, a client acceptance form, and a client continuance form are provided. Documentation of the client acceptance and continuance decisions is an essential quality control procedure.

The opinions of CPA firm partners on selected quality control procedures are presented in Tables 7-1, 7-2, and 7-3. These opinions should provide to practitioners some perspective on what other CPAs are thinking and doing with respect to quality control. For the reader's convenience, all tables and exhibits are presented at the end of the chapter.

OVERVIEW

More and more CPAs are coming to realize the importance of careful selection of audit clients. Too often, disappointed creditors and stockholders of a failing business sue the auditor to recover from their misfortunes. All auditors are familiar with the National Student Marketing,[1] Continental Vending,[2] and Yale Express cases.[3] From the 1136 Tenant's Corporation case,[4] CPAs learned the importance of using an engagement letter for all clients. While the Hochfelder case provides some hope of relief from third-party actions against auditors, the need for client acceptance and continuance policies is not diminished.

A decision to accept a new client or to continue serving a current client entails both practice management and business management considerations. The practice management considerations, as the term is used in this book, should be reflected in the firm's quality control policies and procedures. An auditor wants to avoid being associated with the financial statements of a company with a management of dubious integrity. If a client's management has a reputation for being unscrupulous, this can demean the auditor's reputation. Other practice management considerations include independence, appropriate audit expertise, capability to staff the engagement, reasons for changing auditors, and auditability.

For the business management aspect of client acceptance and continuance decisions, the focus is on profitability. Most CPA firms want a continuous flow of new clients in order to achieve their growth goals. The more satisfied clients, the more new client referrals there will be. Desirable new engagements are those which can be profitably billed at standard rates, where the client is growing, and where there is a promising opportunity for additional accounting and Management Advisory Service (MAS) services in the future. In addition to this basic profile, a client's desirability can be judged by the amount of its cooperation in providing information, its promptness in paying fees, the number of referrals by the client, the client's attitude toward the firm's staff, and the client's economic stability. Each CPA has his or her own level of tolerance for dealing with clients.

While peer reviewers examine only the practice management aspects of client acceptance and continuance, there is no reason why business management objectives and procedures must be segregated from practice management in developing procedures. In fact, one benefit of devising a new client acceptance and continuance system is to improve business management. Forms used in the client acceptance process can include space for business management factors to be evaluated. To meet quality assurance standards, the firm must have formalized procedures. The procedures must be adequately documented and communicated to professional personnel. This documentation requires some forms or a client file. The responsibility for client acceptance and continuance decisions must be fixed within the management group.

AUTHORITATIVE POLICIES AND PROCEDURES

The AICPA quality control policies and procedures are presented in Exhibit 7-5. The first objective covers acceptance of clients; the second covers continuance of clients. The same client selection criteria should be reflected in the procedures under both objectives. Examples of procedures are identified in Exhibit 7-5 by letters. Procedures are identified in the text by using the objective number and the letter, and possibly small Roman numerals (1a, (iv) for example). Common procedures and the peer reviewer's approach are discussed below for each objective.

Evaluate Prospective Clients

Objective 1: ESTABLISH PROCEDURES FOR EVALUATION OF PROSPECTIVE CLIENTS AND FOR THEIR APPROVAL AS CLIENTS.

An adequate quality assurance system has formalized procedures for evaluating all prospective accounting and auditing clients. Responsibility for approving new clients should be fixed. Some firms focus too much on the profitability of a prospective client. This may be understandable, since CPA firms, like other professionals, are in business to earn money. A quality assurance system should, however, cause a systematic evaluation of all pertinent factors.

Criteria

Obtaining financial information on a client (1a(i)) makes sense since the firm wants to appraise the nature of the accounting or auditing engagement. Also, CPA firms are careful in dealing with financially troubled organizations. Checking business references (1a(ii)) is a reasonable way of obtaining information on the prospective client's reputation. The extent of the investigation depends on the prospective client and the results of initial contacts. Generally, the investigation is easier for small clients. Documentation of phone calls and letters should be kept on file to allow for verification by peer reviewers. AICPA's *Communication Between Predecessor and Successor Auditors,* SAS No. 7, requires a successor auditor to attempt certain communications with the predecessor auditor. Thus procedure 1a(iii) seems appropriate for the quality control document.

Audit risk is an important consideration in assessing the possibility of future litigation arising out of a relationship with a prospective client. Procedure 1a(iv) suggests that criteria be developed for this analysis. Exhibit 7-1 is a check list of factors worthy of consideration, and a firm would want to include some of these criteria in its quality control document. Since an absolute measurement of risk is not possible, a firm must rely on careful evaluation of the criteria it establishes. Procedures 1a(v) and 1a(vi) are little more than common sense, but are nonetheless worthy of note. Client acceptance procedures might be stated in a firm's accounting and auditing manual rather than in its quality control document, with appropriate reference.

Table 7-1 presents CPAs' opinions on several sample procedures. Part 1a shows that the importance score for evaluating financial information increases with the size of the respondent's firm. Some of this difference can be attributed to the types of clients smaller firms have — small clients have less complex businesses, and their financial condition is easier to assess. Usage was estimated in the "occasional" range, except for the "more than 80" group. For references by bankers, lawyers, etc., the importance and usage scores were slightly higher for the "1 to 5" and "6 to 20'' groups. Independence considerations received higher importance and usage scores for all groups.

Documentation

Accounting and auditing client evaluation procedures should be documented in such a way that reviews can verify compliance. Although a memo is probably adequate, a form is a more effective method. Exhibit 7-2 is a very comprehensive client acceptance form that would be completed for every client. It shows that the information for audit clients and publicly-held clients would be more extensive than for other types of clients. In adopting this form, a firm would make additions or deletions to suit its practice. For example, check list items in Exhibit 7-1 could be incorporated into this form, or the form could refer to the check list.

Part 2 of Table 7-1 indicates CPAs' lack of enthusiasm for documenting the evaluation process. Again, the importance increases with firm size. The estimated usage was low, except for the largest firms. Thus, this is an area where many firms will be making significant changes.

Responsibility for obtaining new client information and approving the acceptance decision (1b) must be assigned. Referring to the bottom of Exhibit 7-2, note that the engagement partner provides the information on the form. Approval is required by the management committee in some cases; for example, for all audit engagements or for all publicly-held corporations. Exhibit 7-3 illustrates a shorter form that may be more suitable for smaller firms. This form follows the procedures specified by 1a(i) through (vi) in Exhibit 7-5.

Second Partner Approval

Whether written approval by the engagement partner and at least one other partner is required is an interesting question. I have found no definite statement in the professional standards or peer review manuals that two partners must approve engagements. However, the AICPA sample quality control documents have two partners approving all engagements.[5]

Table 7-1, part 3 sheds some light on this issue. Only CPAs from the largest firms viewed written authorization by second partners to be of great importance for all audits, and the usage among the largest firms was estimated to be high. The estimated usage was "occasional" for the smallest firms, and in the "rare" range for the "6 to 20" and "20 to 80" groups. (Note how the coefficient of variation is highest for the "1 to 5" group. Remember that the higher the coefficient, the greater the diversity of the responses within the group.)

The CPAs viewed second partner approval to be more important for risky audit engagements. The usage scores were higher in all cases, but they still were only in the "occasional" range, except for the largest firms. These responses seem to indicate that most firms will incorporate, at a minimum, second partner approval of risky audit engagements; this will be a significant change in procedure for many firms. In addition to this receptiveness to second partner approval, all of the quality control documents I have seen contain this procedure. Therefore (1) it seems advisable to have second partner approval of at least "risky" engagements, and (2) extending this approval requirement to all engagements seems appropriate in all but unusual cases.

Views on second partner approval for unaudited engagements are presented in parts 3c and 3d of Table 7-1. The importance and usage scores are just slightly lower than the results for audit engagements. Second partner approval of risky unaudited engagements seems to be a minimum level of quality assurance.

If a firm is contemplating a merger with another CPA firm, the quality control document might require that the acceptance criteria be applied to new clients gained from the merger. If not stated, this would be assumed anyway.

Communication and Monitoring

The need to communicate acceptance policies and procedures is obvious (1c). The quality control document or accounting and auditing manual would be used for this purpose. A sole practitioner, of course, need not bother with communication procedures.

Responsibility for administering and monitoring client acceptance procedures must be assigned. In a smaller firm, the same partner or committee could take both responsibilities. The partner with administrative responsibilities does not have to be the second partner who approves new clients. However, some segregation of responsibilities is generally desirable, so that a single partner does not have approval, administrative, and monitoring power. (Special circumstances might justify a departure from this rule.) To have a committee of partners perform all three functions is more understandable. The procedures for monitoring — such as an annual review of new clients — should be stated in the quality control document.

Peer Reviewers

External peer reviewers examine client acceptance policies and procedures to assess their adequacy. The documentation for a sample of new clients is reviewed to test compliance. Responsibility for approval, administration and monitoring are reviewed to determine whether these tasks are assigned to appropriate personnel.

Reevaluate Clients

Objective 2: EVALUATE CLIENTS AT THE END OF SPECIFIC PERIODS OR UPON THE OCCURRENCE OF SPECIFIED EVENTS TO DETERMINE WHETHER THE RELATIONSHIPS SHOULD BE CONTINUED.

Client continuance procedures are required because the client's circumstances might become unfavorable. The basic criteria for judging continuance should be the same as for acceptance. After the first audit, the auditor has better information for decision making. Procedure 2a suggests periodic reevaluation, and three years seems common. Since an auditor should be constantly alert to changes in circumstances, reevaluation might be confined to the occurrence of specified events, examples of which are specified under procedure 2a(ii). Other significant events might arise out of the most recent engagement, such as major disagreements with the client or suspicions about the client's integrity. A change in the independence of a client or an employee might cause reevaluation. An independence question might arise out of a merger by the CPA firm or the client. Procedure 2a(iii) requires consistency between acceptance and continuance criteria.

Responsibility for the continuance decision should be fixed (2b). The engagement partner can make this decision, because there is a monitoring process. Alternatively, the engagement partner could provide information and a recommendation to another partner or a committee for final approval. Whatever the procedure, the reevaluation and the conclusion reached must be documented.

Documentation

Exhibit 7-4 shows how the business management and practice management aspects of client review can be integrated. The instructions are on the form. The first five items cover business management. Item 6 requires consideration of the changes listed under 2a(ii) in Exhibit 7-5. This is an essential element of client continuance documentation. Note the documentation of the decision at the bottom. Priority A clients — the risky or publicly-held clients, or clients identified under a procedure like 2a(iii) — receive annual consideration. The form is generally included in the client's permanent file. An alternative is to document the review on the client record in the client master file. This record could be the original client acceptance form or some version of it. A second alternative is to have the client acceptance form reviewed or remade periodically. Another consideration is documentation for SEC-regulated clients. SEC's Form 8-K requirements might be stated in the quality control document, or referred to in the accounting and auditing manual.

Since the in-charge accountant and other staff members may contribute information to the client review process, it is important to communicate policies and procedures (2c).

Responsibility for administration and monitoring must be assigned (2d). A separation of these functions is desirable.

Peer Reviewers

The adequacy of continuance procedures and criteria are evaluated by reviewers. Compliance is tested by reviewing documentation. Remember, the design of the system should consider the reviewer's point of view. Documentation that is too elaborate causes problems for the reviewer. Unnecessary questions may be raised.

Not knowing the client, and being unable to talk to references, the reviewer is generally unable to duplicate the firm's feel for the client and its circumstances. Conversely, there are circumstances where client rejection is the obvious decision. This is a judgmental area of quality control, and the CPA firm has the right to make those judgments. If those judgments are wrong, the CPA firm must face the consequences, not the reviewer. The reviewer can only judge the system to see whether it is consistent with professional standards and is being followed.

Reviewers check the means for communicating policies and procedures. The assignment of responsibility for the continuance decision, administration, and monitoring are evaluated, based on the appropriateness of the personnel selected. Authority must be commensurate with responsibility.

GENERAL DESIGN

A sample general design for acceptance and continuance of clients is shown in Exhibit 7-6. The responsibilities for operating, communicating, and monitoring are divided among several partners. Partners A and B are a committee with authority to approve all client acceptance and continuance decisions. The accounting and auditing manual contains criteria, and serves as a communication function. Once approved by the partners, the general design can be converted into a section of the quality control document.

Client acceptance and continuance is an area where most firms need major modification to reach an adequate quality control system. The usage data in Table 7-1 suggested this; the data in Table 7-2 confirm it. The general lack of acceptance criteria is evidenced by the percentages for parts a and c in Table 7-2. Looking at part b, note that documentation is also uncommon. Part d reveals second partner authorization to be uncommon. Consistent with Table 7-1 data, usage of these procedures was common for the largest firms.

While use of the profession's new client acceptance and continuance procedures is not common in local firms, CPAs seem receptive to this change. This is evidenced by Table 7-3. A significant majority of respondents in all groups agreed that formal procedures will improve the decision process.

A summary of AICPA objectives and sample procedures to implement them is shown in Table 7-4. A procedure's applicability according to firm size is a generalization based upon current standards. Standards will evolve as the profession becomes more experienced with external peer reviews. Several characteristics of firms are recognized in the accounting profession's quality control programs as determinants of the appropriate quality control policies and procedures for CPA firms. Therefore, a firm should consider all of its characteristics in designing procedures and assigning responsibilities. Similarly, forms, check lists, and other documentation shown in this book and elsewhere should be modified to fit the individual firm's needs. Table 7-5 summarizes documentation.

Exhibit 7-1 Check List of Factors to Consider in Assessing Audit Risk of Clients and Prospective Clients

Instructions: Factors receiving "Yes" answers require further evaluation in making a decision.

1. Is the firm a publicly-held corporation?_____
2. Have any audit opinions in recent years not been unqualified?_____
3. Is the firm new in its industry?
4. Is the industry unstable or declining?_____
5. Is the firm financially unstable as indicated by:
   a. coverage ratios?_____
   b. favorable cash flow?_____
   c. debt/equity ratio?_____
   d. liquidity ratios?_____
   e. profit margins?_____
6. Is the firm experiencing problems obtaining new outside financing?_____
7. Has significantly new collateral been pledged to support existing obligations?_____
8. Do existing loan agreements restrict needed financing?_____
9. Has the firm's sales order backlog declined?_____
10. Has the industry's/competitive situation unfavorably changed recently?_____
11. Have the firm's customers, or a class of its customers, experienced difficulties as evidenced by smaller sales orders or slow payment of accounts receivable?_____
12. Do recent economic developments adversely affect this firm?_____
13. Has the firm ventured into new speculative projects?_____
14. Does management seem to desire to take all possible steps to have a favorable earnings picture?_____
15. Is management prone to too much secrecy?_____
16. Have there been significant tax adjustments by the IRS in recent years?_____
17. Have regulatory agencies imposed sanctions or penalties on the firm in recent years?_____
18. Does it appear that the firm will lose any significant lawsuits?_____
19. Is the firm involved in any new litigation?_____
20. Do the firm's accounting policies differ significantly from other firms in the industry?_____
21. Do changes in operating management, directors, or ownership indicate that the firm's operations or management have been adversely affected?_____
22. Has there been an unexplained change in legal counsel?_____
23. Has the scope of the auditor's work been limited by the firm's actions?_____
24. Are there major weaknesses in the internal control system?_____
25. Are there any unusual related-party transactions?_____

Exhibit 7-2 Sample New Client Acceptance Form

```
(Specific firm information deleted.)
Section A:  For all new clients
  1. Client Name_____
  2. Address_____
  3. Nature of Business_____
  4. Date Business Started_____Fiscal Year End_____
  5. Type of Client:
        _____Individual       _____Partnership     _____Corporation
        _____Trust            _____Estate          _____Exempt
        _____Pension/Profit Sharing
  6. Nature of Engagement:
        _____Opinion Audit         _____Tax Return Preparation
        _____Unaudited Statements  _____MAS
        _____Business Consulting   _____Accounting Services
        _____Tax Planning & Consulting
        _____Other (Describe)_____
  7. Estimated Fee $_____ How Determined (Book, Fixed fee, Discount,
     etc.)
     _____
  8. Billing arrangement (retainer, monthly, annual, etc.)_____
  9. Estimate of manpower requirements (Grade of personnel & time of year)____
     _____
 10. Nature of Referral:
        Referred by_____Business_____
        Relationship to firm_____
        Other matters with referrer_____
 11. Attorneys_____
     Other Outside Advisers_____
 12. Can we expect to be retained on a continuing basis?
     Yes_____ No_____
 13. Will any other of our offices also be servicing the client?
     Yes_____ No _____
     If yes, list offices and degree of participation_____
     _____
 14. Have client's returns been examined by IRS? (For tax and accounting
     clients)_____
     If known, state last year examined and nature of significant changes for
     the past few years, if any_____
```

```
Section B:  For audit clients
  1. Name of Principals:
```

			Previous Business
Name	Title	% Owned	(if known)
_____	_____	_____	_____
_____	_____	_____	_____
_____	_____	_____	_____

```
  2. Previous relationship with principals_____
  3. Any known independence problems?_____
  4. If proposed client is not publicly held, submit copy of recent financial
     statements._____Check if client has not completed initial year of business.
```

Exhibit 7-2 continued

5. If last annual report is not available, list for last two years gross
   revenues and net income.

Period	Gross Revenues	Net Income After Tax

   Equity $_____(latest year end)
6. Is the client required to report to any governmental agency? (other than
   tax)
   _____

7. Subsidiaries:

Name	Fiscal Year	Nature of Business	Audited by firm or others

8. Accountants being replaced_____
9. Why?_____
10. Will previous accountants cooperate with us?   Yes____   No____
11. Give details of communication with prior accountants (dates, method, etc.)
    and state whether they indicated any accounting or professional problems
    prior to their replacement. (Attach copy of correspondence with prior
    accountants or memorandum of conversation with prior accountants--See SAS #7.)
    _____

12. Does the company appear to have a "going concern" problem?
    Yes____   No____   N/A____
13. Have previous accountants been paid?
    Yes____   No____   N/A____
14. Condition of books and records (based on inquiry and review)
    Excellent____   Good____   Fair____   Bad____
    Our Responsibility to set up____
15. Are books susceptible to audit of prior year?_____
    Yes____   No____   N/A____
16. Do any accounting or auditing problems appear to exist?_____
17. Have we any knowledge of charges of violation of state or federal
    securities or tax laws (other than normal tax exams) which have ever been
    made against the company or any of its principals?_____
    If yes, set forth details and outcome_____

18. Have we knowledge of any significant litigation or other legal proceedings
    pending against the company or any of its principals?   Yes____   No____
    If yes, set forth nature of material items and possible outcome_____

19. Investigative reports and references:
    Obtain a D&B or information from a similar reference source
    Banks (name)_____
    Other_____

Exhibit 7-2 continued

Section C: For Audits of Publicly Held Companies
1. Is client a public company?   Yes_____   No_____   If listed, give
   exchange_____
   If yes, give a summary of outstanding securities including ownership of
   control group

_____

2. Submit copy of last annual report or Form 10-K. (Also prospectus, if
   issued during the last two years.)
3. Has necessary Form 8-K information been filed regarding replacement of
   accountants?   Yes_____   No_____   If no, comment_____
4. Obtain and submit (at a later date, if necessary) copy of accountants'
   letter accompany Form 8-K.
5. Names of Professional Advisers:
   Underwriter_____
   Attorney-SEC (if different)_____
Comments:_____

_____

Submitted by:_____   _____
                        Partner   Date
Approved:_____   _____
            Management Committee (if applicable)   Date

_____

Management Committee Partner or Office Managing Partner   Date

Source: Reprinted with permission from the *CPA Journal*, published by the New York State Society of
Certified Public Accountants.

Exhibit 7-3 Acceptance Form for Accounting and Auditing Clients

Client Name_____

Nature of Business_____

Nature of Engagement_____

_____ Year End_____

Referred by_____

Client Evaluation ("Yes" answers should be explained on the back of this form if additional space is needed):

1. Does available financial information on the client indicate any problems of an accounting, auditing, or solvency nature?_____
2. Do the client's tax returns indicate any problems?_____
3. Have inquiries to the following indicated any potential problems? (Indicate the date of the inquiry in the bracketed space.)
   a. Attorneys(____) _____
   b. Bankers(____) _____
   c. Credit sources(____) _____
   d. Predecessor accountants(____) _____
   e. _____(____) _____
4. Are there any unusual risks associated with this client?_____
5. Are there any independence problems?_____
6. Are there any foreseeable problems in servicing the client?_____
7. Will accepting the client violate any regulatory agency requirements?___
8. Is the client involved in litigation that will affect the fairness of the financial statements or complicate the audit?_____

Submitted by_____ _____
                                                              Date

Approved by_____ _____
                                                              Date

Engagement letter mailed _____
                               Date

Exhibit 7-4 Client Continuance Form

(This form is to be completed tri-annually for priority B clients
and annually for priority A clients. Complete it at the end of
the client's fiscal year prior to the preparation of an engagement
letter for the new year. The completed form is to be discussed at
the partners' meeting.)

Client Name_____ Number_____
Nature of Services: Fees Collected-Past two years
                                                     (approximately)

_____   _____

	Circle one number
Evaluation criteria:	Poor				Good
1. Potential for upgrading of--					
a. Services	1	2	3	4	5
b. Fees	1	2	3	4	5
2. Collection of fees--					
a. Collection of full amount billed	1	2	3	4	5
b. Collection period	1	2	3	4	5
3. Potential that our exposure as to liability will be minimal (considering nature of services).	1	2	3	4	5
4. Client's promotion of our firm to others.	1	2	3	4	5
5. Client's attitude as to our--					
a. Professional Personnel	1	2	3	4	5
b. Firm as a whole	1	2	3	4	5

6. Since the last evaluation, have there been any significant changes in
management, directors, ownership, legal counsel, financial condition,
litigation status, nature of the client's business, or scope of the
engagement? If yes, explain the change and any adverse effect on
client continuance._____

_____

_____

Prepared by _____ Date _____

Results of Consideration:
  1. Opinion of person in charge of engagement_____

_____

  2. Results of discussion at partners' meeting - Agree with opinion of in-
    charge accountant_____
    Other_____

Exhibit 7-5 AICPA Quality Control Policies and Procedures for Acceptance and Continuance of Clients

1. **Establish procedures for evaluation of prospective clients and for their approval as clients.**
   a. Consider evaluation procedures such as the following before accepting a client:
      (i) Obtain and review available financial information regarding the prospective client, such as annual reports, interim financial statements, registration statements, Forms 10-K, other reports to regulatory agencies, and income tax returns.
      (ii) Inquire of third parties as to any information regarding the prospective client and its management and principals which may have a bearing on evaluating the prospective client. Inquiries may be directed to the prospective client's bankers, legal counsel, investment banker, underwriter, and others in the financial or business community who may have such knowledge. Credit reports may also be useful.
      (iii) Communicate with the predecessor auditor as required by auditing standards. Inquiries should include questions regarding facts that might bear on the integrity of management, on disagreements with management as to accounting principles, auditing procedures, or other similarly significant matters, and on the predecessor's understanding as to the reasons for the change of auditors.
      (iv) Consider circumstances which would cause the firm to regard the engagement as one requiring special attention or presenting unusual risks.
      (v) Evaluate the firm's independence and ability to service the prospective client. In evaluating the firm's ability, consider needs for technical skills, knowledge of the industry, and personnel.
      (vi) Determine that acceptance of the client would not violate applicable regulatory agency requirements and the codes of professional ethics of the AICPA or a state CPA society.
   b. Designate an individual or group, at appropriate management levels, to evaluate the information obtained regarding the prospective client and to make the acceptance decision.
      (i) Consider types of engagements that the firm would not accept or which would be accepted only under certain conditions.
      (ii) Provide for documentation of the conclusion reached.

Source: Copyright © 1976, 1978 by the American Institute of Certified Public Accountants, Inc. Reprinted, with permission, from *Voluntary Quality Control Review Program for CPA Firms.*

   c. Inform appropriate personnel of the firm's policies and procedures for accepting clients.

   d. Designate responsibility for administering and monitoring compliance with the firm's policies and procedures for acceptance of clients.

2. **Evaluate clients at the end of specific periods or upon the occurrence of specified events to determine whether the relationships should be continued.**

   a. Specify conditions which require evaluation of a client to determine whether the relationship should be continued. Conditions could include —
   - (i) The expiration of a time period.
   - (ii) A significant change since the last evaluation, including a major change in one or more of the following:
     - (a) Management.
     - (b) Directors.
     - (c) Ownership.
     - (d) Legal counsel.
     - (e) Financial condition.
     - (f) Litigation status.
     - (g) Nature of the client's business.
     - (h) Scope of the engagement.
   - (iii) The existence of conditions which would have caused the firm to reject a client had such conditions existed at the time of the initial acceptance.

   b. Designate an individual or group, at appropriate management levels, to evaluate the information obtained and to make continuance decisions.
   - (i) Consider types of engagements that the firm would not continue or which would be continued only under certain conditions.
   - (ii) Provide for documentation of the conclusion reached.

   c. Inform appropriate personnel of the firm's policies and procedures for continuing clients.

   d. Designate responsibility for administering and monitoring compliance with the firm's policies and procedures for continuance of clients.

Exhibit 7-6 Example of General Design for Acceptance and Continuance of Clients

Operational Responsibilities:

The engagement partner is responsible for completing the new client acceptance form and making a recommendation. Partner A and Partner B must approve all new clients. Partner B is responsible for administering new client acceptance, which includes a review of the engagement letter. The engagement partner is responsible for completing the client continuance form (when required) and making a recommendation. Partner A and Partner B make the continuance decision. Partner B is responsible for administering client continuance.

Communication:

The accounting and auditing manual contains procedures for client acceptance and continuance. Partner B is responsible for maintaining this section of the manual.

Monitoring:

Partner A is responsible for making an annual review of client acceptance and continuance during the month of December. A report is made at the December partners' meeting.

Documentation:

1. Accounting and auditing manual — contains criteria for client acceptance and continuance, audit risk check list, procedures for client review
2. Engagement letter
3. New client acceptance form
4. Client continuance form
5. Minutes of partners' meetings

NOTE: The profile firm is described in Appendix A.

Table 7-1 Opinions on Acceptance and Continuance of Clients' Policies and Procedures

Quality Control Policy or Procedure	Number of Professional Personnel in Firm							
	1 to 5		6 to 20		20 to 80		More than 80	
	Mean	CV	Mean	CV	Mean	CV	Mean	CV
(1) The firm has procedures for evaluating prospective clients on the basis of:								
a. Financial information								
Importance	2.65	48%	3.34	26%	3.71	29%	4.53	14%
Usage	2.50	55%	2.61	50%	2.75	43%	4.53	17%
b. References by bankers, lawyers, etc.								
Importance	3.09	39%	3.63	25%	3.64	28%	4.53	17%
Usage	2.86	47%	2.90	39%	2.75	35%	4.45	20%
c. Independence considerations								
Importance	3.79	34%	4.05	18%	4.29	17%	4.71	12%
Usage	3.41	42%	3.39	38%	3.00	35%	4.65	14%
(2) The firm documents the evaluation process for new clients.								
Importance	2.61	56%	3.20	32%	3.57	34%	4.47	24%
Usage	2.26	65%	2.10	57%	1.75	45%	4.33	26%
(3) For accounting firms that are partnerships, written authorization of acceptance of new clients is required by at least the engagement partner and one other partner for:								
a. All audit engagements								
Importance	2.68	53%	2.80	41%	3.00	43%	4.47	20%
Usage	2.44	61%	1.81	57%	1.84	50%	4.43	24%
b. Just risky audit engagements								
Importance	3.44	40%	3.49	34%	3.85	23%	4.61	21%
Usage	2.89	54%	2.35	61%	2.76	54%	4.60	22%
c. All unaudited engagements								
Importance	2.69	48%	2.71	44%	2.85	40%	4.18	26%
Usage	1.95	57%	1.74	58%	1.51	35%	4.05	32%
d. Just risky unaudited engagements								
Importance	3.33	39%	3.35	35%	3.46	30%	4.18	27%
Usage	2.91	51%	2.23	56%	2.24	55%	3.98	33%
Number of respondents	16		42		15		39	

Table 7-1 continued

NOTE: The mean responses are based on a five-point scale. They can be interpreted according to where they fall within the following ranges:

Importance	Range	Usage	Range
Unimportant	1.00-1.5	Rare	1.25-1.88
Little importance	1.51-2.5	Occasional	1.89-3.13
Some importance	2.51-3.5	Common	3.14-4.38
Important	3.51-4.5	Almost always	4.39-5.00
Essential	4.51-5.0		

For example, an importance score of 1.81 indicates that the respondents viewed the procedure as being of little importance. CV represents coefficient of variation. The higher the coefficient of variation, the greater the variability in the responses of the CPA firm partners in a particular group. See Appendix C for a description of the study.

Table 7-2 Attitudes Toward Quality Control Procedures

Question	Affirmative Responses Grouped by Number of Professional Personnel in Firm			
	1 to 5	6 to 20	20 to 80	More than 80
Does your firm have formal procedures for acceptance and continuance of clients that:				
a. Establish criteria for acceptance?	21%	22%	13%	88%
b. Require documentation of acceptance for some clients?	29%	20%	27%	95%
c. Require identification of high-risk clients?	36%	33%	20%	90%
d. Acceptance of a client requires authorization by at least two partners?	18%	13%	13%	80%

Table 7-3 Client Acceptance and Continuance Procedures Improving the Decision Process

Statement	Number of Professional Personnel in Firm				
	1 to 5	6 to 20	20 to 80	More than 80	Total
Requiring firms to establish formal policies and procedures on the acceptance and continuance of clients will improve the decision process.					
Strongly agree	26.9	35.6	57.1	60.0	44.0
Agree	53.8	57.8	42.9	35.0	48.0
No opinion	11.5	4.4	0.0	2.5	4.8
Disagree	3.8	0.0	0.0	2.5	1.5
Strongly disagree	3.8	2.2	0.0	0.0	1.6
Mean	3.96	4.24	4.57	4.53	4.31
Number of CPAs responding	28	45	15	40	128

NOTE: All numbers, except means, are stated as a percentage of the total responding. The means are based on a scale of 1 to 5, where "strongly disagree" is 1 and "strongly agree" is 5. See Appendix C for a description of the study.

Table 7-4 Acceptance and Continuance of Clients. Summary Evaluation of Quality Control Policies and Procedures (for inclusion in a firm's quality control document).

Summarized AICPA Objective/Procedures to Implement	Procedure's Applicability to Firm					Comments
	N	R	LL	SL	SP	
1. Establish procedures for evaluation of prospective clients and for their approval.						
a. Sample evaluation procedures						
(i) Review available financial information about prospective clients.	H	H	H	H	H	Document the analysis
(ii) Reference inquiries are made to bankers, attorneys, and others.	H	H	H	H	H	Extent depends on client; document references
(iii) Inquiries appropriate under GAAS are made to predecessor auditors.	H	H	H	H	H	Document inquiries
(iv) The risk associated with the client is assessed (refer to firm guidelines, if any).	H	H	H	H	H	Document analysis
(v) The firm's independence and ability to adequately serve potential clients are evaluated.	H	H	H	H	H	Document evaluation
(vi) Prospective clients should be reviewed to assure that acceptance will not violate professional ethics or regulatory requirements.	H	H	H	H	H	Document evaluation
b. Responsibility for administering the acceptance of clients is fixed (state who).	H	H	H	H	H	Document conclusions
c. Inform appropriate personnel.	H	H	H	H	NA	

	N	R	LL	SL	SP	
d. Responsibility for administering and monitoring compliance is assigned (state who).	H	H	H	H	NA	
2. Clients are evaluated periodically or upon the occurrence of certain events to determine whether the relationship should be continued.						
a. Periodic reevaluations are made of existing clients.	H	H	H	H	H	Frequency depends on risk and other characteristics
b. Responsibility for continuance decisions is fixed (state who).	H	H	H	H	H	Document decision
c. Inform appropriate personnel.	H	H	H	H	NA	
d. Adherence to continuance policies and procedures is monitored (state how).	H	H	H	H	NA	

N = National or international firm
R = Regional firm
LL = Large Local firm (possibly two or three offices)
SL = Small Local firm (one office)
SP = Sole Practitioner (possibly one part-time staff member)

H= High
M= Medium
L= Low

Table 7-5 Summary of Acceptance and Continuance of Clients Documentation

Documentation — Purpose	AICPA Procedures
Quality control document — informs staff of policies and procedures	all
Accounting and auditing manual — contains criteria for client acceptance and continuance, procedures for client review	1a,1b 1c 2a,2c
New client acceptance form — document and guide new client evaluation	1a, 1b
Client continuance form — document periodic reevaluation of clients	2b
Minutes of partners' meetings — record monitoring process	2d
Engagement letter — document scope and terms of engagement	1b

NOTES

1. United States v. Natelli (2nd Cir. 1975).
2. United States v. Simon, 425 F.2d 796 (2nd Cir. 1969).
3. Fischer v. Kletz, 266 F. Supp. 180 (S.D.N.Y. 1967).
4. 1136 Tenants' Corp. v. Max Rothenberg and Co., 27 A.2d 830, 277 N.Y.S.2d 996 (N.Y. Ct. App. 1967).
5. American Institute of Certified Public Accountants, *Sample Quality Control Documents for Local CPA Firms* (New York, N.Y.: AICPA, 1977), p. 17, 36.

BIBLIOGRAPHY

AICPA. *Sample Quality Control Documents for Local CPA Firms.* New York, N.Y.: AICPA, 1977.

Block, Max. "Engagement and Alternative Letters." *New York CPA Journal,* 1973, pp. 45-48.

Block, Max. "Screening Prospective Clients." *The CPA Journal,* August 1974, pp. 67-69.

Foundation for Accounting Education. *Engagement and Alternative Letters.* New York, N.Y.: Foundation for Accounting Education, 1978.

Grimsley, James. "Client Evaluation." *Journal of Accountancy,* November 1975, pp. 86-88.

The Practical Accountant. "When to Fire a Client." *The Practical Accountant,* November/December 1977, pp. 47-48.

Chapter 8

Hiring

This chapter analyzes the three AICPA objectives for hiring. The AICPA quality control policies and procedures stating the objectives and sample procedures are reprinted in Exhibit 8-5 and summarized with comments in Table 8-2. An example of a professional employment application, an interview evaluation form, a staff orientation check list, and a personnel manual check list are provided. Hiring documentation is summarized in Table 8-3.

Since a sole practitioner has no employees, the hiring element can be omitted from the firm's quality control document. If part-time or per diem professionals are used, procedures for hiring them should be documented.

OVERVIEW

The supply of new accountants is increasing each year. Many traditional liberal arts colleges have now established accounting curricula. More and better students are being attracted to the long-established accounting programs at colleges and universities. The AICPA's figures on the supply and demand for accounting graduates have shown an increasing excess supply in recent years. There also seems to be a better supply of experienced personnel. It is becoming common to see staff personnel move from larger firms to smaller ones after gaining several years of experience. While there is still competition for the best accounting graduates, recruiting has never been better for firms.

Since most firms have established procedures for hiring, the major effect of the profession's quality control standards is to require more documentation. A firm should plan to meet personnel needs at all levels. Qualifications and guidelines for evaluating personnel must be established. An orientation program or procedure for new personnel must be developed. These basic procedures are needed to assure that qualified personnel are available to perform client services. A sole practitioner can omit hiring from his or her quality control document if there are no plans to hire professional personnel.

AUTHORITATIVE POLICIES AND PROCEDURES

The AICPA quality control policies and procedures are shown in Exhibit 8-5. Firms should establish policies and procedures to accomplish the three objectives listed. Examples of procedures are identified in Exhibit 8-5 by letters, and are identified in the text by using the objective number, a letter, and Roman numerals (1b(ii), for example). Hiring is the easiest element of quality control to handle because procedures are well-established in firms. Common procedures and the peer reviewer's approach are discussed below for each objective.

Maintain a Program

Objective 1: MAINTAIN A PROGRAM DESIGNED TO OBTAIN QUAL-IFIED PERSONNEL BY PLANNING FOR PERSONNEL NEEDS, ESTAB-LISHING HIRING OBJECTIVES, AND SETTING QUALIFICATIONS FOR THOSE INVOLVED IN THE HIRING FUNCTION.

Having a system for hiring qualified personnel is necessary for a firm's continuity and growth. The degree of formality in planning (1a) for personnel needs increases with the firm's size, because it is easier for large firms to quantify and predict personnel needs. An office with 200 professional personnel may be able to predict that it will need 30 entrants for the coming year. On the other hand, an office with 12 professional personnel probably can only guess that its needs will be "one or two people." A firm's program for achieving hiring objectives (1b) need not be very formalized for smaller firms. It could simply be one item on the agenda of partners' meetings. For larger firms with more people involved in recruiting, the program should be more formalized, so that an organized recruiting effort is possible. It would include the number of staff to be hired at each level and possibly a recruiting brochure. Persons involved in hiring should be informed of the firm's personnel needs and hiring objectives (1c). For smaller firms, written communication is not necessary.

In all firms, responsibility for recruiting decisions must be assigned (1d). If a hiring element exists, a sole practitioner obviously has this responsibility, Many firms have a personnel partner with this responsibility, although other partners in these firms interview prospective applicants and make recommendations. Sometimes, the responsibility for a decision depends on the staff level of the position opening. A monitoring process must also be followed (1e). A committee approach might be followed, or recruiting might be discussed periodically at partners' meetings.

Table 8-1 presents the survey data on hiring. Only 100 of the questionnaires mailed to the CPA firm partners contained queries on hiring, because it is an uncomplicated element of quality control. Most of the responses were by CPAs in the "6 to 20" group, and the analysis here focuses on these. The respondents in the "6 to 20" group viewed a documented formal hiring program to be of "some importance." However, the estimated usage was in the "rare" range. Making a periodic review of hiring results to evaluate the accomplishment of hiring goals and personnel needs was viewed to be of greater importance. The estimated usage was viewed to be "occasional." For the four respondents from the largest firms, these scores were very high; For the three respondents from the smallest firms, the scores were very low.

Peer Reviewers

Reviewers check to see if responsibility for hiring decisions is clearly fixed with persons in positions of adequate authority. Methods for planning and monitoring are reviewed for adequacy.

Establish Qualifications

Objective 2: ESTABLISH QUALIFICATIONS AND GUIDELINES FOR EVALUATING POTENTIAL HIREES AT EACH PROFESSIONAL LEVEL.

In making a hiring decision, an interviewee is evaluated on the basis of established standards. It is not possible to make an intelligent hiring decision without some desired qualifications in mind. Objective 2 requires the establishment of qualifications and guidelines at each professional level. These qualifications are embodied in job descriptions for each staff level. Typically, the job descriptions are contained in a personnel manual, but they can be included in a quality control document. Examples are included in the AICPA sample documents.[1] Other examples are referred to in the bibliography.

Documentation

While job descriptions show necessary qualifications, specific personal attributes and credentials must be identified. These should be summarized in the quality control document. They are evidenced in a firm's application form and interview evaluation form. Exhibit 8-1 presents a very comprehensive application form from the *MAP Handbook*. It covers all of the examples listed under procedure 2b, and more. As with all forms, the application form should be adapted to meet a firm's needs. For example, Exhibit 8-1 does not provide a specific space for hobbies and personal interests. Instead, this information can be volunteered in the "Comments" section on page 2. A possible reason for this design is that the interviewer naturally asks about these attributes.

Exhibit 8-2 is an interview evaluation form. It contains common characteristics sought in professionals. In designing its form, a firm should take note of all characteristics that seem important. These characteristics should reflect the firm's recent hiring decisions, and be consistent with advancement criteria.

The opinions on documentation in part 3 of Table 8-1 are somewhat surprising. The importance score for the "6 to 20" group is in the "important" range. The usage was estimated at the bottom of the "occasional" range.

Atypical Situations

Having procedures for resolving atypical situations is suggested by procedure 2c. Rather than have an elaborate set of guidelines, these situations can be referred to a committee or to a partners' meeting for resolution on the basis of their individual merits. For example, Partner X might be authorized to hire all staff personnel. However, when considering relatives of staff members, clients, former employees, and client employees, Partners X, Y and Z might comprise a committee with final authority to make a decision.

Table 8-1 reports on hiring policies to cover atypical situations. These procedures were viewed as "important" by the CPAs in the "6 to 20" group. The estimated usage was only "occasional" for the smaller firms.

Documentation and Procedures

Common sense would dictate that an applicant's credentials be documented. Everyone has heard stories of faked credentials — such as "scientists" who never actually received a Ph.D. Typical credentials are shown under procedure 2d.

In Table 8-1, we see that the documenting of credentials was viewed as "important" by all CPAs. However, usage was estimated to be only "common," which indicates a need for new procedures in some firms.

Procedure 2e calls for a description of a firm's interviewing procedures. Typically, an interviewee talks to several people, and comments are made to the partner with the authority to make the hiring decision. Alternatively, a vote might be taken at a partners' meeting. If a firm has a history of mergers — or if a merger is likely — the quality control document might describe the procedures for evaluating the personnel of the merged firm.

Peer Reviewers

To evaluate hiring criteria, reviewers examine interview forms and application forms. They review personnel files to see the correlation between these criteria and the people hired. As evidence of this correlation, firms should consider retaining the application and rating forms of those not hired. Retaining these for a year or two will also be evidence of the firm's total hiring effort. While desirable, this procedure does not seem to be required at this time. Personnel files are reviewed to determine if there has been compliance with the firm's procedures, as well as adequate documentation.

Communicate Personnel Policies

Objective 3: INFORM APPLICANTS AND NEW PERSONNEL OF THE FIRM'S POLICIES AND PROCEDURES RELEVANT TO THEM.

Personnel policies and procedures must be effectively communicated if they are to be meaningful and effective. I have often talked with new employees of smaller firms who do not understand their firms' personnel policies. They do not know about all the employee benefits. Some do not even understand how overtime is handled in computing compensation. This situation is undesirable because it creates uncertainty. Studies have found that entrants — whether or not they've been informed about their firm's personnel policies — have great anxiety about their initial accounting job.[2] Firms should make efforts to avoid creating any unnecessary uncertainty.

A personnel manual is a handy device for accomplishing the third objective. Even a short manual is helpful for a small firm. Logically, the detail of the manual would increase with firm size, so that everyone would know what the rules are. If a rule is written in the manual, a staff person cannot argue convincingly that he did not know about that rule. The survey questionnaire asked the CPA firm partners to indicate whether their firm had a personnel manual. Grouped by the number of professional personnel in the respondents' firms, the number of affirmative responses were:

1 to 5	36%
6 to 20	67%
20 to 80	67%
More than 80	100%

Personnel manuals seem to be very common for all but the smallest firms.

Exhibit 8-3 is an example of a staff orientation check list. While an orientation check list does not have to be this comprehensive, this example covers most relevant areas.

Exhibit 8-4 is a personnel manual check list. It includes items for possible inclusion in a personnel manual. All of these would not have to be covered. Again, what is included depends on the firm, and size is a major factor.

Peer Reviewers

Peer reviewers check to see whether the communication of personnel policies and procedures is effective. If a firm has a personnel manual, it is examined for adequacy. If a firm has no manual, recent hirees may be interviewed. The adequacy of the orientation process is evaluated.

GENERAL DESIGN

A general design for hiring is shown in Exhibit 8-6. Partner A has the primary recruiting responsibility, and the other partners participate in the process. While Partner C is responsible for maintaining the manual, the other partners must approve changes. After approval by the partners, this general design can be converted into the hiring section of the quality control document.

A summary of the AICPA objectives, and sample procedures to implement them, is shown in Table 8-2. Each procedure's applicability according to firm size is a generalization based upon current standards. Standards will evolve as the profession becomes more experienced with external peer reviews. Several characteristics of firms are recognized in the accounting profession's quality control programs as determinants of the appropriate quality control policies and procedures for CPA firms. Therefore, a firm must consider all of its characteristics in designing procedures and assigning responsibilities. Similarly, forms, check lists, and other documentation shown in this book and elsewhere must be modified to fit the individual firm's needs. Table 8-3 summarizes documentation.

Exhibit 8-1 Professional Employment Application
(Firm name) Certified Public Accountants

(Firm name) **Certified Public Accountants**
Professional Employment Application

(Please print in ink.)

Name

Present address	Last		First			Middle	
Permanent address	No. and street	City	State	Zip code	(Area code)	Telephone	
	No. and street	City	State	Zip code	(Area code)	Telephone	

Personal

Social security no. _____

Have you ever been bonded? ☐ Yes ☐ No

Has your application for bond ever been rejected?
☐ Yes ☐ No

Have you ever been arrested, summoned, or arraigned in a court *(other than for a traffic misdemeanor)?*
☐ Yes ☐ No
(If yes, please explain either under Comments or in an attachment.)

Have you ever been denied government security clearance?
☐ Yes ☐ No *(If yes, please explain either under Comments or in an attachment.)*

Military

Military record *(Armed Forces—United States)*:

Service and branch _____

Date entered _____ Date discharged _____

Primary function _____

Final rank _____

Active reserve obligation remaining _____ years

Interests

What is your primary field of interest?
☐ Accounting and auditing ☐ Taxes
☐ Management advisory services
☐ Other *(indicate)* _____

What are your location preferences?
1st choice _____ 2nd _____ 3rd _____

Indicate extent to which you are willing to travel _____

Are you willing to work overtime? ☐ Yes ☐ No

Annual compensation expected $ _____

On what date are you available to begin employment? _____

Referred to us by? _____

Physical data

Condition of health _____

_____

_____

_____

_____

_____

Vision _____

Employment data

Previous employment *(List chronologically with most recent employment first—include both permanent and part-time.)*

Name and address of employer	Dates		Kind of work	Compensation		Immediate supervisor	Reason for leaving
	From	To		Start	End		

References
(Include only one college faculty member; do not include former employers or relatives.)

	Name	Address	Title or occupation	Years known
1.				
2.				
3.				

10/77 Rev.

Source: Copyright © 1975, 1976, 1977 by the American Institute of Certified Public Accountants, Inc. Reprinted, with permission, from *Management of an Accounting Practice Handbook.*

Exhibit 8-1 continued

Education			
High school	**College or university**	**College or university**	**College or university**
Name	Name	Name	Name
City and state	City and state	City and state	City and state
From___ To___ Attended	From___ To___ Attended	From___ To___ Attended	From___ To___ Attended
Mo. and yr. of grad.	Degree — Mo. and yr. of grad.	Degree — Mo. and yr. of grad.	Degree — Mo. and yr. of grad
☐ Top 10 percent	Major	Major	Major
☐ Top 25 percent	Grade point averages: Overall ___	Grade point averages: Overall ___	Grade point averages: Overall ___
☐ Top 50 percent	Major ___	Major ___	Major ___
☐ Lower 50 percent	Accounting ___	Accounting ___	Accounting ___
of class of ___ Number	Grade point equivalent of "A" ___	Grade point equivalent of "A" ___	Grade point equivalent of "A" ___
	Rank in class: ___ out of ___	Rank in class: ___ out of ___	Rank in class: ___ out of ___

Distribution of grades expressed in hours.	Grades	Acctg.	English	Other	Acctg.	English	Other	Acctg.	English	Other
	A or B									
	C or lower									
		Semester hours ☐ Quarter hours ☐			Semester hours ☐ Quarter hours ☐			Semester hours ☐ Quarter hours ☐		

No. of hours worked per week in outside employment while in college _____ Percent of college expenses earned _____ percent
AICPA test scores: Orientation ___ Level I ___ Level II ___   College board scores: Verbal ___ Math ___ Total ___
Graduate school entrance scores: Verbal _____ Math _____ Other graduate entrance scores _____

(Please fill in sections on Distribution of Grades, AICPA Test scores, and Board scores to the best of your ability; explain under Comments if you do not have your records immediately at hand. In reference to your Test and Board scores, it would be helpful if you could note whether they are "raw" or "percentile" scores.)

Attainments	**Activities**
Scholarships and awards _____	Participation in school activities (e.g., class organizations, athletics, publications and offices held in each):
Honors: ☐ Beta Gamma Sigma ☐ Phi Beta Kappa ☐ Beta Alpha Psi ☐ Other _____	_____
CPA status: Have taken exam ☐ Yes ☐ No	_____
If yes, indicate: State _____ Date _____	_____
Subjects passed: ☐ Auditing ☐ Law ☐ Problems ☐ Theory	_____
CPA certificate State of _____ Year ___ If no, indicate semester credit hours:	_____
Business Law ___ Finance ___ Economics ___	_____
Other professional achievements _____	_____

Comments
Use this space for further information you wish to give: _____

Have you previously applied to our firm for a position? ☐ Yes ☐ No If yes, give city or school _____ and year_____
Do you have any employment commitment? ☐ Yes ☐ No If yes, explain _____
In making this application for employment with _____ (Firm name) _____ I grant permission for the firm to contact all references and former employers and to obtain school transcripts.

_____ (Signature)   _____ (date)

We are an Equal Opportunity Employer.

10/77 Rev.

108

Exhibit 8-2 Interview Evaluation Form

Name_____ Date_____

Current Address_____ Tel. No._____

_____ Available_____

Rating Category	Poor	Avg.	Good	Very Good	Excel.
Appearance	1	2	3	4	5
Communication	1	2	3	4	5
Intelligence	1	2	3	4	5
Motivation	1	2	3	4	5
Leadership Potential	1	2	3	4	5
Personality	1	2	3	4	5
Maturity	1	2	3	4	5
Experience	1	2	3	4	5
Alertness	1	2	3	4	5

Comments_____

_____

_____

_____

Disposition_____

Interviewer_____

Exhibit 8-3 Staff Orientation Check List — (Permanent Employees)

STAFF ORIENTATION

CHECK LIST — (Permanent Employees)

Date
Received

1. Forms to be completed:
   Income tax w/h
   Federal _____ _____
   State _____ _____
   City _____ _____
   Insurance forms
   Hospitalization _____ _____
   Major Medical (3 months), if applicable _____ _____
   Life (1 year) _____ _____
   Personnel profile _____ _____

2. Photograph & History _____ _____

3. Assignment of employee number _____ _____

4. Items to be distributed:
   Keys _____ _____
   Staff guide _____ _____
   Technical Manuals:
   Report guide _____ _____
   Model workpapers _____ _____
   Model permanent file _____ _____
   Manual of outside
   verification procedure _____ _____
   Manual of special forms and
   related instructions _____ _____
   Model 1120 _____ _____
   Model 1040 _____ _____
   Tax handbook _____ _____
   Building I.D. Card _____ _____
   List of personnel _____ _____
   Other items: _____ _____
   _____ _____

5. Assignment of mail box _____ _____

6. Firm business cards, if applicable _____ _____

_____
(Signed by Staffman)

N/A = not available   I/A = inapplicable

Source: Reprinted from *Quality Control Documentation in the Local CPA Firm* by California CPA Foundation for Education and Research, © 1978.

Exhibit 8-3 continued

**STAFF ORIENTATION
PROGRAM**

FIRST DAY

Morning:

Initial "WELCOME" visit, tour of office & introductions.
See check list for forms to be completed, items to be distributed.

For remainder of morning:
Period of completing forms and reviewing manuals and guides.
Bookkeeping to instruct on payroll and preparation of time and expense reports.
Request a staffman to see that coffee break and lunch are covered.
This will be someone who can also answer questions on parking, etc.

Afternoon:

1. Review manuals.
2. Review staff guide.
3. Review practice and professional development programs.
4. Review files, library, forms supply and duplicating process.
5. Review S & S publications.
6. Review internal organization.

SECOND DAY (Optional)

Morning:

Sample grouping and write up of statements.

Afternoon:

Tax Department personnel to:
1. Review Tax Manual.
2. Review Model 1120 and 1040.
3. Explain completion of tax returns with appropriate "who done it"
   form and filing instructions.
4. Review of references in library.
5. Review of tax department and files.
6. Instructions on grouping for completion of sample 1120.

THIRD DAY (Optional)

Morning:

Complete grouping of sample 1120

Afternoon:

Review of groupings with audit and tax principal.
Review of questions which have arisen during first two and one-half days.

Exhibit 8-4 Personnel Manual Check List

I. Purpose of Manual

II. Firm Objectives
   a. Growth and service _____
   b. Technical competence _____
   c. Service to the profession _____

III. Management of the firm
   a. Organization charts _____
   b. Partner positions _____
   c. Staff positions _____
   d. Advancement procedures _____
   e. Significance of quality control policies
      and procedures _____

IV. Employment Practices
   a. College graduate _____
   b. Equal opportunity _____
   c. Social, religious, civic, and educational Life _____
   d. Professional meetings _____
   e. Accounting work for others _____
   f. Team approach _____
   g. Advancement _____

V. Employee Compensation
   a. Basic compensation _____
   b. Overtime compensation _____
   c. Holidays _____
   d. Sick leave _____
   e. Vacations _____
   f. Time off _____
   g. Travel time _____
   h. Reimbursement for travel and other expenses _____
   i. Continuing professional education _____
   j. Tax season _____
   k. CPA exam _____

VI. Employee Benefits
   a. Social security _____
   b. Unemployment _____
   c. Workers' compensation _____
   d. Group life insurance _____
   e. Long-term disability income plan _____
   f. Hospitalization and major medical _____
   g. Group travel and accident insurance _____
   h. Retirement planning _____
   i. Night school _____
   j. Jury duty _____
   k. Moving expenses _____

Exhibit 8-4 continued

VII. Personal Conduct
    a. Professional bearing and attitude _____
    b. Dress and grooming _____
    c. Smoking _____
    d. Drinking _____
    e. Drugs _____
    f. Relations with client personnel _____
    g. Relations with other staff members and partners _____
    h. Professional societies _____
    i. Work outside firm _____
    j. Public speeches and writing for publication _____
    k. Confidentiality of client information _____
    l. Criticism of client's accounting system or management _____
    m. Discovery of possible defalcation _____
    n. Physical fitness _____

VIII. Office Practices
    a. Relations with staff _____
    b. Checking with receptionist _____
    c. Work assignments _____
    d. Unassigned personnel _____
    e. Personal calls to office _____
    f. Stationery policies _____
    g. Briefcases _____
    h. Preparation of working papers and forms _____
    i. Care of firm property _____
    j. Time reporting _____
    k. Client's office rules _____
    l. Use of copying equipment _____
    m. Conference room use _____
    n. Library _____
    o. Mail and postage _____
    p. Telephones _____
    q. Keys _____
    r. Bulletin boards _____

IX. Professional Practices
    a. Care of clients' records _____
    b. Copying clients' records _____
    c. Calls at clients' offices _____
    d. Use of clients' telephones _____
    e. Client irregularities _____
    f. Standards of professional work _____
    g. Job evaluations _____
    h. Personnel evaluations _____
    i. Client entertainment _____
    j. Assignment procedures _____
    k. Removing records from clients' offices _____
    l. Relations with EDP service bureau _____

Exhibit 8-5 AICPA Quality Control Policies and Procedures for Hiring

1. **Maintain a program designed to obtain qualified personnel by planning for personnel needs, establishing hiring objectives, and setting qualifications for those involved in the hiring function.**

   a. Plan for the firm's personnel needs at all levels and establish quantified hiring objectives based on current clientele, anticipated growth, personnel turnover, individual advancement, and retirement.

   b. Design a program to achieve hiring objectives which provides for —
      (i) Identification of sources of potential hirees.
      (ii) Methods of contact with potential hirees.
      (iii) Methods of specific identification of potential hirees.
      (iv) Methods of attracting potential hirees and informing them about the firm.
      (v) Methods of evaluating and selecting potential hirees for extension of employment offers.

   c. Inform those persons involved in hiring as to the firm's personnel needs and hiring objectives.

   d. Assign to authorized persons the responsibility for employment decisions.

   e. Monitor the effectiveness of the recruiting program.
      (i) Evaluate the recruiting program periodically to determine whether policies and procedures for obtaining qualified personnel are being observed.
      (ii) Review hiring results periodically to determine whether goals and personnel needs are being achieved.

2. **Establish qualifications and guidelines for evaluating potential hirees at each professional level.**

   a. Identify the attributes to be sought in hirees, such as intelligence, integrity, honesty, motivation, and aptitude for the profession.

   b. Identify achievements and experiences desirable for entry-level and experienced personnel. For example,
      (i) Academic background.
      (ii) Personal achievements.
      (iii) Work experience.
      (iv) Personal interests.

Source: Copyright © 1976, 1978 by the American Institute of Certified Public Accountants, Inc. Reprinted, with permission, from *Voluntary Quality Control Review Program for CPA Firms.*

Exhibit 8-5 continued

    c. Set guidelines to be followed when hiring individuals in atypical situations such as —
- (i) Hiring relatives of personnel or relatives of clients.
- (ii) Rehiring former employees.
- (iii) Hiring client employees.

    d. Obtain background information and documentation of qualifications of applicants by appropriate means, such as —
- (i) Resumes.
- (ii) Application forms.
- (iii) Interviews.
- (iv) College transcripts.
- (v) Personal references.
- (vi) Former employment references.

    e. Evaluate the qualifications of new personnel, including those obtained from other than the usual hiring channels (for example, those joining the firm at supervisory levels or through merger or acquisition), to determine that they meet the firm's requirements and standards.

3. Inform applicants and new personnel of the firm's policies and procedures relevant to them.

    a. Use a brochure or another means to so inform applicants and new personnel.

    b. Prepare and maintain a manual describing policies and procedures for distribution to personnel.

    c. Conduct an orientation program for new personnel.

Exhibit 8-6 Example of General Design for Hiring

Operational Responsibilities:

Partner A has the responsibility for hiring new staff accountants. All partners must approve the decision to hire managers and in charge accountants. Planning personnel needs is periodically done in partners' meetings. An employment offer cannot be extended unless at least two partners interview the applicant. Atypical situations are resolved at partners' meetings. Partner A is responsible for orientation of new personnel.

Communication:

Partner C is responsible for maintaining the personnel manual. Changes in the personnel manual must be approved by the partners.

Monitoring:

The effectiveness of the recruiting program is periodically discussed at partners' meetings.

Documentation:

1. Personnel manual, job descriptions, operating personnel procedures as per outline
2. Professional employment application
3. Interview evaluation forms
4. Staff orientation check list
5. Minutes of partners' meetings

NOTE: The profile firm is described in Appendix A.

Table 8-1 Opinions on Hiring Policies and Procedures

Quality Control	Number of Professional Personnel in Firm							
	1 to 5		6 to 20		20 to 80		More than 80	
Policy or Procedure	Mean	CV	Mean	CV	Mean	CV	Mean	CV
(1) The firm has designed and documented a formal program to achieve hiring objectives.								
Importance	1.00	0%	3.40	27%			4.40	13%
Usage	1.25	0%	1.66	47%			3.38	16%
(2) Hiring results are periodically reviewed to determine whether goals and personnel needs are being achieved.								
Importance	1.00	0%	3.80	18%			4.20	20%
Usage	1.25	0%	2.50	47%			4.25	26%
(3) The firm has documented attributes and achievements sought in hires.								
Importance	1.50	47%	3.67	25%			3.40	45%
Usage	1.25	0%	1.91	48%			3.25	34%
(4) The firm has developed hiring policies to avoid personnel and independence problems.								
Importance	3.00	47%	3.80	27%			4.60	12%
Usage	2.09	69%	2.16	60%			4.50	15%
(5) The credentials and references of hires are documented.								
Importance	4.50	16%	3.80	25%			4.20	20%
Usage	3.75	33%	3.16	42%			4.00	26%
Number of respondents	3		15		0		5	

NOTE: The mean responses are based on a five-point scale. They can be interpreted according to where they fall within the following ranges:

Importance	Range	Usage	Range
Unimportant	1.00-1.5	Rare	1.25-1.88
Little importance	1.51-2.5	Occasional	1.89-3.13
Some importance	2.51-3.5	Common	3.14-4.38
Important	3.51-4.5	Almost always	4.39-5.00
Essential	4.51-5.0		

For example, an importance score of 1.81 indicates that the respondents viewed the procedure as being of little importance. CV represents coefficient of variation. The higher the coefficient of variation, the greater the variability in the responses of the CPA firm partners in a particular group. See Appendix C for a description of the study.

Table 8-2 Hiring. Summary Evaluation of Quality Control Policies and Procedures (for inclusion in a firm's quality control document).

AICPA Policy/Procedure	Procedure's Applicability to Firm					Comments
	N	R	LL	SL	SP	
1. Maintain a program designed to obtain qualified personnel.						
a. Plan for the firm's personnel needs at all levels, and establish quantified hiring objectives.	H	H	H	H	L	Formality of plan increases with firm size
b. Design a program to achieve hiring objectives.	H	H	H	M-L	NA	Hiring program and recruiting materials
c. Inform personnel involved in hiring about the firm's personnel needs and objectives.	H	H	H	H-M	NA	
d. Assign responsibility for recruiting decisions.	H	H	H	H	NA	
e. Monitor effectiveness of recruiting program to determine whether:						
(i) Policies and procedures are being followed.	H	H	H	M	L	
(ii) Goals and personnel needs are achieved.	H	H	H	M	L	
2. Establish qualifications and guidelines for evaluating potential hirees at each professional level.						
a. Identify personal attributes sought in hirees (state attributes).	H	H	H	H	L	Includes interns and part-time employees

	N	R	LL	SL	SP	
b. Identify criteria for evaluating applicants.	H	H	H	M	L	Academic, achievements, experience, personal interests
c. Set guidelines for atypical situation.	H	H	H	M	L	Relatives, former employees, client employees
d. Document qualifications.	H	H	H	H	L	Résumés, application forms, interviews, college transcripts, personal references, employment references
e. Evaluate qualifications of applicants (state how).	H	H	H	H	L	Specify firm's interview procedures
3. Inform applicants and new personnel of the firm's policies and procedures applicable to them.						
a. Inform applicants and new personnel.	H	H	H	H	H	Personnel manual or recruiting brochure
b. Maintain and distribute a personnel manual.	H	H	H	M	NA	Specify responsibility
c. Orient new personnel.	H	H	H	H	H	Specify responsibility

Key:

H	= High	
M	= Medium	
L	= Low	
NA	= Not Applicable	

N	= National or international firm
R	= Regional firm
LL	= Large Local firm (possibly two or three offices)
SL	= Small Local Firm (one office)
SP	= Sole Practitioner (possibly one part-time staff member)

119

Table 8-3 Summary of Hiring Documentation

Documentation — Purpose	AICPA Procedures
Quality control document — informs staff of policies and procedures	all
Professional employment application — document qualifications	2b
Interview evaluation form — guide interviewer and document hiring process	2a, d, e
Staff orientation check list — document orientation process	3c
Personnel manual — document personnel policies and procedures	3a, b, c
Minutes of partners' meetings — record monitoring process	1e, 2c

NOTES

1. AICPA, *Sample Quality Control Documents for Local CPA Firms* (New York, N.Y.: AICPA, 1977). pp. 39-41.
2. Wayne G. Bremser and Paul E. Dascher, "Accounting Careers in Perspective," *The CPA Journal*, January 1975, pp. 46-48.

BIBLIOGRAPHY

AICPA. *Sample Quality Control Documents for Local CPA Firms.* New York, N.Y.: AICPA, 1977.

Bremser, Wayne G. and Dascher, Paul E. "Accounting Careers in Perspective." *The CPA Journal*, January 1975, pp. 46-48.

Knezel, Jeffrey. "Successful Small Firm Recruiting." *Journal of Accountancy*, April 1977, p. 49.

Lawson, J.W. II. *How to Develop a Company Personnel Policy Manual.* Chicago, Illinois: Dartnell, 1974.

Magasum, Arnold W. "Requirements for a Personnel Manual." *Attorney – CPA*, Winter 1974, p. 5.

Parsons, John W. "Testing Job Applicants." *Journal of Accountancy*, March 1977, p. 47.

Chapter 9

Advancement

This chapter analyzes the three AICPA objectives for advancement. The AICPA quality control policies and procedures are reprinted in Exhibit 9-5 and summarized with comments in Table 9-3. An example of a check list of personnel rating criteria, an assignment performance evaluation questionnaire, and a knowledge and skill form are provided. Recommended advancement documentation is summarized in Table 9-4.

The opinions of CPA firm partners on selected quality control procedures are presented in Tables 9-1 and 9-2. These opinions should provide to practitioners some perspective on what other CPAs are thinking and doing with respect to advancement. It is unnecessary for a sole practitioner to include advancement in the firm's quality control document. For the reader's convenience, all tables and exhibits are presented at the end of the chapter.

OVERVIEW

CPA firms should have procedures to assure that qualified personnel are selected for advancement. Accountants want to progress to positions of greater responsibility and compensation. Personnel experts advise all professionals to have a planned career path with well-defined, measurable objectives. An accountant's objectives might be stated in terms of compensation, position, type of work, autonomy, certification, or even a planned progression out of public accounting. My frequent discussions with entry-level accountants from many firms and many different universities reveal that an increasing number are planning to leave public accounting after two or three years. Advancement policies and procedures must consider both the firm's needs and the individual's needs and feelings.

For the advancement element, qualifications must be established for various levels. Less detail is normally required in smaller firms than in larger firms, because smaller firms have fewer levels, and because advancement decisions are made on a more personal level. One would expect an articulation between the criteria used for evaluating hirees and making advancement decisions. However, when making advancement decisions, more information about the individual is known. From a business management point of view, an effective evaluation and counseling process promotes job satisfaction and provides motivation for staff members.

AUTHORITATIVE POLICIES AND PROCEDURES

The AICPA quality control policies and procedures are shown in Exhibit 9-5. Procedures are identified by letters. When necessary, procedures are identified in the text with the objective number and the letter, and possibly small Roman numerals (2a(i), for example). Common procedures and the peer reviewer's approach are discussed below for each objective. For this element, firm size and personalities in the firm are very important in designing procedures.

Establish Qualifications

Objective 1: ESTABLISH QUALIFICATIONS DEEMED NECESSARY FOR THE VARIOUS LEVELS OF RESPONSIBILITY WITHIN THE FIRM.

If a CPA firm has levels other than "partners" and "staff," the qualifications for each level should be documented. The extent of job descriptions varies among firms. A list of credentials, responsibilities, and duties is adequate.[1] Firms that have only two levels — partner and staff — will face the question of whether to define several staff levels. In making this decision, these firms should recognize that an informal system of staff levels already exists.

Staff Levels

An informal system is always established by the staff and the partners. Staff personnel judge levels based on credentials and rewards. Rewards are based on compensation, duties and responsibilities, who an individual works for, client assignments, and the way information is shared. The association between staff level and compensation, credentials, and duties and responsibilities is obvious, and is generally deliberate and controlled by a firm's management. A staff member may be elevated in the eyes of his peers if he or she usually works for a partner who is considered by the staff to be the head partner, the "sharpest" partner, the best partner to work for, or the partner with the best clients. This may be an unintended effect. The effect of the way information is shared may also be unintended, but it has an effect because staff personnel generally attach prestige to those who know what is going on in the firm.

Many firms have found significant advantages in having different staff levels clearly defined in writing. Clearly defined levels help in administering the compensation of staff members, provide objectives for staff members to incorporate in their career paths, and eliminate some of the unintended effects of the informal system. For example, the partners can make better decisions on the way information is shared.

The views of CPA firm partners on written job descriptions are contained in Table 9-1, part 1. "Some importance" is reflected by the scores of the "6 to 20" group and the "20 to 80" group. The partners of the largest firms indicate that the procedure is "important" to them. However, the usage of job descriptions was estimated to be low, except for the "20 to 80" group.

Performance Criteria

If different staff levels exist, criteria for evaluating performance must be identified. Some examples are identified under procedure 1b in Exhibit 9-5. Even if only one staff level exists, evaluation criteria are appropriate. It is good personnel management to let employees know what is expected of them for advancement, and how they are doing. The lack of this communication can create uncertainties, having undesirable effects on job performance. A check list of common personnel rating criteria is presented in Exhibit 9-1. The applicability of the criteria listed under "administrative abilities" obviously depends on staff level. Some of the criteria are purposely redundant to allow choices in terminology. The number of criteria used should be minimized, since an excess could make them all incomprehensible. To satisfy procedure 1c, criteria may be communicated to personnel orally or in writing.

Part 2 of Table 9-1 shows the respondents' views on the need to identify evaluation criteria in writing. Considerable importance is indicated by scores ranging from 3.55 to 4.56, except for the smallest firms (2.56). The lower score is understandable because these small-firm CPAs might feel the need to keep evaluation criteria on a personal level, to be communicated from time to time as the opportunity arises. However, this does not justify excluding the criteria from the quality control document. Usage was estimated to be "frequent" in the "20 to 80" and "more than 80" groups.

Peer Reviewers

Reviewers examine job descriptions and the appropriateness of qualifications for each. If a personnel manual is not used to communicate advancement policies and procedures, the method used is evaluated for adequacy and compliance.

Periodically Evaluate Performance

Objective 2: EVALUATE PERFORMANCE OF PERSONNEL AND PERIODICALLY ADVISE PERSONNEL OF THEIR PROGRESS. MAINTAIN PERSONNEL FILES CONTAINING DOCUMENTATION RELATING TO THE EVALUATION PROCESS.

Having periodic evaluations of all personnel is widely accepted as good personnel management. Evaluations provide an opportunity for bosses to communicate their perceptions of subordinates' performance. They can satisfy an employee's need to know where he or she stands. They provide an opportunity to tell an employee what should be done for improvement. However, these potential benefits are not always achieved. The evaluation system might be poor, or the evaluator might be unskilled.

Evaluation Forms

The basic elements of an evaluation system are listed under procedure 2a. Annual evaluations are common. Sometimes evaluations are made after relatively large engagements. In a formalized evaluation system, an evaluation form is essential. (A possible exception is a sole practitioner who feels that a memo is sufficient because he only has one or two staff members.)

The importance scores in part 3 of Table 9-1 indicate some resistance by smaller firms to using evaluation forms. The estimated usage was only in the "occasional" range for the two smaller groups.

Two excellent evaluation forms taken from the *MAP Handbook* are shown as Exhibits 9-2 and 9-3. A form like Exhibit 9-2 would be used after major engagements. Exhibit 9-3 can be used after an engagement or as an annual evaluation form for a local firm. The performance criteria and the form should be modified to fit the firm (see Exhibit 9-4). A firm can make the following test. When completed, will the documentation reflect the criteria used in making past advancement decisions? Firms want to avoid the situation where it looks as if Harry should have been promoted to manager instead of Janet.

Counseling

Procedure 2b advocates evaluation and counseling for all personnel. The benefits of communicating evaluations were discussed above, and Table 9-1, part 4, indicates considerable support for this idea from CPAs. However, the usage was estimated to be only "occasional" in the smallest firms and "common" in the "6 to 20" group.

Procedure 2b(ii) might seem a novel idea to some CPAs. To some extent, partner evaluation is done informally in all firms. National firms have an obvious need for a formal evaluation process, because they have a large number of partners. Formal evaluation of partners seems to be slowly gaining acceptance.[2] However, a firm might omit this procedure for fear of stirring up resentments among partners. This reason is very logical, and defensible for small firms.

In Table 9-1, part 6, we see that the CPAs generally viewed evaluation of partners to be of "some importance." However, the usage of partner evaluation by superiors was estimated to be "rare" or "occasional" at best, except for the largest firms. These results seem to indicate that increased use of this procedure can be expected.

All CPAs surveyed were asked whether a formal evaluation process is an effective way of improving staff performance. In Table 9-2, we see considerable agreement with the notion that improvement of staff performance is a benefit because standards are known. Agreement increases with firm size. These results may encourage firms to formalize their evaluation process. Mixed opinions were given on whether improvement of staff performance would result because staff would know they were to be evaluated.

The need for monitoring the evaluation system is suggested in procedure 2b(iii). A good procedure is to have the system discussed annually at a partners' meeting. A committee approach is an alternative.

Peer Reviewers

External peer reviewers examine the appropriateness of evaluation methods. This obviously involves considerable judgment. To check compliance, personnel files are reviewed for completeness. Some personnel might be interviewed in making these tests. The firm's system for monitoring its evaluation system is reviewed.

Assign Responsibilities

Objective 3: ASSIGN RESPONSIBILITY FOR MAKING ADVANCEMENT DECISIONS.

The responsibility for advancement decisions might be assigned to an individual or to a group. These responsibilities should generally be consistent with the hiring responsibilities. For example, if a manager can be hired only with the approval of three partners, this same approval should be required to promote someone to manager.

A periodic study of the firm's advancement experience can help forecast personnel problems. The formality of this study would vary with firm size, as indicated by the responses in Table 9-1, part 5. A large firm might require a written report. In a smaller firm, a discussion at a partners' meeting would be adequate. Procedures 2b(iii) and 3c are obviously related.

Peer Reviewers

Reviewers ascertain the appropriateness of responsibilities assigned for the various steps in the evaluation process. The functioning of the process is usually discussed with these individuals. The firm's conclusions about its experience are reviewed.

GENERAL DESIGN

A general design for advancement is shown in Exhibit 9-6. Partner C has the primary responsibility for the evaluation system. Annual and engagement evaluations are used. Promotions must be approved by all partners.

A summary of the AICPA objectives and sample procedures is shown in Table 9-3. Since advancement is a very personalized and sensitive area, the applicability of these procedures varies. Each procedure's applicability according to firm size is a generalization based upon current standards. Standards will evolve as the profession becomes more experienced with external peer reviews. Several characteristics of firms are recognized in the accounting profession's quality control programs as determinants of the appropriate quality control policies and procedures for CPA firms. Therefore, a firm must consider all of its characteristics in designing procedures and assigning responsibilities. Similarly, forms, check lists, and other documentation shown in this book and elsewhere must be modified to fit the individual firm's needs. Table 9-4 summarizes documentation.

Exhibit 9-1 Check List of Personnel Rating Criteria

A. Administrative abilities
   1. Planning and organization _____
   2. Evaluation of internal control _____
   3. Adherence to budgets _____
   4. Practice development _____
   5. Problem solving _____
   6. Leadership _____
   7. Efficient use of staff _____
   8. Training of assistants _____
   9. Use of client personnel _____
   10. Handling personnel problems _____

B. Technical ability
   1. Knowledge of GAAP _____
   2. Knowledge of GAAS _____
   3. Knowledge of the firm's accounting and auditing procedures _____
   4. Dealing with tax matters _____
   5. Dealing with IRS agents _____
   6. Computer systems _____
   7. Computer auditing _____
   8. Statistical sampling _____
   9. Working paper preparation techniques _____
   10. Financial statement preparation _____
   11. Ability to review work of others _____

C. Professional and personal
   1. Inquisitiveness _____
   2. Creativity _____
   3. Enthusiam _____
   4. Written communication _____
   5. Oral communication _____
   6. Motivation _____
   7. Ability to relate to clients _____
   8. Industry _____
   9. Keeps superiors informed _____
   10. Willingness to accept responsibility _____
   11. Ability to follow instructions _____
   12. Work habits _____
   13. General business knowledge _____
   14. Leadership _____
   15. Administrative ability _____
   16. Appearance _____
   17. Attitude _____
   18. Maturity _____

Exhibit 9-2 Assignment Performance Evaluation Questionnaire

Assignment Performance Evaluation Questionnaire

Staff member _____ Yrs. of experience _____

Assignment/client _____ Number staff supervised _____

Period of report: From _____/_____/19____ to ____/____/19____ Hours worked _____

Assigned duties _____

Were functions performed on this assignment compatible with the individual's ability?   Yes ☐   No ☐   { Above ☐ / Below ☐ }

Classification:	Manager	Supervisor	In-charge accountant ☐ Senior consultant ☐	Staff assistant ☐ Consultant ☐	Other
Used on this assignment as:					
Based on performance. rated as:					

Performance Rating:
(Evaluate staff member by checking applicable box. If not applicable. leave blank.)

	Outstanding	Satisfactory	Needs improvement
Administrative skill:			
1. Ability to organize and plan work	☐	☐	☐
2. Ability to train and develop assistants	☐	☐	☐
3. Ability to meet scheduled deadlines and time estimates	☐	☐	☐
4. Communication with superiors and subordinates	☐	☐	☐
5. Ability to supervise and direct work of others	☐	☐	☐
Technical skills:			
6. Knowledge of client's accounting system	☐	☐	☐
7. Working paper preparation/review techniques	☐	☐	☐
8. Knowledge of accounting theory/practice *(SAPs, APBs, SEC)*	☐	☐	☐
9. Knowledge of federal state and local tax laws	☐	☐	☐
10. Ability to apply tax knowledge to client problems	☐	☐	☐
Professional and general skills:			
11. Understands assignment and follows instructions	☐	☐	☐
12. Accuracy of work including neatness and clarity	☐	☐	☐
13. Ability to work independently and adhere to time budget	☐	☐	☐
14. Ability to analyze complex matters	☐	☐	☐
15. Ability to make decisions	☐	☐	☐
16. Relations with client personnel and firm associates	☐	☐	☐
17. Communication capabilities in writing and speech	☐	☐	☐
18. Creativity. initiative, and enthusiasm demonstrated	☐	☐	☐
Personal characteristics:			
19. Responsibility—trustworthy and conscientious	☐	☐	☐
20. Integrity—loyal, sincere, reliable, and punctual	☐	☐	☐
21. Appearance—attire. neatness. and grooming	☐	☐	☐
22. Attitude—cooperative. courteous. friendly. and professional	☐	☐	☐
23. Bearing—maturity. poise. and tact	☐	☐	☐
24. Ambition—professional interest and competitiveness	☐	☐	☐

How do you evaluate this staff member's overall performance? *(Highlight strengths and weaknesses.)*

10/77 Rev.

Source: Copyright 1975, 1976, 1977 by the American Institute of Certified Public Accountants, Inc. Reprinted, with permission, from *Management of an Accounting Practice Handbook.*

Exhibit 9-2 continued

General Appraisal:
(Give specific reasons for your answers.)

Would you accept this individual on another of your engagements?   Yes ☐   No ☐
Reason _____
_____
_____

Is the staff member capable of more advanced assignments?   Yes ☐   No ☐
Explain _____
_____
_____

How would you evaluate the staff member's potential for advancement in the firm?
Explain on short-term and long-range basis _____
_____
_____
_____

Comments:
(Give your general impression and describe here any other observations that will assist in appraising this staff member.)

_____
_____
_____
_____
_____
_____

Counseling:
(Review evaluation with staff member.)

On-the-job training requires that a staff member's performance on each assignment be discussed as the work progresses and in summary at the end of the assignment. A meeting must be scheduled with the staff member for the purpose of discussing good work or his poor performance pointing out his weaknesses and suggesting means of correcting them.

Topics discussed during meeting	Staff member's reaction
_____	_____
_____	_____
_____	_____
_____	_____

Evaluated by _____Staff level _____ Date _____
Reviewed by partner/manager _____ Date _____

4/76 Rev.

Exhibit 9-3 Knowledge and Skill Form
(and Profile of Management Role Performance)

Knowledge and Skill Form

(and Profile of Management Role Performance)

Staff member evaluated   Date

Evaluator

(Only one check in cols. 1 and 5 because they are extremes. All other checks enter in cols. 2, 3, and 4.)

(Circle at least two but no more than four in each section.)			If you wish, add your own words.	Effectiveness				
				Least				Most
				1	2	3	4	5
Planner								
Careful	Sloppy	Thorough						
Imaginative	Foresighted	Infrequent						
Routine	Erratic	Last-minute						
Constant	Cautious	Meticulous						
Problem solver								
Analytical	Consistent	Superficial						
Critical	Faulty	Routine						
Hasty	Creative	Reliable						
Slow	Quick	Successful						
Communicator								
Warm	Sloppy	Cold						
Inhibited	Weak	Unstructured						
Thorough	Receptive	Patient						
Expressive	Efficient	Precise						
Leader								
Dominating	Excitable	Partial						
Uncertain	Permissive	Energetic						
Weak	Fair	Heavy-handed						
Loose	Amiable	Sure						
Decision maker								
Decisive	Lone	Delayer						
Slow	Avoider	Reliable						
Quick	Seldom	Participative						
Frequent	Rash	Dependent						
Trainer								
Systematic	Unprepared	Conscientious						
Patient	Efficient	Knowledgeable						
Sloppy	Diligent	Disinterested						
Off-on	Slow	Enthusiastic						
Team-member								
Cooperative	Unreliable	Independent						
Influential	Divisive	Undisciplined						
Conformist	Reliable	Contributing						
Forceful	Reluctant	Welcome						
Innovator								
Original	Appropriate	Consistent						
Infrequent	Clever	Sensible						
Unnecessary	Creative	Unimaginative						
Constant	Disruptive	Rash						
Job expertise								
Amateur	Improving	Too technical						
Obsolete	Mediocre	Disinterested						
Masterful	Balanced	Lagging						
Versatile	Up-to-date	Thorough						

4/76 Rev.

Source: Copyright 1975, 1976, 1977, by the American Institute of Certified Public Accountants, Inc. Reprinted, by permission, from *Management of an Accounting Practice Handbook.*

Exhibit 9-4 Annual Evaluation Form

Name_____

Staff Level_____ Years of experience _____

	Circle one		
Performance Criteria	Outstanding	Good	Needs Improvement
Administrative ability	1	2	3
Knowledge of GAAP	1	2	3
Knowledge of GAAS	1	2	3
Knowledge of taxes	1	2	3
Motivation	1	2	3
Relationships with clients	1	2	3
Overall performance	1	2	3

Potential for advancement_____

_____

_____

Summary of counseling_____

_____

_____

Use reverse side for other remarks.

Evaluator_____

Exhibit 9-5 AICPA Quality Control Policies and Procedures for Advancement

1. Establish qualifications deemed necessary for the various levels of responsibility within the firm.

   a. Prepare guidelines describing responsibilities at each level and expected performance and qualifications necessary for advancement to each level, including —

     (i) Titles and related responsibilities.

     (ii) The amount of experience (which may be expressed as a time period) generally required for advancement to the succeeding level.

   b. Identify criteria which will be considered in evaluating individual performance and expected proficiency, such as —

     (i) Technical knowledge.

     (ii) Analytical and judgmental abilities.

     (iii) Communicative skills.

     (iv) Leadership and training skills.

     (v) Client relations.

     (vi) Personal attitude and professional bearing (character, intelligence, judgment, and motivation).

     (vii) Possession of a CPA certificate for advancement to a supervisory position.

   c. Use a personnel manual or other means to communicate advancement policies and procedures to personnel.

2. Evaluate performance of personnel and periodically advise personnel of their progress. Maintain personnel files containing documentation relating to the evaluation process.

   a. Gather and evaluate information on performance of personnel.

     (i) Identify evaluation responsibilities and requirements at each level indicating who will prepare evaluations and when they will be prepared.

     (ii) Instruct personnel on the objectives of personnel evaluation.

     (iii) Utilize forms, which may be standardized, for evaluating performance of personnel.

     (iv) Review evaluations with the individual being evaluated.

     (v) Require that evaluations be reviewed by the evaluator's superior.

     (vi) Review evaluations to determine that individuals worked for and were evaluated by different persons.

     (vii) Determine that evaluations are completed on a timely basis.

Exhibit 9-5 continued

b. Periodically counsel personnel as to their progress and career opportunities.

   (i) Review periodically with personnel the evaluation of their performance, including an assessment of their progress with the firm. Considerations should include the following:

      (a) Performance.

      (b) Future objectives of the firm and the individual.

      (c) Assignment preferences.

      (d) Career opportunities.

   (ii) Evaluate partners periodically by means of counseling, peer evaluation, or self appraisal, as appropriate, as to whether they continue to have the qualifications to fulfill their responsibilities.

   (iii) Review periodically the system of personnel evaluation and counseling to ascertain that —

      (a) Procedures for evaluation and documentation are being followed on a timely basis.

      (b) Requirements established for advancement are being achieved.

      (c) Personnel decisions are consistent with evaluations.

      (d) Recognition is given to outstanding performance.

3. Assign responsibility for making advancement decisions.

a. Assign responsibility to designated persons for making advancement and termination decisions, conducting evaluation interviews with persons considered for advancement, documenting the results of the interviews, and maintaining appropriate records.

b. Evaluate data obtained giving appropriate recognition in advancement decisions to the quality of the work performed.

c. Study the firm's advancement experience periodically to ascertain whether individuals meeting stated criteria are assigned increased degrees of responsibility.

Exhibit 9-6 Example of General Design for Advancement

Operational Responsibilities:

Partner C is responsible for the evaluation system. Partner C is assisted by Partner A in making annual evaluations of personnel and counseling. Partners, managers, and accountants in charge are responsible for evaluating subordinates when an engagement assignment exceeds five days. All partners are responsible for making an annual self-evaluation and maintaining files on these. Promotions must be approved by all partners. An employee cannot be terminated by a partner without the approval of another partner.

Communication:

Partner C is responsible for maintaining the personnel manual. Changes in the advancement procedures stated in the personnel manual must be approved by all partners.

Monitoring:

The effectiveness of the evaluation program is discussed at the June partners' meeting. Partner C makes a report.

Documentation:

1. Personnel manual, job descriptions and qualifications, advancement and evaluation procedures
2. Assignment performance evaluation questionnaire
3. Annual evaluation form
4. Minutes of partners' meetings

NOTE: The profile firm is described in Appendix A.

Table 9-1 Opinions on Advancement of Personnel Policies and Procedures

		Number of Professional Personnel in Firm						
Quality Control		1 to 5		6 to 20		20 to 80		More than 80
Policy or Procedure	Mean	CV	Mean	CV	Mean	CV	Mean	CV
(1) Job titles and descriptions of responsibilities are written.								
Importance	2.22	37%	3.05	31%	3.00	94%	4.13	22%
Usage	2.16	53%	1.81	46%	2.50	50%	4.06	35%
(2) Criteria to be considered in evaluating performance are identified in writing.								
Importance	2.56	48%	3.55	27%	4.50	16%	4.56	13%
Usage	2.29	59%	2.21	46%	3.75	33%	4.54	25%
(3) Personnel evaluation forms are used periodically.								
Importance	2.78	53%	3.30	33%	4.50	16%	4.69	10%
Usage	2.16	64%	2.45	58%	4.16	17%	3.69	12%
(4) Evaluations are communicated with personnel periodically.								
Importance	3.25	51%	4.20	17%	5.00	0%	4.75	9%
Usage	2.63	61%	3.53	28%	4.59	16%	4.76	10%
(5) The firm's advancement experience should be formally appraised.								
Importance	2.56	44%	3.25	26%	3.00	47%	4.19	18%
Usage	2.16	58%	2.08	45%	2.91	66%	3.75	32%
(6) Partners are evaluated by:								
a. Superiors								
Importance	2.57	38%	2.95	37%	3.00	47%	4.63	13%
Usage	1.61	38%	1.61	60%	2.50	50%	4.06	31%
b. Peers								
Importance	2.67	33%	3.50	25%	2.50	28%	3.13	40%
Usage	1.80	51%	2.09	54%	2.50	50%	2.04	50%
Number of respondents	10		21		5		32	

NOTE: The mean responses are based on a five-point scale. They can be interpreted according to where they fall within the following ranges:

Importance	Range	Usage	Range
Unimportant	1.00-1.5	Rare	1.25-1.88
Little importance	1.51-2.5	Occasional	1.89-3.13
Some importance	2.51-3.5	Common	3.14-4.38
Important	3.51-4.5	Almost always	4.39-5.00
Essential	4.51-5.0		

For example, an importance score of 1.81 indicates that the respondents viewed the procedure as being of little importance. CV represents coefficient of variation. The higher the coefficient of variation, the greater the variability in the responses of the CPA firm partners in a particular group. See Appendix C for a description of the study.

Table 9-2 Formal Evaluation and Staff Performance

Statement	Number of Professional Personnel in Firm				
	1 to 5	6 to 20	20 to 80	More than 80	Total
The existence of a formal evaluation process is an effective way of improving staff performance because:					
— Standards are known					
Strongly agree	11.5	8.9	21.4	45.0	22.4
Agree	26.9	48.9	28.6	40.0	39.2
No opinion	23.1	15.6	21.4	7.5	15.2
Disagree	26.9	20.0	21.4	5.0	16.8
Strongly disagree	11.5	6.7	7.1	2.5	6.4
Mean	3.00	3.33	3.36	4.20	3.54
— Staff members know they will be evaluated.					
Strongly agree	3.7	13.3	0.0	10.3	8.8
Agree	44.4	26.7	28.6	38.5	34.4
No opinion	33.3	17.8	14.3	15.4	20.0
Disagree	11.1	35.6	50.0	25.6	28.8
Strongly disagree	7.4	6.7	7.1	10.3	8.0
Mean	3.26	3.04	2.64	3.13	3.07
Number of CPAs responding	28	45	15	40	128

NOTE: All numbers, except means, are stated as a percentage of the total responding. The means are based on a scale of 1 to 5, where "strongly disagree" is 1 and "strongly agree" is 5. See Appendix C for a description of the study.

Table 9-3 Advancement. Summary Evaluation of Quality Control Policies and Procedures (for inclusion in a firm's quality control document).

AICPA Policy/Procedure	Procedure's Applicability to Firm					Comments
	N	R	LL	SL	SP	
1. Establish qualifications deemed necessary for various levels of responsibility within the firm.						
a. Prepare job descriptions.	H	H	H	H-M	NA	Less detail for smaller firms
b. Identify criteria to be considered in evaluating an individual's qualifications.	H	H	H	H	NA	See Exhibit 9-1
c. Communicate advancement policies and procedures.	H	H	H	H	NA	Could be oral for SP
2. Evaluate performance of personnel and periodically advise personnel of their progress. Keep files.						
a. Evaluate personnel.	H	H	H	H	NA	State frequency and outline the procedure; it could be on an engagement and/or a periodic basis
(i) Assign responsibilities.	H	H	H	H	NA	
(ii) Delineate objectives to all personnel.	H	H	H	H	NA	
(iii) Use evaluation forms.	H	H	H	H	NA	
(iv) Discuss with evaluated person.	H	H	H	H	NA	
(v) Review evaluations.	H	H	H	M	NA	
(vi) Rotate supervisors and evaluators.	H	H	H	M	NA	
(vii) Make timely evaluations.	H	H	H	H	NA	

Table 9-3 continued

AICPA Policy/Procedure	Procedure's Applicability to Firm					Comments
	N	R	LL	SL	SP	
b. Periodically counsel personnel on their career opportunities.	H	H	H	H	NA	
(i) Periodically counsel staff on their progress and opportunities.	H	H	H	H	NA	
(ii) Periodically evaluate partners.	H	H	M	M-L	NA	Could be self-appraisal or peer evaluation
(iii) Monitor evaluation system for effectiveness and fairness.	H	H	H	M	NA	
3. Assign responsibility for advancement decisions.						
a. Assign responsibility for advancement and termination decisions and related procedures.	H	H	H	H	NA	Be consistent with hiring
b. Give appropriate recognition to quality of work performed.	H	H	H	H	NA	
c. Monitor advancement experience.	H	H	M	M	NA	

Key:

H	= High	N	= National or international firm
M	= Medium	R	= Regional firm
L	= Low	LL	= Large Local firm (possibly two or three offices)
NA	= Not Applicable	SL	= Small Local firm (one office)
		SP	= Sole Practitioner (possibly one part-time staff member)

Table 9-4 Summary of Advancement Documentation

Documentation — Purpose	AICPA Procedures
Quality control document — informs staff of policies and procedures	all
Assignment performance evaluation questionnaire — evaluation	2a, b
Annual evaluation form — evaluation	2a, b
Minutes of partners' meetings — record monitoring process	2b(iii), 3c

NOTES

1. For example see AICPA, *Sample Quality Control Documents for Local CPA Firms* (New York, N.Y.: AICPA, 1977), pp. 39-41.
2. Donald B. Scholl, "Preventing a Problem Partner," *Pennsylvania CPA Spokesman*, September 1974, pp. 12-16.

BIBLIOGRAPHY

AICPA. *Sample Quality Control Documents for Local CPA Firms.* New York, N.Y.: AICPA, 1977.

Pearson, Michael A. "Eight Ways to Increase Staff Turnovers." *Journal of Accountancy,* October 1977, p. 50.

Rachlin, Norman S. "Advice for Prospective Merger Partners." *Journal of Accountancy,* June 1977, p. 36.

Rachlin, Norman S. "How to Develop a Program to Motivate Your Staff." *The Practical Accountant,* September/October 1975, pp. 45-50.

Scholl, Donald B. "Preventing a Problem Partner." *Pennsylvania CPA Spokesman,* September 1976, pp. 12-16.

Stouffer, C. David. "How Not to Motivate Your Staff." *Journal of Accountancy,* September 1977, p. 67.

Chapter 10

Professional Development

A growing number of states require a minimum number of professional development hours for licensed CPAs. The AICPA quality control policies and procedures for professional development are covered in this chapter. An example of an annual report of Continuing Professional Education (CPE) hours, a history of CPE hours form, a CPE program participant's evaluation form, and a check list summary of standards for formal group study and self-study programs are provided. Professional development documentation is summarized in Table 10-4.

The opinions of CPA firm partners on selected quality control procedures are presented in Tables 10-1 and 10-2. These opinions should provide to practitioners some perspective on what other CPAs are thinking and doing with respect to quality control. For the reader's convenience, all tables and exhibits are presented at the end of the chapter.

OVERVIEW

Every CPA has the continuing obligation to expand his or her professional competence. Our world is very dynamic and that means that education must be a life-long process. In accounting there are almost constant changes in auditing and accounting standards, the business system, regulatory statutes, computer technology, taxes, and other parts of the CPA's environment. In an effort to keep the CPA informed, there is a growing accounting literature and a proliferation of CPE courses. In 1971, the AICPA Council passed a resolution urging states to require CPE as a condition for renewing CPA licenses. This resolution recommended 120 hours of CPE over a three-year period. During the 1970s, many states adopted mandatory CPE. It is likely that this trend will continue.

The professional development element of quality control poses a new practice management challenge to many accounting firms. They will have to provide a relevant CPE program to all professional personnel. While many firms in nonmandatory CPE states have followed the AICPA's 120-hour guidelines for CPAs, the requirement of the Division for CPA Firms is 120 hours every three years for *all* professional personnel. This additional expense poses a management challenge: to provide effective programs that will pay off in terms of better and more efficient services to clients.

AUTHORITATIVE POLICIES AND PROCEDURES

The AICPA quality control policies and procedures in Exhibit 10-6 outline the essentials for a firm's CPE program. The four objectives are followed by sample procedures, which are identified by letters. In the text, a procedure is identified by its objective number, the letter, and possibly small Roman numerals (2b(i), for example). Common procedures and the peer reviewer's approach are discussed below for each objective.

Establish Guidelines and Requirements

Objective 1: ESTABLISH GUIDELINES AND REQUIREMENTS FOR THE FIRM'S PROFESSIONAL DEVELOPMENT PROGRAM AND COMMUNICATE THEM TO PERSONNEL.

A firm should have an organized professional development program, stated in terms of hours and acceptable programs. The hours should be based on the AICPA guidelines of 120 hours every three years. A minimum of 20 hours per year is required by both Sections of the Division for CPA Firms. Acceptable programs include those sponsored by the AICPA, state CPA societies, and other professional organizations, and should be relevant to the CPA's expertise. The AICPA Council's resolution said that it should be a "formal program of learning which contributes directly to the professional competence of the individual."[1]

Formal programs requiring class attendance qualify if:

- An outline is prepared in advance, and preserved.
- The program is at least one hour (50-minute period) in length.
- The program is conducted by a qualified instructor.
- A record of registration or attendance is maintained.[2]

In-house programs meeting the above criteria are acceptable, as are both formal group study and self-study programs. Records should be maintained for five years. Standards for CPE programs are presented as a check list in Exhibit 10-5. Large firms have the capability to provide a large number of in-house programs. For smaller firms, the appropriate strategy is to use a combination of the alternative forms.

Looking at the survey data in Table 10-1, part 1, we see widespread acceptance of the CPE obligation by the respondents. As expected, the importance and usage scores increase with firm size.

Procedure 1a in Exhibit 10-6 requires an assignment of responsibility for a firm's CPE program. This same individual or group would likely perform the monitoring function suggested by procedure 1b.

Orientation

The orientation program specified by procedure 1c overlaps with the hiring element. The orientation program check list, presented in Exhibit 8-3, describes the basic elements of an orientation program.

Part 2 of Table 10-1 shows a deficiency in the use of orientation programs. Usage was estimated to be "occasional" in all but the largest firms, where it was "almost always." The importance scores show a general recognition of an orientation program's usefulness. Some of the low usage responses may be due to varying interpretations of "formalized." Formalized means systematic, like the program outlined in Exhibit 10-4, but it does not require classroom training. While a small firm can have an effective orientation without a detailed program or check list, the orientation process should be described in its quality control document. Part 3 of Table 10-1 shows estimated usage of formal staff training for inexperienced personnel to be "common" for all but the smallest firms. The very small firms rely more on on-the-job training. Since the Division for CPA Firm's minimum CPE requirements cover all professional personnel, more firms will use AICPA and state society courses, which are excellent.

Planning and Monitoring

Procedure 1d suggests the need for systematic CPE planning. The educational needs of managers are different from those of junior accountants. A convenient way of meeting this objective is to formulate an individualized CPE plan on an annual basis during the formal evaluation process. Referring back to the chapter on advancement, counseling was suggested in procedure 2b. This counseling logically should include a discussion of CPE objectives. This counseling also fits in with the monitoring requirement (1e).

The responses summarized in Table 10-2 indicate that CPAs view an individual's CPE record as an effective measure of ability. Eighty-six percent of the respondents agreed with this concept to some extent, and only 7.2 percent disagreed to some extent. It is very surprising that this result is so strong. It indicates that CPAs almost universally view CPE as necessary and beneficial.

The monitoring process requires recordkeeping. Exhibit 10-2 illustrates an annual report that would be submitted by all staff members. The information contained in the form reflects the recordkeeping specified by AICPA standards. Evidence of attendance includes grades, certificates and program materials. Incidentally, the retention period should be five years. Since the 120-hour standard covers three years, a record like Exhibit 10-3 provides a useful summary history for an individual. It records the type of educational program; a mixture is desirable.

An evaluation form like the one in Exhibit 10-4 should be used for in-house programs. This feedback mechanism helps instructors improve their performance and aids in the revision of program objectives and content.

Peer Reviewers

Reviewers analyze whether those responsible for professional development actually influence the firm's CPE program. A reviewer's check list is presented in Exhibit 10-1. Although it is oriented toward an international CPE firm, it does reflect what a reviewer looks for. Parts II, III, IV, and VI would be applied to a sample of courses. Firm records and interviews are used to make judgments. For example, in evaluating the orientation program, the orientation check list would be reviewed, and new personnel would be interviewed to see if it had been followed. A firm's CPE requirements, hours, and content are reviewed for adequacy. The means used by the firm to encourage CPE — such as paying for courses, professional dues, and meetings — are evaluated. A firm's monitoring procedures can be evaluated by reviewing records of participation for compliance with standards, and by evaluating the counseling procedures followed. Reviewers want to be sure that adequate action is taken if a firm's requirements are not met by an individual. The SEC Practice Section and the Private Companies Practice Section require an annual CPE report to be filed, and this might be verified by reviewers.

Provide Technical Updates

Objective 2: MAKE AVAILABLE TO PERSONNEL INFORMATION ABOUT CURRENT DEVELOPMENTS IN PROFESSIONAL TECHNICAL STANDARDS AND MATERIALS CONTAINING THE FIRM'S TECHNICAL POLICIES AND PROCEDURES AND ENCOURAGE PERSONNEL TO ENGAGE IN SELF-DEVELOPMENT ACTIVITIES.

Since the FASB, the Auditing Standards Executive Committee, the SEC, and other authoritative bodies are continually developing new standards, a system for advising personnel of current technical developments is needed. While large firms can use newsletters and firm publications, smaller firms have to rely on more economically feasible methods such as routing sheets and bulletin boards. In order to avoid an information overload, firms should be selective about the material routed to staff members. One possible system is to place information that "may be of interest" in a designated place (a clip board or file basket might be used) for a period of 30 days. The responsibility for distributing various types of materials should be assigned. Since the estimated usage responses in part 4 of Table 10-1 indicate that formal distribution systems are common, this procedural requirement should have minimal impact on firms.

Procedure 2b points out that a firm's CPE programs are an important means for disseminating information. The examples listed under 2b reflect the AICPA standards. These standards are summarized in Exhibit 10-5.

Peer Reviewers

Peer reviewers analyze the distribution system to determine whether information is effectively communicated. They check for timeliness and for comprehensiveness of coverage of current developments. A firm's training programs on current developments are evaluated for compliance with AICPA standards for CPE programs, in the same manner discussed under objective 1.

Provide Specialized Programs

Objective 3: PROVIDE, TO THE EXTENT NECESSARY, PROGRAMS TO FILL THE FIRM'S NEEDS FOR PERSONNEL WITH EXPERTISE IN SPECIALIZED AREAS AND INDUSTRIES.

The third objective reflects the need for customized CPE for specialists. The specialist must assume a considerable amount of individual responsibility for meeting this objective. In large firms, in-house programs are feasible (3a), but small firms must rely on outside programs (3b). A firm can encourage specialties by paying for training, educational materials, and memberships in specialized professional associations (3c and 3d).

Peer Reviewers

A firm's specialized training programs are evaluated by reviewers for adequacy. The CPE records for specialists might be reviewed to see whether specialized training is reflected. For example, you would expect to find computer audit specialists attending some programs on computer-related topics. Some specialized technical materials might be reviewed.

Provide On-the-Job Training

Objective 4: PROVIDE FOR ON-THE-JOB TRAINING DURING THE PER-
FORMANCE OF ENGAGEMENTS.

The importance of on-the-job training is firmly imbedded in the minds of
practitioners. It has its roots in the days when accounting was taught by the
apprenticeship method. To maximize the effectiveness of on-the-job training,
engagement supervisors and their assistants must be reminded of its importance.
One procedure is to include on-the-job training in the engagement planning check
list. Having staff evaluations after all long engagements is a means of emphasizing
on-the-job training. In their evaluation of engagement working papers, reviewers
check for the on-the-job training dimension of engagement management.

Procedure 4b suggests the need for formal management training of supervisory
personnel. While a supervisory person's college education might include formal
management training, some evidence of additional training may be desirable on an
individual's CPE record.

Procedure 4d suggests a monitoring process for important measurable aspects of
on-the-job training. This would normally be integrated with the career counseling
process, discussed in the chapter on advancement. Thus, responsibilities for these
functions should be coordinated.

In part 5 of Table 10-1, the responses indicate a receptiveness to monitoring
personnel assignments. The lowest importance score is 3.5. However, the estimated usage is only in the "occasional" range for the smallest firms and the "20 to
80" group.

Peer Reviewers

Part IX indicates the major review procedures. Reviewers might also check
efforts to rotate staff among types of engagement work and among supervisory
personnel.

GENERAL DESIGN

A general design for professional development is shown in Exhibit 10-7. Partner
C has the primary responsibility for the system. All supervisory personnel have
on-the-job training responsibilities. Personnel are counseled on their individual
CPE responsibilities during the annual evaluation process. Thus, the annual
evaluation form is pertinent documentation.

A summary of AICPA objectives and sample procedures to implement them is
presented in Table 10-3. Each procedure's applicability according to firm size is a

generalization based upon current standards. Several characteristics of firms are recognized in the accounting profession's quality control programs as determinants of the appropriate quality control policies and procedures for CPA firms. Therefore, a firm must consider all of its characteristics in designing procedures and assigning responsibilities. Similarly, forms, check lists, and other documentation shown in this book and elsewhere must be modified to fit the individual firm's needs. Table 10-4 summarizes professional development documentation.

Exhibit 10-1 Reviewer's Check List for Evaluating Audit Training

I. Evaluation of training philosophy, goals, and objectives.
____A. Gain an understanding of the mission, organization, policies, and responsibilities of the individuals charged with the audit training responsibility.
____B. Study the overall operation of the training program.
____C. Compare the training philosophy, goals, and objectives with:
____(1) the profession's standards (e.g., GAAS, SAS No. 4, Voluntary Quality Control Review Programs for CPA Firms).
____(2) the firm's audit training philosophy and objectives.
____D. Determine if audit training philosophy, goals, and objectives are being implemented.
____E. Determine if firm monitors whether goals and objectives are being met.

II. Review training curriculum for:
____A. Completeness and relevance.
____B. Currency.
____C. Location of courses.
____D. Internal monitoring system.

III. Review selected courses for:
____A. Content.
____B. Delivery system.

IV. Review quality of instruction in firm programs with respect to:
____A. Instructor selection.
____B. Instructor training.
____C. Instructor preparation.
____D. Instructor evaluation.
____E. Instructor recognition.

V. Evaluate the training information system with respect to:
____A. Recordkeeping for the firm's purposes.
____B. Recordkeeping for the benefit of regulatory groups or associations.

VI. Evaluate the training facilities:
____A. Physical facilities.
____B. Training equipment.
____C. Library resources.

VII. Evaluate the administration of training, including:
____A. The training organization.
____B. Policies as to training.
____C. Partner participation and supervision.

VIII. Evaluate participants:
____A. Matching participants with the appropriate course.
____B. Ascertaining if participant's performance is reviewed.

IX. Review on-the-job training:
____A. Review policies and procedures relating to on-the-job training.
____B. Determine firm's commitment to on-the-job training (e.g., whether it is emphasized in staff evaluations).
____C. Determine if staff is formally trained on how to conduct on-the-job training.
____D. Determine ability of firm's executives to monitor effectiveness of the on-the-job training.

Source: Anthony T. Kryzstofits, Stephen E. Loeb, Doyle Z. Williams, "How to Review Audit Training," *The CPA Journal,* July 1978, p. 12. This is reprinted with permission from the *CPA Journal,* published by the New York State Society of Certified Public Accountants.

Exhibit 10-2 Annual Report of CPE Hours

NAME_____   YEAR_____

Summary of CPE Hours: CPE Hours Guidelines:

1. In-house _____   Credit Courses: Each semester-hour credit equals 15 CPE hours.
2. External _____   Each quarter-hour credit equals 10 CPE hours.
3. Self-study _____   Noncredit Courses: Each classroom hours equals one CPE hour
4. Group-study _____   (50-minute hours).
    Instructors: CPE hours can be granted on a 3 for 1 basis.

School, Firm or Sponsoring Organization Conducting Program	Date and Location	Title of Program or Description of Content	Principal Instructor	Evidence Retained	CPE Hours Firm	External
				yes no		
				yes no		
				yes no		
				yes no		
				yes no		
				yes no		
				yes no		
				yes no		
				yes no		
				TOTALS		

The above statement reflects my CPE performance for the year.

Signed_____

Exhibit 10-3 History of CPE Hours

Name_____   Staff No. _____

Year	Programs Attended		Self-study Programs	Group Study	Annual Total	3-Year Moving Average
	In-house	External				
___	___	___	___	___	___	___
___	___	___	___	___	___	___
___	___	___	___	___	___	___
___	___	___	___	___	___	___
___	___	___	___	___	___	___
___	___	___	___	___	___	___
___	___	___	___	___	___	___
___	___	___	___	___	___	___
___	___	___	___	___	___	___
___	___	___	___	___	___	___
___	___	___	___	___	___	___
___	___	___	___	___	___	___
___	___	___	___	___	___	___
___	___	___	___	___	___	___
___	___	___	___	___	___	___
___	___	___	___	___	___	___
___	___	___	___	___	___	___
___	___	___	___	___	___	___
___	___	___	___	___	___	___
___	___	___	___	___	___	___

Exhibit 10-4 CPE Program Participant's Evaluation

NAME OF COURSE_____ DATE_____

LOCATION_____

To help us improve our programs, please complete this form by circling the appropriate number below.

5 = excellent	4 = very good	3 = good
2 = fair	1 = poor	

1. The quality of the materials   1   2   3   4   5

2. Overall effectiveness of the instructors   1   2   3   4   5

    _____

    _____

    _____

3. The instructor's technical competence   1   2   3   4   5
    to teach the course

4. Contribution to your professional   1   2   3   4   5
    competence--conceptual knowledge

5. Contribution to your professional   1   2   3   4   5
    competence--practical knowledge

6. Satisfaction with facilities   1   2   3   4   5

7. Overall satisfaction with the program   1   2   3   4   5

8. Was the course outline followed? _____

9. What specific comments can you provide that will assist us in the future (good things, bad things, new ideas, etc.)? _____

   _____

   _____

   _____

   _____

Signature_____
(optional)

Exhibit 10-5 Check List Summary of Standards for Formal Group and Self-study
Programs

Standards for CPE Program Development

1. The program should contribute to the professional competence of participants.
2. The stated program objectives should specify the level of knowledge the
participant should have attained or the level of competence he should
be able to demonstrate upon completing the program.
3. The education and/or experience prerequisites for the program should be
stated.
4. Programs should be developed by individuals qualified in the subject
matter and in instructional design.
5. Program content should be current.
6. Programs should be reviewed by qualified persons other than the preparers
to ensure compliance with the above standards.

Standards for CPE Program Presentation

1. Participants should be informed in advance of objectives, prerequisites,
experience level, content, advance preparation, teaching methods, and
CPE contact hours credit.
2. Instructors should be qualified both with respect to program content and
teaching methods used.
3. Program sponsors should encourage participation only by individuals with
appropriate education and/or experience.
4. The number of participants and physical facilities should be consistent
with the teaching methods specified.
5. All programs should include some means for evaluating quality.

Fifty Minutes Standards for CPE Program Measurement

1. All programs should be measured in terms of 50-minute contact hours.
The shortest recognized program should consist of one contact hour.
2. When an instructor or discussion leader serves at a program for which
participants receive CPE credit and at a level that increases his or
her professional competence, credit should be given for preparation
and presentation time, measured in terms of contact hours.

Group-study or Self-study Standards for CPE Reporting

1. Participants in group or self-study programs should document their
participation, including: (a) sponsor, (b) title and/or description
of content, (c) dates, (d) location, and (e) number of CPE contact
hours. Documentation should be retained for five years.
2. In order to support the reports that may be required of participants,
the sponsor of group or self-study programs should retain for an
appropriate period: (a) record of participation, (b) outline of the
course (or equivalent), (c) dates, (d) location, (e) instructors, and
(f) number of CPE contact hours.

Source: Reprinted from AICPA *CPE Catalog* 1978-1979 by permission of the AICPA, © 1978.

Exhibit 10-6 AICPA Quality Control Policies and Procedures for Professional
Development

1. **Establish guidelines and requirements for the firm's professional development program and communicate them to personnel.**
   a. Assign responsibility for the professional development function to a person or group with appropriate authority.
   b. Provide that programs developed by the firm be reviewed by qualified individuals. Programs should contain statements of objectives and education and/or experience prerequisites.
   c. Provide an orientation program relating to the firm and the profession for newly employed personnel.
      (i) Prepare publications and programs designed to inform newly employed personnel of their professional responsibilities and opportunities.
      (ii) Designate responsibility for conducting orientation conferences to explain professional responsibilities and firm policies.
      (iii) Enable newly employed personnel with limited experience to attend the AICPA or other comparable level staff training programs.
   d. Establish continuing professional education requirements for personnel at each level within the firm.
      (i) Consider state mandatory requirements or voluntary guidelines in establishing firm requirements.
      (ii) Encourage participation in external continuing professional education programs, including college-level and self-study courses.
      (iii) Encourage membership in professional organizations. Consider having the firm pay or contribute toward membership dues and expenses.
      (iv) Encourage personnel to serve on professional committees, prepare articles, and participate in other professional activities.
   e. Monitor continuing professional education programs and maintain appropriate records, both on a firm and an individual basis.
      (i) Review periodically the records of participation by personnel to determine compliance with firm requirements.
      (ii) Review periodically evaluation reports and other records prepared for continuing education programs to evaluate whether the programs are being presented effectively and are accomplishing firm objectives. Consider the need for new programs and for revision or elimination of ineffective programs.

Exhibit 10-6 continued

2. **Make available to personnel information about current developments in professional technical standards and materials containing the firm's technical policies and procedures and encourage personnel to engage in self-development activities.**

   a. Provide personnel with professional literature relating to current developments in professional technical standards.
      (i)   Distribute to personnel material of general interest, such as pronouncements of the Financial Accounting Standards Board and the AICPA Auditing Standards Executive Committee.
      (ii) Distribute pronouncements in areas of specific interest, such as those issued by the Securities and Exchange Commission, Internal Revenue Service, and other regulatory agencies to persons who have responsibility in such areas.
      (iii) Distribute manuals containing firm policies and procedures on technical matters to personnel. Manuals should be updated for new developments and changing conditions.

   b. For training programs presented by the firm, develop or obtain course materials and select and train instructors.
      (i)   State the program objectives and education and/or experience prerequisites in the training programs.
      (ii) Provide that program instructors be qualified as to both program content and teaching methods.
      (iii) Have participants evaluate program content and instructors of training sessions.
      (iv) Have instructors evaluate program content and participants in training sessions.
      (v)   Update programs as needed in light of new developments, changing conditions, and evaluation reports.

3. **Provide, to the extent necessary, programs to fill the firm's needs for personnel with expertise in specialized areas and industries.**

   a. Conduct firm programs to develop and maintain expertise in specialized areas and industries, such as regulated industries, computer auditing, and statistical sampling methods.

   b. Encourage attendance at external education programs, meetings, and conferences to acquire technical or industry expertise.

   c. Encourage membership and participation in organizations concerned with specialized areas and industries.

   d. Provide technical literature relating to specialized areas and industries.

Exhibit 10-6 continued

4. Provide for on-the-job training during the performance of engagements.

   a. Emphasize the importance of on-the-job training as a significant part of an individual's development.

      (i)   Discuss with assistants the relationship of the work they are performing to the engagement as a whole.

      (ii) Involve assistants in as many portions of the engagement as practicable.

   b. Emphasize the significance of personnel management skills and include coverage of these subjects in firm training programs.

   c. Encourage personnel to train and develop subordinates.

   d. Monitor assignments to determine that personnel —

      (i)   Fulfill, where applicable, the experience requirements of the state board of accountancy.

      (ii) Gain experience in various areas of engagements and varied industries.

      (iii) Work under different supervisory personnel.

Exhibit 10-7 Example of General Design for Professional Development

Operational Responsibilities:

Partner C is responsible for the professional development function, including distribution of technical materials to professional personnel. All partners are responsible for maintaining competence in their designated specialties, and for providing general interest materials on their specialties to Partner C for distribution to all professional personnel. Partners A and C counsel personnel on their CPE needs during the annual evaluation process. All supervisory personnel are responsible for on-the-job training during engagements. As needed, firm personnel take responsibility for in-house CPE programs.

Communication:

The personnel manual contains CPE procedures, including procedures for distribution of materials.

Monitoring:

Partner C monitors the CPE participation by personnel, the firm's CPE programs, and on-the-job training. An annual report is made at the September partners' meeting.

Documentation:

1. Personnel manual; CPE policies and procedures
2. Annual report of CPE hours
3. History of CPE hours
4. CPE program participant's evaluation
5. Annual evaluation form
6. Routing slip
7. Minutes of partners' meetings

NOTE: The profile firm is described in Appendix A.

Table 10-1 Opinions on Professional Development Policies and Procedures

| Quality Control | Number of Professional Personnel in Firm | | | | | | | |
| | 1 to 5 | | 6 to 20 | | 20 to 80 | | More than 80 | |
Policy or Procedure	Mean	CV	Mean	CV	Mean	CV	Mean	CV
(1) The firm establishes a professional development program with guidelines and requirements as to:								
a. Relevant subject matter.								
Importance	3.78	22%	4.50	15%	4.50	16%	4.94	5%
Usage	3.19	41%	3.64	26%	2.91	25%	4.61	16%
b. Hours of participation.								
Importance	3.44	29%	4.25	15%	5.00	0%	4.50	16%
Usage	3.08	49%	3.75	21%	3.34	43%	4.61	16%
c. Acceptable forms of professional development.								
Importance	3.56	32%	4.32	13%	4.50	16%	4.38	25%
Usage	3.19	41%	3.81	24%	3.34	22%	4.25	27%
(2) A formalized orientation program is established for new personnel.								
Importance	2.78	35%	3.50	24%	4.50	16%	4.50	16%
Usage	2.50	50%	2.50	44%	2.50	50%	4.61	19%
(3) Inexperienced personnel must have formal staff training when hired.								
Importance	3.11	30%	3.60	33%	3.50	61%	4.25	29%
Usage	2.61	55%	3.19	46%	3.75	58%	4.29	28%
(4) A formal system of distributing materials on new technical developments is used. Materials include articles, pronouncements, etc.								
Importance	3.44	39%	4.15	18%	3.50	20%	4.69	13%
Usage	3.19	44%	3.41	32%	4.16	17%	3.54	22%
(5) The assignment of personnel to engagements is monitored to assure that on-the-job training is being provided.								
Importance	3.67	38%	4.30	20%	3.50	20%	4.67	13%
Usage	2.73	54%	3.70	30%	2.91	25%	4.25	27%
Number of Responses	10		21		5		32	

Table 10-1 continued

NOTE: The mean responses are based on a five-point scale. They can be interpreted according to where they fall within the following ranges:

Importance	Range	Usage	Range
Unimportant	1.00-1.5	Rare	1.25-1.88
Little importance	1.51-2.5	Occasional	1.89-3.13
Some importance	2.51-3.5	Common	3.14-4.38
Important	3.51-4.5	Almost always	4.39-5.00
Essential	4.51-5.0		

For example, an importance score of 1.81 indicates that the respondents viewed the procedure as being of little importance. CV represents coefficient of variation. The higher the coefficient of variation, the greater the variability in the responses of the CPA firm partners in a particular group. See Appendix C for a description of the study.

Table 10-2 Questionnaire Responses

Statement	Number of Professional Personnel in Firm				
	1 to 5	6 to 20	20 to 80	More than 80	Total
The professional development record of an accountant is an effective way of measuring abilities.					
Strongly agree	23.1	26.7	57.1	55.0	38.4
Agree	57.7	57.8	35.7	35.0	48.0
No opinion	7.7	8.9	0.0	5.0	6.8
Disagree	3.8	4.4	7.1	5.0	4.8
Strongly disagree	7.7	2.2	0.0	0.0	2.4
Mean	3.85	4.02	4.43	4.40	4.16
Number of CPAs responding	28	45	15	40	128

NOTE: All numbers, except means, are stated as a percentage of the total column responding. The means are based on a scale of 1 to 5, where "strongly disagree" is 1 and "strongly agree" is 5. See Appendix C for a description of the study.

Table 10-3 Professional Development. Summary Evaluation of Quality Control Policies and Procedures (for inclusion in a firm's quality control document).

AICPA Policy/Procedure	Procedure's Applicability to Firm					Comments
	N	R	LL	SL	SP	
1. Establish guidelines and requirements for the firm's professional development program and communicate them to personnel.						
a. Assign responsibility for the professional development function (state who).	H	H	H	H	NA	
b. Firm-sponsored CPE programs are reviewed by qualified personnel (state who).	H	H	H	M	NA	Keep records of firm's programs for five years
c. Provide orientation program for new personnel.	H	H	H	H	NA	AICPA or firm staff training
d. Establish CPE requirements for all levels of firm professional personnel (state requirements and define acceptable activities).	H	H	H	H	H	Consider AICPA, state, and Division for CPA Firms guidelines; generally at least 20 hrs per year and 120 hrs for 3 years
e. Monitor CPE programs and maintain records.	H	H	H	H	H	Individual records, firm reports, retain for 5 years
(i) Monitor participation by personnel.	H	H	H	H	NA	
(ii) Review program evaluations, etc., and make revisions as necessary.	H	H	H	M	NA	
2. Inform personnel about current technical developments and encourage self-development.						
a. Distribute professional literature about technical developments (state how).	H	H	H	H	H	Indicate responsibilities; update firm manuals

	N	R	LL	SL	SP	
b. Firm training programs are designed to meet professional standards.	H	H	H	M	L	See Exhibit 10-4
3. The firm provides programs to fill its needs for specialists.						
a. In-house programs are used.	H	H	M	L	L	See Exhibit 10-4
b. Outside programs are used.	H	H	H	H	H	
c. The firm encourages specialists to participate in specialized organizations.	H	H	H	M	L	Pay dues for professional societies, etc.
d. Individuals (state who) are responsible for acquiring and distributing specialized technical materials.	H	H	H	M	L	
4. Provide for on-the-job training during the performance of engagements.						
a. Emphasize the importance of on-the-job training to supervisors and assistants.	H	H	H-M	M	NA	Guide and rotate assistants
b. Train supervisory people to develop personnel management skills.	H	H-M	H-M	M	NA	
c. Encourage personnel to train and develop subordinates.	H	H	H-M	M	NA	
d. Plan and monitor personnel assignments so that on-the-job training is maximized.	H	H	H-M	H-M	NA	Rotate supervisors and engagements; assignment flexibility decreases with firm size

Key:

H	= High	N	= National or international firm
M	= Medium	R	= Regional firm
L	= Low	LL	= Large Local firm (possibly two or three offices)
NA	= Not Applicable	SL	= Small Local firm (one office)
		SP	= Sole Practitioner (possibly one part-time staff member)

Table 10-4 Summary of Professional Development Documentation

Documentation — Purpose	AICPA Procedures
Quality control document — informs personnel of policies and procedures	all
Annual report of CPE hours — document hours	1e
History of CPE hours — analyzes hours	1e
CPE program participants' evaluations — control program quality	1e,2b
Annual evaluation form — record CPE counseling	1d
Routing slip — distribution	2a
Minutes of partners' meetings — record monitoring process	1e

NOTES

1. AICPA Council, *Resolution on Continuing Education* (New York, N.Y.: AICPA, 1971), p. 1.
2. Ibid.

BIBLIOGRAPHY

AICPA Council. *Resolution on Continuing Education*. New York, N.Y.: AICPA, 1971.

Axline, Larry L. "How to Measure and Improve Your Professional Staff's Performance." *The Practical Accountant,* March/April 1977, pp. 39-44.

Cass, Martin and Kronstadt, Norman. "In-House CPE Program." *Journal of Accountancy,* October 1977, p. 52.

Grollman, William. "Professional Development for Smaller Firms." *The CPA Journal,* May 1976, pp. 29-33.

Kryzstofits, Anthony T. and Loeb, Stephen E. and Williams, Doyle Z. "How to Review Audit Training." The *CPA Journal,* July 1978, pp. 11-15.

May, Gordon. "Professional Development in Medium-Size Firms." *The CPA Journal,* March 1976, pp. 35-39.

Sprague, W.D. "The Case for Universal Professional Development." *The CPA Journal,* September 1973, pp. 747-753.

White, Gary E. and Buchman, Thomas A. "Continuing Education Requirement: How Effective?" *The CPA Journal,* December 1977, pp. 11-15.

Chapter 11

Supervision

Supervision is the most important element of quality control. It covers planning, directing and reviewing engagements. The AICPA supervision quality control policies and procedures stating the objectives and sample procedures are reprinted in Exhibit 11-7 and summarized with comments in Table 11-3. An example of an audit engagement planning check list, an audit pre-planning check list, and a work paper review check list are provided. Relevant documentation is summarized in Table 11-4.

The opinions of CPA firm partners on selected quality control procedures are presented in Tables 11-1 and 11-2. These opinions should provide to practitioners some perspective on what other CPAs are thinking and doing with respect to quality control. For the reader's convenience, all tables and exhibits are presented at the end of the chapter.

OVERVIEW

The supervision element covers all aspects of engagement management. It requires adequate engagement planning, staffing, directing, and controlling. While supervision techniques can be taught to engagement management personnel, experience, judgment, and effective firm procedures are important factors. This element includes the review process for working papers, financial reports, and audit reports. For audit engagements with SEC-regulated clients, a second partner with no direct responsibility for the engagement should make a review. For other engagements, the extent of review varies with the difficulty, the risk, the competence of those doing the work, etc.

In developing quality control policies and procedures for supervision, a firm should seriously consider the use of an accounting and auditing manual, which would contain guidelines for engagement management, working paper content, and review procedures. It would also include check lists and instructions for various segments of the audit engagement. Since the detailed contents of an accounting and auditing manual can be extensive — and can vary by firm — only the most important contents of an audit manual are discussed in this book. The bibliography provides references to other sources of useful materials. The Private Companies Practice Section makes a model audit manual available to its members.

AUTHORITATIVE POLICIES AND PROCEDURES

Three objectives are contained in the AICPA quality control policies and procedures in Exhibit 11-7. A firm's accounting and auditing procedures should be designed to accomplish these objectives. Examples of procedures are identified in Exhibit 11-7 by letters and Roman numerals, and are identified that way in the text (3a(ii), for example). For each objective, common procedures and the external peer reviewer's likely approach are discussed below.

Engagement Planning Procedures

Objective 1: PROVIDE PROCEDURES FOR PLANNING ENGAGEMENTS.

Careful planning is the key to effective engagement management. In SAS No. 22 the need for planning is mandated:

> In planning his examination, the auditor should consider the nature, extent, and timing of work to be performed and should prepare a written audit program (or a set of written audit programs). An audit program aids in instructing assistants in the work to be done. It should set forth in reasonable detail the audit procedures that the auditor believes are necessary to accomplish the objectives of the examination. The form of the audit program and the extent of its detail will vary.[1]

Plans can be changed as the examination progresses. According to procedure 1a in Exhibit 11-7, responsibilities for planning must be clearly assigned to the various levels of management. For example, the engagement manager may be responsible for drafting a plan if the budgeted engagement hours exceed a certain minimum or if the engagement is for a new client. A review of this plan by the engagement partner would be required before implementation.

Successful engagement planning starts with adequate background information (1b). The next step is a detailed plan, including work programs, staff requests, budgets, etc. (1c). The extent of planning depends on the engagement's scope, size, risk, and other factors. Planning is obviously easier for repeat engagements. Some firms use standardized work programs and modify them to suit the specific client. The detail of these programs varies by firm. They are several pages long, and can be obtained from several sources (see bibliography). Instead of a long work program, the firm might use a shorter engagement planning check list, which has the advantage of guiding the CPA's plan without too much rigidity. It can be used alone or on shorter engagements. An example is shown in Exhibit 11-2.

The audit pre-planning check list in Exhibit 11-3 can be used with a detailed work program. The form indicates that it should be prepared by a manager or senior accountant and be reviewed by a manager or partner. A space for partner approval is at the bottom.

The importance of engagement planning is emphasized by the survey data in Table 11-1, part 1. Parts a and b show high importance scores for requiring formalized planning to cover specified areas of audit engagements. The scores increase in importance with firm size, because the complexity of a firm's largest audits generally increases with the size of the firm. The usage scores for formalized audit planning are in the "common" range except in the largest firms, where it is in the "almost always" range. Part c shows lower scores for unaudited engagements, which is to be expected because they are less complex than audits. The coefficients of variation for part c are higher than the coefficients for parts a and b. This suggests greater diversity among firms in the planning procedures used for unaudited engagements.

Peer Reviewers

During their inspection of engagement working papers, reviewers check for the adequacy of engagement planning. They are concerned with whether planning responsibilities have been appropriately assigned and plans have been properly approved. They look for adequate background information on the client in the working papers. The comprehensiveness of the plan is considered, and the causes of significant deviations from plans are investigated.

Maintain the Firm's Standards of Quality

Objective 2: PROVIDE PROCEDURES FOR MAINTAINING THE FIRM'S STANDARDS OF QUALITY FOR THE WORK PERFORMED.

The second objective covers a significant portion of a firm's accounting and auditing operations. Firms should seriously consider preparing some form of accounting and auditing manual, which should cover all the objectives and sample procedures under the supervision element. It could include standard audit plans, internal control evaluation, check lists, reviewing, etc. The details can vary, according to the firm's practice. Since a small firm has less complex audits than a national firm, it could just include some check lists, questionnaires, and outlines of procedures.

The CPA firm partners were asked whether their firm used an auditing manual. The "Yes" responses, by firm size, were as follows:

1 to 5	36%
6 to 20	38%
20 to 80	67%
More than 80	100%

We can expect more smaller firms to use audit manuals in the future, but there is some discretion under current quality control standards.

An obvious perspective is that working paper guidelines should be coordinated with or based on the engagement check list used by peer reviewers. These check lists are readily available from the AICPA. One possible short cut is to alter a copy of this check list, and use it as the guidelines. Another possible short cut is to designate certain sets of client working papers as examples of a firm's standards. For smaller firms, the guidelines can be broader than for larger firms because partners can give personal instructions to all staff members.

In some firms, each partner has his or her own way of doing working papers. This is one characteristic of Whipple's "his firm/my firm" setup. How much diversity will reviewers tolerate? While an exact answer is not yet available, a logical approach would be for reviewers to expect at least some conformity to a firm's general guidelines. We should expect a greater demand for uniformity within a firm as time passes.

The estimated usage of guidelines for working paper form and content (Table 11-1, part 2), is in the "common" range for all four groups. The importance scores are in the 3.67 to 4.64 range. Since firms should have some guidelines, some improvement is needed.

The use of standardized forms, check lists, and questionnaires is encouraged by procedure 2c. While many are available from numerous sources, firms must be selective. A good compromise is to have a few check lists for all engagements, and others to be used as needed.

The key audit check list areas indicated by the Private Companies Practice Section's compliance review program guidelines are internal control, audit planning and programs, financial statement disclosures, time budgets, and reviews of field work. A common problem with check lists is their tendency to become outdated upon the issuance of new authoritative pronouncements.

SAS No. 22 provides guidance for when there are differences in opinion among audit personnel:

The auditor with final responsibility for the examination and assistants should be aware of the procedures to be followed when differences of opinion concerning accounting and auditing issues exist among firm personnel involved in the examination. Such procedures should enable an assistant to document his disagreement with the conclusions reached if, after appropriate consultation, he believes it necessary to disassociate himself from the resolution of the matter. In this situation, the basis for the final resolution should also be documented.[2]

A firm's procedures for resolving differences of professional judgment among members of the engagement team must naturally be linked to its chain of command. Typically, one partner or a committee has the ultimate authority. Some firms require a memo for the files to document the resolution of significant disputes. According to procedure 1d, the quality control document should describe the procedure in general terms. Peer reviewers judge the adequacy of supervision by the overall content of selected engagement working papers. The qualifications of the supervisory personnel on particular engagements is another factor. Working paper guidelines and check lists are evaluated for appropriateness to a firm's practice and AICPA standards; compliance is tested. The effectiveness of procedures for resolving judgmental differences among engagement personnel are also examined for compliance.

Procedures for Reviewing Working Papers and Reports

Objective 3: PROVIDE PROCEDURES FOR REVIEWING ENGAGEMENT WORKING PAPERS AND REPORTS.

A firm's third objective for the supervision element is to develop guidelines for the review of working papers and reports. SAS No. 22 states:

The work performed by each assistant should be reviewed to determine whether it was adequately performed and to evaluate whether the results are consistent with the conclusions to be presented in the auditor's report.[3]

These firm guidelines can be stated in terms of (1) who does the reviewing and (2) the coverage of the review. The coverage of the review can be documented by a reviewer's check list.

Procedure 3a covers working papers, and procedure 3b covers reports. This division is important because procedure 3b(iii) — under which someone with no other responsibility for the engagement reviews the report — is an important quality control issue. The SEC requires this review — commonly called a "second partner review" — for all publicly-held companies' audits. When this second reviewer has only minimal knowledge of the client's business, it is called by some a "cold review." This second reviewer normally uses a shorter check list (if any) than the one used by engagement management personnel.

Primary Review

An example of a working paper review check list is presented in Exhibit 11-4. It indicates that the review process is a team effort, progressing from lower-level engagement managers to a partner. In addition to signing the check list, each reviewer should initial some of the working papers as evidence of the review process. While the accountant in charge may be able to initial all work papers, upper-level reviewers should not attempt to do this, since a review of all working papers would be too time-consuming.

Upper-level reviewers have to be selective in their review efforts. They want to focus on key engagement areas. An advantage of this sample check list is its conciseness. I have talked to many reviewers, and several have said that lengthy check lists are a burden except for new clients. In a small firm, the engagement partner often does the entire check list because the other levels of engagement management do not exist.

The disclosure check list (item 6, Manager/Supervisor Review of Exhibit 11-4) is a commonly used device. Disclosure check lists indicate crucial disclosures, with references to authoritative pronouncements. The AICPA check lists for audited and unaudited engagements (contained in *Technical Practice Aids*), include disclosure check lists.

In talking to practitioners I have encountered various ideas on how the primary review should be handled. There are many different check lists in use. Some CPAs do not use a review check list. Some do not use a check list on "easy audits" that only have a few crucial areas. Engagement complexity, and the perceived competence of staff members assigned to the engagement, typically affect the reviewer's depth of investigation.

In an article in *The CPA Journal*, Joseph V. Bencivenga described his method for reviewing working papers and reports. It is worthwhile reading for anyone doing engagement reviews. Bencivenga's summary of his views appears in Exhibit 11-1. According to item 3, he views the reviewer's function as developing an exception report. While he recommends doing the review in the client's office, many practitioners prefer to work at the CPA firm's office. In item 14, he recommends that review notes on what must be done should be discarded at the conclusion of the engagement. This is a common practice. The notes have no potential future benefit to the CPA, and could harm him if the engagement becomes subject to litigation. The last point in the guidelines is to have a second reviewer.

The CPA firm partners were asked their views on guidelines for reviewing working papers and documenting the review. The results appear in part 4 of Table 11-1. The importance scores, ranging from 4.04 for the smallest firms to 4.79 for the largest, indicate an overall receptiveness to this procedure by all groups of CPAs. The coefficients of variation show more diversity in response among the smaller firm CPAs as to importance. The estimated usage scores indicate this procedure to be in the "common" range except for the largest firms which are in the "almost always" range. Thus, we can expect the need for some firms to develop guidelines for reviewing working papers. Systematic reviewing by others of auditing and accounting work is one of the major objectives of the profession's quality control program. In my interviews with quality control specialists, the failure to review some engagements was commonly cited as a major problem in some CPA firms. One major concern of external peer reviewers is to see whether the reviewed firm has an adequate review mechanism.

Second Reviewer

The second reviewer's purpose is to ascertain that the work was done, generally accepted auditing standards and accounting principles were followed, and the audit report is justified. The second reviewer generally uses a shorter check list (if any) than the primary reviewer. A good idea is to include new technical developments on this check list, because the greatest chance of error is in new areas. Second reviewers look for reporting deficiencies, and do not try to rewrite reports so that they conform with their personal style. The second reviewer might not be a partner: in some firms, the second reviewer must be a partner only for risky or complex engagements. The second reviewer procedure can be eliminated for low-risk engagements. There is, of course, an element of judgment in determining risk.

Some offices have a reviewer specialist — not necessarily a partner — who reviews all audit engagements to some extent before a report is released. Typically, this specialist is also responsible for keeping up with current technical developments and for modifying the firm's manuals accordingly. In a large office, this specialist might have no direct client responsibility.

To control the reports and document the review process, a guide sheet is commonly used. Exhibit 11-5 contains a report guide sheet from the *MAP Handbook*. It provides room for authorizations and clerical matters. This sample form is very extensive, but it points out the need to have established procedures for report processing. Every firm should have a guide sheet in some form, even if only a small slip of paper is used as evidence that the report has gone through the major processing stages — review, typing, proofreading, reproduction, and release. A shorter version of a report guide sheet is presented in Exhibit 11-6. The need to show control over reports and to document the review process cannot be over emphasized.

Opinions on Engagement Review

Table 11-1 presents the CPA respondents' views of primary reviews and second reviews. High importance scores, ranging from 4.33 to 4.84, for primary reviews of all audit engagements are shown in 5a. The estimated usage scores are also high, 4.09 to 4.48. While these usage scores are high, some audit engagements are apparently not reviewed by the engagement partner. Either the respondents do not always follow the procedure in their firms, or they suspect that others do not. This is not necessarily bad. Objective 3 and its sample procedures strongly encourage the review of engagement working papers, but exceptions for very simple engagements seem acceptable. A self-review by the accountant, using a check list, could be acceptable.

The importance and usage scores for risky engagements (5b) were only slightly higher than for all engagements (5a). Some accounting firms do try to distinguish audits by their complexity. The importance and estimated usage scores for 5c are just about the same as 5a, indicating the importance of reviewing unaudited engagements.

Second partner review was not considered as common or as important as primary review. The scores under part 6 of Table 11-1 are noticeably lower than the scores under part 5. For all audit engagements (6a), the estimated usage is in the "occasional" range except for the largest firms, where it is "common." The second partner review importance scores are higher for risky or difficult audited engagements (6b).

Use of Second Reviewers

Table 11-2 provides additional insight into the use of second reviewers. From 58 to 80 percent of the firms in each group used this procedure for all audit engagements. Part b shows second review to be less common for unaudited financial statements, with a range from 20 to 53 percent.

Since second review is a common procedure, all firms should give careful consideration to adopting it, at least on a selective basis. If not followed for all audits, guidelines for its use should be objective. Examples of measurable guidelines are engagement hours, ownership of common stock, and type of business. The client acceptance and continuance criteria should be considered in these guidelines. If these require special approval for a particular client's acceptance or continuance, a second review of the report for this client seems appropriate. This consistency between the risk perceived under client acceptance and continuance procedures and review procedures is important to remember.

Sole Practitioners

A special note on reviewing seems appropriate for sole practitioners. For a primary review, a check list can be used for self-review. This self-review works best if a day or more has elapsed after the report was drafted. For longer or more complex engagements, a second reviewer from outside the firm could be used. Some CPAs have made agreements with other practitioners to conduct reviews on a reciprocal basis. This makes the process more orderly, and minimizes the cost.

Peer Reviewers

External peer reviewers evaluate the adequacy of a firm's review procedures. When examining sample engagements, they check documentation for compliance with procedures. Since they review the engagement, it is natural for them to come to a conclusion as to whether they agree with the firm's reviewer's decision.

GENERAL DESIGN

An example of a general design for supervision is presented in Exhibit 11-8. The field supervisor, who is either an accountant in charge or a manager, prepares the engagement plan and is responsible for all aspects of the engagement. A second review is performed for most engagements. The firm's check lists are included in its accounting and auditing manual. The firm allows some flexibility for engagement planning. The audit pre-planning check list is filled out for all audits, and engagement planning check lists are used for additional guidance. An example of an audit time budget is not included in this book because these are so commonly used and their format is obvious to CPAs. As mentioned above, disclosure check lists are available from the AICPA and other sources. None are included in this book because they become outdated quickly. The second reviewer's disclosure check list would be a shortened version of this, focusing on critical areas.

A summary of AICPA objectives and sample procedures to implement them is presented in Table 11-3. Each procedure's applicability according to firm size is a generalization based upon current standards. Several characteristics of firms are recognized in the accounting profession's quality control programs as determinants of the appropriate quality control policies and procedures for CPA firms. Therefore, a firm must consider all of its characteristics in designing procedures and assigning responsibilities. Similarly, forms, check lists, and other documentation shown in this book and elsewhere must be modified to fit the individual firm's needs. (Table 11-4 summarizes supervision documentation.)

Exhibit 11-1 Helpful Guidelines for Reviews of Audit Engagements

1. The review should be an informed review — not a cold review. The reviewer needs client background before he commences report review.
2. Specialists should be used in the review process, e.g., tax personnel, legal counsel.
3. The reviewer's sole function is to develop an exception report.
4. Keep in mind that excessive time pressure is a principal cause of substandard work.
5. The reviewer's personal characteristics should suit the role he is expected to play.
6. An audit is not complete unless the client is provided with constructive suggestions.
7. Individuals at all levels should review their own work (self-review).
8. The best place to accomplish the review is probably at the client's office.
9. The accountant in charge of field work should prepare a review memorandum for the reviewer's edification.
10. The time spent on the review of the report should not be at the expense of the work paper review.
11. The audit review requires a critical — not a casual — reading of all the work papers.
12. A disclosure check list is a useful tool when reviewing the report.
13. A work paper review check list helps to document your review.
14. Discard review notes at conclusion of the engagement.
15. The reviewer should note for removal from the work papers all irrelevant material.
16. Potential problem areas the reviewer should recognize: relating internal control findings to audit tests and procedures; errors, irregularities and illegal acts; and related party disclosure.
17. The report should be reviewed for completeness, reasonableness, and intelligibility.
18. A second person not associated with the planning or execution of the engagement should review the report before its release.

Source: Joseph V. Bencivenga, "Improving Reviews of Audit Examinations," *The CPA Journal,* April 1978, p. 38. This is reprinted with permission from *The CPA Journal,* published by the New York State Society of Certified Public Accountants.

Exhibit 11-2 Audit Engagement Planning Check List

1. What is the scope of the engagement? Are there any expected problems?

2. What assistance is expected from clients? How will this be organized?

3. What are the names and positions of client personnel important to the audit?

4. What significant auditing, accounting, and tax problems may occur?

5. Has a budget of hours and expected fees been prepared? If there is a major increase from last year, how will the client be advised of this?

6. Has a staff request been submitted for scheduling?

7. What are the responsibilities of:
   a. Partner in charge?
   b. Accountant in charge?
   c. Engagement reviewer?
   d. Tax specialist?
   e. Computer audit specialist?

8. Who will prepare the analysis of internal control? Will a standard questionnaire be used?

9. What are the starting and completion dates for:
   a. Receivable confirmations?
   b. Inventory observation?
   c. Cash and securities counts?
   d. Interim work?
   e. Final work?
   f. Report preparation?
   g. Tax returns?

10. What are the target dates for delivery of audit and management letter reports?

11. Are there any sensitive areas requiring special consideration for this client?

12. Have changed business conditions significantly affected this client's operations so that certain assets (receivables, inventory, investments) might be undervalued, or unrecorded liabilities or contingencies might exist?

13. Are there any contingencies, new disclosures, or subsequent events requiring special consideration?

14. Have the firm's client acceptance and continuance procedures been followed?

15. What are the major on-the-job training objectives for assistants with respect to:
    a. Specific job segments?
    b. Completion of whole areas of the job?
    c. Depth of experience?

Exhibit 11-3 Audit Pre-Planning Check List

CLIENT:_____ PERIOD:_____

	Work Performed By (Mgr. or Sr.)		Work Reviewed By (Mgr. or Partner)	
1. Planning memo written and attached	Initials	Date	Initials	Date
2. Time budget completed and attached	____	____	____	____
3. Request for staff prepared and attached	____	____	____	____

4. Audit program completed as follows:

Area	Not Applicable	Std. Program To Be Used	Tailored Program To Be Prepared By	To Be Used and Approved By
General	____	____	____	____
Cash	____	____	____	____
Confirmation of receivables	____	____	____	____
Receivables	____	____	____	____
Observation of inventories	____	____	____	____
Inventories	____	____	____	____
Prepaid expenses and other assets	____	____	____	____
Property, plant and equipment	____	____	____	____
Investment securities	____	____	____	____
Notes payable	____	____	____	____
Accounts payable	____	____	____	____
Income taxes	____	____	____	____
Accrued expenses and other current liabilities	____	____	____	____
Commitments, claims and contingencies	____	____	____	____
Equity	____	____	____	____
Operations	____	____	____	____
Related party transactions	____	____	____	____
Detailed tests of transactions as follows:				
a. Sales, accounts receivable and cash receipts	____	____	____	____
b. Purchasing, accounts payable and cash disbursements				
c. Payroll	____	____	____	____
d.	____	____	____	____
e.	____	____	____	____
f.	____	____	____	____

Partner approval:_____ Date:_____

Source: Reprinted from *Quality Control Documentation in the Local CPA Firm* by California CPA Foundation for Education and Research, © 1978.

Exhibit 11-4 Work Paper Review Check List

(To be Filed with Workpapers)

Client _____ Period Ended_____

	Yes	No	Comments (An explanation is required here for each "no" answer)
In-Charge Accountant Review			
1. Permanent file of pertinent information established or updated	——	——	
2. Workpapers indexed and crossreferenced	——	——	
3. Responses to audit inquiry letters obtained	——	——	
4. Signed minutes certificate obtained	——	——	
5. Signed representation letter obtained	——	——	
6. Draft letter on internal control weaknesses prepared	——	——	
7. Workpapers include an explanation for each significant variance between time budgeted and time spent	——	——	
8. Workpapers properly headed, initialed and dated by preparer	——	——	
9. Internal control questionnaire completed	——	——	
10. Comparative analysis of income and expense accounts (and balance sheet accounts, if appropriate) included in workpapers and satisfactory explanation given for material increases or decreases	——	——	
11. Audit program completed	——	——	
12. Suggestions for future examinations included in workpapers	——	——	

Signature_____

Date_____

	Yes	No	
MANAGER/SUPERVISOR REVIEW			
1. Workpapers properly headed, initialed, and dated by reviewer	——	——	
2. Income tax accruals reviewed by tax personnel and related workpapers approved by reviewing tax personnel	——	——	
3. Financial and other information in report agrees with client's records and is internally consistent	——	——	
4. Auditor's report and client's financial statements reviewed for completeness, propriety and intelligibility	——	——	
5. All significant open items cleared and pertinent workpapers revised	——	——	
6. Disclosure checklist completed	——	——	
7. Last year's post-issue review comments considered in preparation of current year's report	——	——	
8. Do the language in the report and the presentation of the data meet the tests of accuracy, brevity and clarity?	——	——	

Signature_____

Date_____

Partner Review
Critical accounting and auditing aspects of the engagement have been reviewed and all problems or questionable items have been resolved satisfactorily   —— ——

Signature_____

Date_____

Source: Joseph V. Bencivenga, "Improving Reviews of Audit Examinations," *The CPA Journal,* April 1978, p. 38. This is reprinted with permission from *The CPA Journal,* published by the New York State Society of Certified Public Accountants.

Exhibit 11-5 Report Guide Sheet

Report Guide Sheet

(To be bound with the _____ colored copy of report.)

Engagement Information

Client _____ Date due _____

Assignment number _____ Assignment name _____

Account administrator _____ Manager _____ In-charge accountant _____

☐ Unaudited year-end report   ☐ Audited statements

☐ Interim unaudited   Limited purpose report

☐ Informal interim unaudited   ☐ Other _____

Delivery Instructions:

Name—attention of: _____ ☐ Mail

Address: _____ ☐ Delivery by: _____

Hold Items *(describe):*

	Cleared by	Date

Report Review:

	Signature	Date
In-charge		
Interim review*		
Account administrator		
Review department		
Tax department		
Technical reviewer *(if applicable)*		

*Represents final level of review for interim unaudited and informal interim reports.

Report Processing:

	Signature	Date
Typing department		
Comparing and proofing		
Final reading		

Final Release:

The report(s) described above were released by me after all hold items were cleared. All appropriate levels of review were signed off, and all processing steps completed.

_____   _____

(Signature of Partner or Manager)   *(Date)*

Source: Copyright 1975, 1976, 1977 by the American Institute of Certified Public Accountants, Inc. Reprinted, by permission, from *Management of an Accounting Practice Handbook.*

176

Exhibit 11-5 continued

Report Description *(Exactly as it will appear):*

Title ☐ Financial statements and auditors' report
☐ Unaudited financial statements   ☐ Unaudited financial statements
☐ Other title   *(for internal use only)*

_____

Client _____ Date _____

Report Production:

Covers: ☐ Printed   ☐ Typed   Report: ☐ Multilith   ☐ Other _____

Report Copies:

In covers	Client	Issuing office[a]	Regional office[b]	Executive office[c]			Totals
Standard form							
Long form							
SEC							
_____							
_____							

Uncovered [d]	Work paper copies *(at least two)*	Extra file copies		
Standard form				
Long form				
SEC stapled				
_____				
_____				

Grand total _____

a. One copy of each report should be bound in a _____ colored cover with a completed report guide sheet.
b. The regional office should be sent *only* the following.
   1. All filings and reports for publicly held clients.
   2. All audit reports expressing a qualified opinion, a denial of opinion, or an adverse opinion.
   3. Limited purpose reports.
   4. All unaudited reports where a reservation is expressed.
   5. Budgets and forecasts.
   6. Pro forma financial statements.
c. The executive office should be sent *only* filings and reports on publicly held clients.
d. Except as required for regulatory purposes, uncovered stapled copies should not be released to clients or third parties.

Other Production Instructions:

_____
_____
_____
_____
_____

Exhibit 11-6 Report Routing Sheet

NOTE: This form is to be used for routing of <u>all</u> reports other than tax
returns. It is to be bound with office copy of the report. The
engagement supervisor deletes items 4 and 5 if not needed.

Client Name and Number_____

Report Prepared by_____ Date_____

Mail to: Per attached_____ Other_____

_____   _____
_____   _____
_____   _____

1. Number of copies to client_____Delivery Date_____

2. Calculations verified by_____ Date_____

3. Supervisor's review by_____ Date_____

4. Second review (if needed) by_____ Date_____

5. Tax Dept. review (if needed) by_____ Date_____

6. Typed by_____ Date_____

7. Proofread by_____ Date_____

8. Typed copy added by_____ Date_____

9. Photocopied by_____ Date_____

10. Assembled by_____ Date_____

11. Comments by processing dept._____

12. Special instructions:

13. Approved for mailing by_____ Date mailed_____

Exhibit 11-7 AICPA Quality Control Policies and Procedures for Supervision

1. Provide procedures for planning engagements.

a. Assign responsibility for planning an engagement. Involve appropriate personnel assigned to the engagement in the planning process.

b. Develop background information or review information obtained from prior engagements and update for changed circumstances.

c. Describe matters to be included in the engagement planning process, such as the following:
   (i) Development of proposed work programs.
   (ii) Determination of manpower requirements and need for specialized knowledge.
   (iii) Development of estimates of time required to complete the engagement.
   (iv) Consideration of current economic conditions affecting the client or its industry and their potential impact on the conduct of the engagement.

2. Provide procedures for maintaining the firm's standards of quality for the work performed.

a. Provide adequate supervision at all organizational levels, considering the training, ability, and experience of the personnel assigned.

b. Develop guidelines for the form and content of working papers.

c. Utilize standardized forms, check lists, and questionnaires to the extent appropriate to assist in the performance of engagements.

d. Provide procedures for resolving differences of professional judgment among members of an engagement team.

3. Provide procedures for reviewing engagement working papers and reports.

a. Develop guidelines for review of working papers and for documentation of the review process.
   (i) Require that reviewers have appropriate competence and responsibility.
   (ii) Determine that work performed is complete and conforms to professional standards and firm policy.
   (iii) Describe documentation evidencing review of working papers and the reviewer's findings. Documentation may include initialing working papers, completing a reviewer's questionnaire, preparing a reviewer's memorandum and employing standard forms or check lists.

Source: Copyright © 1976, 1978 by the American Institute of Certified Public Accountants, Inc. Reprinted, with permission, from *Voluntary Quality Control Review Program for CPA Firms.*

Exhibit 11-7 continued

    b. Develop guidelines for review of the report to be issued for an engagement. Considerations in "a" above would be applicable to this review. In addition, the following matters should be considered for these guidelines:

       (i) Determine that the evidence of work performed and conclusions contained in the working papers support the report.

      (ii) Determine that the report conforms to professional standards and firm policy.

     (iii) Provide for review of the report by an appropriate individual having no other responsibility for the engagement.

Exhibit 11-8 Example of General Design for Supervision

Operational Responsibilities:

The field supervisor of an engagement prepares an audit plan for all engagements. Plan detail varies according to engagement characteristics. The engagement partner must approve the audit plan if the budget exceeds 60 hours, if it is a new client, or if last year's engagement planning notes indicate the need for approval. The field supervisor is responsible for all aspects of the engagement. Any differences in professional judgment that cannot be resolved by the engagement team are resolved at a meeting among engagement personnel, Partner A, and Partner B. The engagement partner has ultimate authority; the resolution of the dispute is documented by a memo if Partner A and Partner B do not agree with him. Engagement personnel appropriately complete the working paper review check list.

Communication:

Accounting and auditing procedures are documented in a firm manual which is made available to all personnel. Partner B is responsible for maintaining this manual.

Monitoring:

The engagement partner reviews all engagements. Partner A or Partner B performs a second review for all audit engagements and all unaudited engagements over 60 hours.

Documentation:

1. Engagement planning check lists
2. Audit pre-planning check list
3. Audit time budget
4. Accounting and auditing manual, including check lists
5. Work paper review check list
6. Disclosure check list
7. Reviewer's disclosure check list
8. Report guide sheet
9. Memo to files

NOTE: The profile firm is described in Appendix A.

Table 11-1 Opinions on Supervision Policies and Procedures

Quality Control Policy or Procedure	Number of Professional Personnel in Firm							
	1 to 5		6 to 20		20 to 80		More than 80	
	Mean	CV	Mean	CV	Mean	CV	Mean	CV
(1) The firm requires formalized planning that covers specified areas for:								
a. All audit engagements.								
Importance	4.04	27%	4.07	19%	4.57	14%	4.71	15%
Usage	3.75	35%	3.61	27%	3.34	37%	4.63	19%
b. Selected audit engagements.								
Importance	4.00	32%	4.28	16%	4.36	21%	4.60	20%
Usage	3.75	35%	3.90	26%	3.41	26%	4.50	23%
c. Selected unaudited engagements.								
Importance	3.26	40%	3.53	29%	3.93	31%	3.94	29%
Usage	3.05	44%	2.76	42%	2.59	44%	3.71	38%
(2) The firm has written guidelines for form and content of working papers.								
Importance	3.67	36%	4.07	22%	4.64	11%	4.26	21%
Usage	3.60	42%	3.13	40%	3.84	19%	4.31	26%
(3) Procedures for resolving differences in professional judgment between engagement personnel are formalized.								
Importance	3.33	43%	3.29	37%	4.33	15%	4.58	18%
Usage	2.75	59%	2.39	55%	2.76	44%	4.36	23%
(4) The firm has guidelines for reviewing work papers and documenting the review.								
Importance	4.04	30%	4.34	19%	4.64	14%	4.79	9%
Usage	3.80	34%	3.39	39%	3.59	41%	4.65	16%
(5) The engagement partner reviews to some extent:								
a. All audit engagements.								
Importance	4.33	23%	4.51	16%	4.57	14%	4.84	9%
Usage	4.26	26%	4.25	21%	4.09	27%	4.48	12%
b. Selected (risky or difficult) audit engagements.								
Importance	4.41	29%	4.80	10%	4.79	9%	4.69	23%
Usage	4.33	28%	4.61	14%	4.59	13%	4.75	17%

Table 11-1 continued

Quality Control	Number of Professional Personnel							
	1 to 5		6 to 20		20 to 80		More than 80	
Policy or Procedure	Mean	CV	Mean	CV	Mean	CV	Mean	CV
c. Selected (risky or diffi-cult) unaudited engage-ments.								
Importance	4.14	32%	4.50	15%	4.64	11%	4.84	9%
Usage	3.93	30%	4.25	23%	4.34	15%	4.71	13%
(6) A second partner, with no other responsibility for the engagement, to some extent reviews:								
a. All audit engagements.								
Importance	3.45	43%	3.68	28%	4.07	23%	4.29	24%
Usage	3.08	45%	2.88	46%	2.81	39%	4.14	31%
b. Selected (risky or diffi-cult) audit engagements.								
Importance	4.05	30%	4.21	19%	4.50	14%	4.47	25%
Usage	3.81	37%	3.54	35%	3.50	36%	4.58	23%
c. Selected (risky or diffi-cult) unaudited engage-ments.								
Importance	3.55	39%	3.95	21%	3.71	32%	4.00	32%
Usage	3.24	44%	3.21	40%	2.59	50%	3.63	42%
Number of responses	18		42		17		42	

NOTE: The mean responses are based on a five-point scale. They can be interpreted according to where they fall within the following ranges:

Importance	Range	Usage	Range
Unimportant	1.00-1.5	Rare	1.25-1.88
Little importance	1.51-2.5	Occasional	1.89-3.13
Some importance	2.51-3.5	Common	3.14-4.38
Important	3.51-4.5	Almost always	4.39-5.00
Essential	4.51-5.0		

For example, an importance score of 1.81 indicates that the respondents viewed the procedure as being of little importance. CV represents coefficient of variation. The higher the coefficient of variation, the greater the variability in the responses of the CPA firm partners in a particular group. See Appendix C for a description of the study.

Table 11-2 Use of Second Partner Review

	Affirmative Responses Grouped by Number of Professional Personnel in Firm			
Question	1 to 5	6 to 20	20 to 80	More than 80
Does your firm require a second partner or CPA to review to some extent:				
a. All audit engagements?	61%	58%	80%	80%
b. All unaudited financial statements?	25%	36%	20%	53%

Table 11-3 Supervision. Summary Evaluation of Quality Control Policies and Procedures (for inclusion in a firm's quality control document).

AICPA Policy/Procedure	Procedure's Applicability to Firm					Comments
	N	R	LL	SL	SP	
1. Provide procedures for planning engagements.						
a. Assign responsibility for planning engagements (state who).	H	H	H	H	L	
b. Develop background information.	H	H	H	H	H	
c. Describe engagement planning procedures.	H	H	H	H	H	See engagement planning check list; amount of planning depends on engagement scope, size, risk, etc.
2. Provide procedures for maintaining the firm's quality for work performed.						
a. Provide adequate supervision at all levels.	H	H	H	H	H	
b. Develop guidelines for form and content of working papers.	H	H	H	H	M	Accounting and auditing manual should contain these; could use AICPA engagement review check lists
c. Utilize standardized forms, check lists, and questionnaires where appropriate.	H	H	H	H	H	Available from many sources
d. Provide procedures for resolving differences in professional judgment.	H	H	H	H	L	A memo may be used to document resolution of significant disputes
e. Supervise other offices or correspondent firms.	H	H	H	H	M	

Table 11-3 continued

AICPA Policy/Procedure	Procedure's Applicability to Firm					Comments
	N	R	LL	SL	SP	
3. Provide procedures for reviewing engagement working papers and reports.						
a. Develop guidelines for review of working papers and documenting the review.		H	H	H	H	A sole practitioner can use a check list for self-review or a correspondent firm for critical engagements
(i) Reviewers have appropriate credentials and responsibility.		H	H	H	H	
(ii) Determine that work is complete and technically correct.		H	H	H	H	
(iii) Document review process.		H	H	H	H	Initial work papers, questionnaire, check list, memo
b. Develop guidelines for reviews of reports to be issued.						
(i) Assure that underlying evidence in the work papers supports the report.		H	H	H	H	
(ii) Review the report for conformity to professional standards and firm policy.		H	H	H	H	
(iii) For some engagements, a partner without line responsibility reviews the report.		H	H	H		A sole practitioner can make arrangements with an associated firm for reviews
(iv) Document the review.		H	H	H	H	

Key:

H	= High	NA	= Not Applicable
M	= Medium	N	= National or international firm
L	= Low	R	= Regional firm

LL = Large Local firm (possibly two or three offices)
SL = Small Local firm (one office)
SP = Sole Practitioner (possibly one part-time staff member)

Table 11-4 Summary of Supervision Documentation

Documentation — Purpose	AICPA Procedures
Quality control document — informs personnel of policies and procedures	all
Engagement planning check list — guides planning	1b,c
Audit time budget — engagement planning and control	1c
Audit pre-planning check list — guides planning	1b,c
Accounting and auditing manual — communicates working paper guidelines and procedures	2b,c
Working paper review check list — guides review by engagement personnel	3a
Disclosure check list — guides review by engagement personnel	3a
Reviewer's disclosure check list — guides second reviewer	3b(iii)
Report guide sheet — controls reports	3a,b
Memo to files — documents dispute in professional judgment	2d

NOTES

1. AICPA, *Statement on Auditing Standards No. 4* (New York, N.Y.: AICPA, 1978), p. 3.
2. Ibid., p. 5.
3. Ibid., p. 5.

BIBLIOGRAPHY

AICPA. *Guide for Engagements of CPAs to Prepare Unaudited Financial Statements.* New York, N.Y.: AICPA, 1975.

AICPA. *Planning and Supervision: Statement on Auditing Standard No. 22.* New York, N.Y.: AICPA, 1978.

AICPA. *Technical Practice Aids.* New York, N.Y.: AICPA, 1978.

CPA Journal. "Proofreading Financial Statements." *CPA Journal,* February 1974, p. 59.

Foundation for Accounting Education. *Preparation of Unaudited Financial Statements.* New York, N.Y.: Foundation for Accounting Education, 1978.

Foundation for Accounting Education. *Financial Statement Review Checklist.* New York, N.Y.: Foundation for Accounting Education, 1978.

Foundation for Accounting Education. *Audit Program.* New York, N.Y.: Foundation for Accounting Education, 1978.

Jackson, Steve. "Operations Manual for Staff." *Journal of Accountancy,* May 1977, p. 42.

Simon, Joel. "Office Control for the Preparation and Processing of Financial Statements." *The CPA Journal,* March 1972, pp. 241-242.

The Practical Accountant, "How to Improve Control over Audit Reports." *The Practical Accountant,* July/August 1974, p. 37.

The Practical Accountant. "A Checklist for Evaluating Internal Control." *The Practical Accountant,* May/June 1976, pp. 35-50.

The Practical Accountant. "A Financial Reporting Checklist to Help You Comply with the Disclosure Requirements." *The Practical Accountant,* January/February, pp. 35-51.

Wendell, Paul and Wakely, Maxwell. *Modern Accounting and Auditing Checklists.* New York, N.Y.: Warren Gorham and Lamont, 1977.

Chapter 12

Consultation

This chapter analyzes the three AICPA objectives for consultation. In complicated situations, the results of consultation should be documented in the working papers. Exhibit 12-1 is a consultation log, and Exhibit 12-3 outlines the general design for consultation. The AICPA quality control policies and procedures stating the objectives and sample procedures are reprinted in Exhibit 12-2 and summarized with comments in Table 12-2. Table 12-3 gives a summary of the consultation documentation.

The opinions of CPA firm partners on selected quality control procedures are presented in Table 12-1. These opinions should provide to practitioners some perspective on what other CPAs are thinking and doing with respect to quality control. For the reader's convenience, all tables and exhibits are presented at the end of the chapter.

OVERVIEW

Accounting has become extraordinarily complex in recent years. The result is that many CPAs now specialize in one or two areas of practice. There is even some discussion within the profession about the possibility of certifying specialists. Common specialties include tax, SEC, industry, computer audit, and systems. In order to maximize a firm's technical capabilities, its specialists must be identified and made accessible to other personnel for consultation. The technical areas covered by a firm's specialists influence, to some extent, the composition of its clientele. While the consultation element covers the use of specialists, it is also relevant to firms with no designated specialists. If experienced senior partners or outside consultants are consulted on difficult technical matters, consultation procedures are required to document their opinions in certain situations. Consultation also encompasses having an adequate technical library for reference purposes.

In general, the number of specialists can be expected to increase with firm size. A firm with only eight or ten professional personnel might have only a tax specialist. Another firm of similar size, however, might have four specialists. This difference could reflect differences in the partners' interests and philosophies, or differences in the two firms' clienteles.

Some firms have increased their technical capabilities by entering into consultation agreements with other firms. These are sometimes arranged through associations of CPA firms. Having other specialists available allows a firm to accept some clients that might otherwise have to be rejected because of uncertainties about the firm's technical competence.

AUTHORITATIVE POLICIES AND PROCEDURES

The AICPA quality control policies and procedures for consultation are presented in Exhibit 12-2. The objectives cover the identification of specialists, procedures for consultation, and appropriate documentation. Sample procedures for each objective are identified by letters, and are identified in the text by the objective number, the procedure letter, and possibly small Roman numerals (1b(i), for example). Common procedures and the external peer reviewer's likely approach are discussed below for each objective.

Identify Specialized Situations

Objective 1: IDENTIFY AREAS AND SPECIALIZED SITUATIONS WHERE CONSULTATION IS REQUIRED AND ENCOURAGE PERSONNEL TO CONSULT WITH OR USE AUTHORITATIVE SOURCES ON OTHER COMPLEX OR UNUSUAL MATTERS.

The first objective suggests that the need for consultation can be defined according to a technical area or by specific circumstances. In a specialized area, a firm's policies can prescribe consultation according to the circumstances. For example, a tax specialist commonly reviews tax accruals. For SEC-regulated clients, a SEC specialist is typically consulted. A firm's consultation policies and procedures are usually in the form of general guidelines, since consultation judgment by staff personnel cannot be eliminated from the process. Consultation procedures typically require staff members to follow the chain of command upward in seeking advice. For example, the engagement manager might be designated as the one who is authorized to seek advice from a specialist. In smaller firms, guidelines can be less formalized because fewer people are involved. The areas identified under 2b in Exhibit 12-2 are common areas of difficulty. Most firms include these areas in their quality control documents as examples of when a specialist is needed, and include a broad statement that consultation should be sought when difficult areas are encountered.

The views of CPA partners on the desirability of having documented policies and procedures for consulting with specialists are shown in Table 12-1. CPAs from the largest firms gave this idea high importance scores (4.27). The scores for the smaller firms were markedly lower — 2.6, 3.29, and 3.17. The estimated usage scores are low for all but the largest firms (4.38). They were in the middle of the "occasional" range for the "1 to 5" and "6 to 20" groups, and in the "rare" range for the "20 to 80" group. The most likely explanation for these findings is that consultation in many smaller firms occurs on an informal basis. Also, many small firms do not have designated audit specialists.

Use of Specialists

One of the questions asked of all respondents was: "Does your firm have any personnel that are designated as specialists in particular auditing areas?" The percentages of firms having designated specialists were:

1 to 5	36%
6 to 20	40%
20 to 80	67%
More than 80	98%

Thus, most firms do not have designated audit specialists. There is no reason to suspect that a significant increase will result from AICPA quality control policies and procedures.

Firms should not feel compelled to identify area specialists just to have a more impressive quality control document. However, firms with SEC-regulated clients are advised to have a SEC specialist or a consultation arrangement with an outside SEC specialist.

Library

A CPA firm must maintain an adequate technical reference library to support its practice. Given that thousands of accounting and tax books are available, the need to be selective is obvious. Essential components of any firm's library are:

- *AICPA Professional Standards* (3 Volumes)
- *AICPA Technical Practice Aids*
- *Journal of Accountancy*
- A tax service
- Firm manuals

- A comprehensive auditing reference book
- A comprehensive accounting reference book

In addition to these, a firm's library should include other publications appropriate for the firm's practice. Firms should consider using a log for checking out materials. While responsibility for the library should be assigned to one individual, all professional personnel should have the opportunity to make recommendations for new acquisitions.

Another source of expertise is outside consultants (1c(iii)). Most firms try to avoid using outside consultants because of their cost. However, formal or informal reciprocal consultation agreements can minimize the cost, and they are becoming more common. If a firm uses outsiders, quality control policies and procedures would specify who is authorized to seek help from outside consultants. The AICPA Technical Information Service is a valuable benefit to members. Some state societies have similar services.

Peer Reviewers

A firm's consultation policies and procedures are evaluated by reviewers for clarity and appropriateness to the firm. Some firm personnel might be interviewed to test their knowledge of procedures and to check for compliance. The adequacy of a firm's library as a reference source is evaluated. Obviously, the composition of a firm's practice is a factor in library evaluation. The library's operating procedures for updating, acquisition, distribution, and deletion of materials is considered, including the assignment of responsibilities.

Designate Specialists and Define Their Authority

Objective 2: DESIGNATE INDIVIDUALS AS SPECIALISTS TO SERVE AS AUTHORITATIVE SOURCES AND DEFINE THEIR AUTHORITY IN CONSULTATIVE SITUATIONS. PROVIDE PROCEDURES FOR RESOLVING DIFFERENCES OF OPINION BETWEEN ENGAGEMENT PERSONNEL AND SPECIALISTS.

If specialists are identified for consultation purposes, the problem arises as to their authority. In some situations, a specialist can provide an indisputable solution to a problem. For other problems, a specialist can only point out the major factors to be considered, and make a recommendation. If the engagement partner disagrees with the specialist, an authority problem exists, the resolution of which depends on the authority structure of the firm. If the firm has an executive partner, he or she might make the final decision. If the firm's partners believe in a maximum amount of autonomy, the engagement partner would have the ultimate authority.

Whatever the procedures are, they should be specified in the quality control document or in a firm's accounting and auditing manual. The procedures will delineate the authority of specialists. Procedure 2d in Exhibit 12-2 indicates the need to document the resolution of differences in opinion between specialists and engagement personnel. This documentation is most common in large firms who have many specialists. Many firms do not require documentation of the issues and opinions unless a compromise cannot be reached. When a memo documenting the results of consultation is prepared, one copy is usually placed in the working papers and another copy is often placed in a subject file for future reference.

Looking at the survey results on clearly defining the authority of specialists (Table 12-1, part 2) we see that the importance scores are in the middle range except for the largest firms. The estimated usage scores are in the "occasional" range except for the largest firms, where it is in the "common" range. These results can be explained, in part, by the survey statistics on the use of specialists, shown above.

Looking at part 3 of Table 12-1, on the documentation of differences, the importances scores are only slightly higher for part 3b than for 3a, except for the largest firms. The importance scores generally increased gradually with firm size, but were significantly lower for the smallest firms. This result, and the high coefficient of variation for the smallest firms, can be attributed to the infrequent use of specialists. The estimated usage scores also reflect the infrequent use of specialists by smaller firms.

Peer Reviewers

The method of identifying specialists and delineating their authority is evaluated by external peer reviewers. Specialists functioning as specialists is analyzed. A specialists's professional development record should reflect training in the designated area of professional expertise. Procedures for documenting differences in opinion are evaluated for adequacy and compliance.

Document Consultation

Objective 3: SPECIFY THE EXTENT OF DOCUMENTATION TO BE PRO-VIDED FOR THE RESULTS OF CONSULTATION IN THOSE AREAS AND SPECIALIZED SITUATIONS WHERE CONSULTATION IS REQUIRED. SPECIFY DOCUMENTATION, AS APPROPRIATE, FOR OTHER CONSULTATIONS.

The third objective suggests documentation of the consultation function. For smaller firms we would expect little, if any, documentation, except when an outside consultant is used. The simplest type of documentation is a consultation log for recording minimal details of requests and their resolution. An example is presented in Exhibit 12-1.

For complicated consultation requests, one might prepare a consultation summary for the working papers and possibly for subject file. This only seems appropriate for complex situations or when an outside consultant is used. It would be done when the specialist's or CPA's professional judgment deems it necessary.

Peer Reviewers

External peer reviewers evaluate the adequacy of a firm's documentation for consultation. If required, documentation and subject files might be reviewed.

GENERAL DESIGN

An example of a general design for consultation is presented in Exhibit 12-3. In accordance with Appendix A, each partner has a designated specialty. The firm uses a consultation log and a subject file.

A summary of AICPA objectives and sample procedures to implement them is presented in Table 12-2. Each procedure's applicability according to firm size is a generalization based upon current standards. Several firm characteristics of firms are recognized in the accounting profession's quality control programs as determinants of the appropriate quality control policies and procedures for CPA firms. Therefore, a firm must consider all of its characteristics in designing procedures and assigning responsibilities. Similarly, forms, check lists, and other documentation shown in this text and elsewhere must be modified to fit the individual firm's needs. Table 12-3 summarizes consultation documentation.

Exhibit 12-1 Consultation Log

Date	Mode of Communication	Client	Office	Request	Response	Memorandum Required Yes/No	Date Rec'd

Exhibit 12-2 AICPA Quality Control Policies and Procedures for Consultation

1. **Identify areas and specialized situations where consultation is required and encourage personnel to consult with or use authoritative sources on other complex or unusual matters.**

   a. Inform personnel of the firm's consultation policies and procedures.

   b. Specify areas or specialized situations requiring consultation because of the nature or complexity of the subject matter. Examples include —

      (i) Application of newly issued technical pronouncements.

      (ii) Industries with special accounting, auditing, or reporting requirements.

      (iii) Emerging practice problems.

      (iv) Choices among alternative generally accepted accounting principles when an accounting change is to be made.

      (v) Filing requirements of regulatory agencies.

   c. Maintain or provide access to adequate reference libraries and other authoritative sources.

      (i) Establish responsibility for maintaining a reference library in each practice office.

      (ii) Maintain technical manuals and issue technical pronouncements, including those relating to particular industries and other specialties.

      (iii) Maintain consultation arrangements with other firms and individuals where necessary to supplement firm resources.

      (iv) Refer problems to a division or group in the AICPA or state CPA society established to deal with technical inquiries.

   d. Maintain a research function to assist personnel with practice problems.

2. **Designate individuals as specialists to serve as authoritative sources and define their authority in consultative situations. Provide procedures for resolving differences of opinion between engagement personnel and specialists.**

   a. Designate individuals as specialists for filings with the Securities and Exchange Commission and other regulatory agencies.

   b. Designate specialists for particular industries.

   c. Advise personnel of the degree of authority to be accorded specialists' opinions and of the procedures to be followed for resolving differences of opinion with specialists.

   d. Require documentation as to the considerations involved in the resolution of differences of opinion.

Exhibit 12-2 continued

3. **Specify the extent of documentation to be provided for the results of consultation in those areas and specialized situations where consultation is required. Specify documentation, as appropriate, for other consultations.**

   a. Advise personnel as to the extent of documentation to be prepared and the responsibility for its preparation.

   b. Indicate where consultation documentation is to be maintained.

   c. Maintain subject files containing the results of consultations for reference and research purposes.

Exhibit 12-3 Example of General Design for Consultation

Operational Responsibilities:

All professional personnel are required to seek consultation in complex situations or when specified by firm manuals. All partners and managers are required to provide consultation as needed to professional personnel, and to prepare consultation summaries as needed. Partner A is responsible for maintaining the firm library, and all personnel should make acquisition recommendations.

Communication:

The accounting and auditing manual identifies situations where the use of specialists is appropriate.

Monitoring:

Outside consultants cannot be hired without the approval of two partners.

Documentation:

1. Accounting and auditing manual, identify areas and situations and specialists
2. Consultation log
3. Subject file memos
4. Consultation summaries
5. Library log

NOTE: The profile firm is described in Appendix A.

Table 12-1 Opinions on Consultation Policies and Procedures

Quality Control Policy or Procedure	Number of Professional Personnel in Firm							
	1 to 5		6 to 20		20 to 80		More than 80	
	Mean	CV	Mean	CV	Mean	CV	Mean	CV
(1) The firm documents policies and procedures for when specialists within the firm should be consulted.								
Importance	2.60	60%	3.29	36%	3.17	40%	4.27	23%
Usage	2.41	60%	2.56	51%	1.66	49%	4.38	25%
(2) The authority of specialists is clearly defined.								
Importance	2.80	59%	3.43	34%	3.17	40%	4.36	17%
Usage	2.91	53%	2.73	52%	2.09	47%	3.96	32%
(3) The considerations involved in resolving differences of opinion with specialists are documented in:								
a. All cases.								
Importance	2.93	62%	3.75	33%	3.82	26%	4.64	23%
Usage	3.21	50%	2.50	53%	2.39	37%	4.48	25%
b. Cases where a consensus is not achieved.								
Importance	3.08	65%	3.67	38%	4.09	25%	4.31	35%
Usage	2.69	65%	2.90	45%	3.08	33%	4.38	34%
Number of Responses	9		20		13		23	

NOTE: The mean responses are based on a five-point scale. They can be interpreted according to where they fall within the following ranges:

Importance	Range	Usage	Range
Unimportant	1.00-1.5	Rare	1.25-1.88
Little importance	1.51-2.5	Occasional	1.89-3.13
Some importance	2.51-3.5	Common	3.14-4.38
Important	3.51-4.5	Almost always	4.39-5.00
Essential	4.51-5.0		

For example, an importance score of 1.81 indicates that the respondents viewed the procedure as being of little importance. CV represents coefficient of variation. The higher the coefficient of variation, the greater the variability in the responses of the CPA firm partners in a particular group. See Appendix C for a description of the study.

Table 12-2 Consultation. Summary Evaluation of Quality Control Policies and Procedures (for inclusion in a firm's quality control document).

AICPA Policy/Procedure	Procedure's Applicability to Firm					Comments
	N	R	LL	SL	SP	
1. Identify areas and specialized situations where consultation is required, and encourage personnel to consult with sources on complex matters.						
a. Inform personnel of documented consultation policies and procedures.	H	H	H	H	L	
b. Identify specialized situations requiring consultation.	H	H	H	M	L	
c. Maintain or provide access to libraries and authoritative sources.	H	H	H	H	H	Includes outside consultants and professional associations
d. Maintain a research function to assist personnel with practice problems.	H	H	M	L	L	
2. Specialists are identified, and their responsibility and authority is defined.						
a. Specialists are designated.	H	H	H	M	NA	SEC, computer audit, tax, etc.
b. Designate industry specialists.	H	H-M	M	L	NA	Depends on firm goals
c. Define the authority of specialists.	H	H	H	M	NA	
d. Procedures for documenting the resolution of differences with specialists are defined.	H	H	H-M	M	NA	

200

3. Specify the extent of documentation to be provided for the results of consultation.

	N	R	LL	SL	SP	
a. Indicate the type and extent of documentation to be used.	H	H	H	H	H	Consultation includes firm personnel and outsiders, such as AICPA services
b. Indicate where consultation documentation is to be maintained.	H	H	H	L	H	
c. Maintain subject files of consultation results.	H	M	L	L	L	File consultation summaries

Key:

H	= High	N	= National or international firm
M	= Medium	R	= Regional firm
L	= Low	LL	= Large Local firm (possibly two or three offices)
NA	= Not Applicable	SL	= Small Local firm (one office)
		SP	= Sole Practitioner (possibly one part-time staff member)

Table 12-3 Summary of Consultation Documentation

Documentation — Purpose	AICPA Procedures
Quality control document — informs staff of policies and procedures	all
Accounting and auditing manual — identifies areas and situations requiring consultation; identifies specialists	1a,b
Consultation log — documents consultation process	3a,b
Subject file memos — reference source	3c
Consultation summaries — document research	3a
Library log — controls distribution of materials	1c

Chapter 13

Assigning Personnel to Engagements

Efficient auditing depends on sound procedures for assigning personnel to engagements. The relevant AICPA quality control policies and procedures stating the objectives and sample procedures are reprinted in Exhibit 13-5 and summarized with comments in Table 13-3. An example of a scheduling request form, a scheduling master plan, a client history of personnel assigned form, and a history of staff assignments form are provided. Documentation is summarized in Table 13-4.

A survey of scheduling lead time is presented in Table 13-2. The opinions of CPA firm partners on selected quality control procedures are presented in Table 13-1. These opinions should provide to practitioners some perspective on what other CPAs are thinking and doing with respect to quality control. For the reader's convenience, all tables and exhibits are presented at the end of the chapter.

OVERVIEW

Every firm has a system for assigning personnel to engagements. For practice management purposes, effective scheduling is necessary to assure that the necessary technical competence is available for engagements. In addition, a firm wants to rotate its personnel among clients, engagement areas, and supervisors in order to enhance their development. From a business management viewpoint, the objective is to make the best possible use of available human resources, thereby minimizing staff requirements. Since low overtime rates for staff are being replaced by straight time or overtime premiums, firms want to minimize overtime.

Since firms are necessarily experienced with scheduling, documenting policies and procedures should be a relatively easy task. However, before preparing a quality control document in this area, a firm might be wise to look at its current system and ask whether it can be improved. Various scheduling techniques are explained in the accounting and management literature. Undoubtedly some firms can make changes that will enhance their use of staff and foster the development of personnel.

AUTHORITATIVE POLICIES AND PROCEDURES

The three objectives under the AICPA quality control policies and procedures are shown in Exhibit 13-5. Sample procedures are indicated by letters. Procedures are identified in the text by using the objective number, the procedure letter, and sometimes Roman numerals (1d(iii), for example). Common assignment procedures and the peer reviewer's approach are discussed below for each objective.

Delineate the Firm's Approach

Objective 1: DELINEATE THE FIRM'S APPROACH TO ASSIGNING PERSONNEL, INCLUDING THE PLANNING OF OVERALL FIRM AND OFFICE NEEDS AND THE MEASURES EMPLOYED TO ACHIEVE A BALANCE OF ENGAGEMENT MANPOWER REQUIREMENTS, PERSONNEL SKILLS, INDIVIDUAL DEVELOPMENT, AND UTILIZATION.

The first objective encourages the firm to plan personnel assignments carefully. This emphasis on planning is designed to assure the availability of competent professional personnel to perform engagements. From a business management point of view, firms want to avoid having personnel do work that could be handled by lower-level staff. CPA firms have assignment criteria based on the following:

- Engagement size and complexity
- Personnel availability
- Special expertise required
- Timing of the work to be performed
- Continuity and periodic rotation of personnel
- Opportunities for on-the-job training

They try to schedule personnel accordingly. These criteria should be included in a firm's quality control document. However, less than optimal results are often achieved because of conflicting scheduling requests.

Budgets and Schedules

Engagement time budgets and schedules of field work are the building blocks of a firm's plan for assigning personnel to engagements (1c). A scheduling request like Exhibit 13-1 can then be used to identify needs on a timely basis (1b). This sample scheduling request includes space for making specific personnel requests. It shows the scheduled work dates, type of work, experience level needed, and the total hours. If these requests are made on a timely basis, someone can integrate the needs into a scheduling master plan, as suggested by procedure 1a.

Scheduling master plans like the one in Exhibit 13-2 are commonly used because they facilitate the reconciliation of requests and available hours. This time, recorded by category and person, can be useful for future planning of staff needs and job dates.

Survey Data

Firms vary in their scheduling methods and lead times. There are many efficient systems in use. Computerized techniques will become more common as more firms acquire in-house computers. Generally, scheduling lead time increases with firm size, as shown in Table 13-2. The most common period is 8 to 21 days for the smallest firms. This increases to 22 to 42 days for medium-sized firms. It increases again for the largest firms, to more than 42 days. This widespread use of advance scheduling indicates that most firms probably have adequate quality control policies and procedures for assigning personnel. The data in Table 13-2 can be used as a guide in estimating a reasonable lead time for a quality control document.

In Table 13-1, part 1, we see the CPAs' views toward the usefulness of formal projections like scheduling master plans. The importance score for firms periodically preparing written formal projections of staffing requirements increases from 2.93 for the smallest firms to 4.73 for the largest. Overall, these projections are viewed to be quite useful. The estimated usage was only in the "occasional" range for the smallest firms, the "common" range for the medium-sized firms, and the "almost always" range for largest firms. The low estimated usage for the smallest firms is understandable because a sole practitioner or a two- or three-person firm can operate effectively with little formalized planning.

The responses in part 2 are at the engagement level. The importance and usage scores for parts 2a and 2b are very close to each other, and they are close to the scores in part 1 for the firm level.

Peer Reviewers

Overall, external peer reviewers try to determine whether engagement assignment planning is adequately comprehensive to assure that sufficient technical expertise is assigned to engagements. Thus, in reviewing engagements they check the time budgets and personnel assignments. They check the firm's scheduling request files to see if these are being used in accordance with firm policy and being submitted on a timely basis. Thus, the lead scheduling time in the quality control document should be realistic. External reviewers compare the firm's scheduling criteria with those listed under 1d in Exhibit 13-5. Accordingly, firms are advised to incorporate these criteria in their quality control document and use them in scheduling. Reviewers usually check to see whether staffing requirement projections influence hiring.

Assign Responsibilities

Objective 2: DESIGNATE AN APPROPRIATE PERSON OR PERSONS TO BE RESPONSIBLE FOR ASSIGNING PERSONNEL TO ENGAGEMENTS.

Effective management requires that responsibility for assigning personnel be clearly assigned. In some smaller firms, partners take joint responsibility for this task, which might be accomplished at weekly, bi-weekly, or monthly partners' meetings. This procedure allows for less detailed scheduling requests. As a firm's size increases, it is likely that one individual can more effectively schedule staff members through written requests.

Additional factors to be considered in scheduling include:

- Staffing and timing requirements of the specific engagement
- Evaluations of the qualifications of personnel as to experience, position, background, and special expertise
- The planned supervision and involvement by supervisory personnel
- Projected time availability of individuals assigned
- Situations where possible independence problems and conflicts of interest may exist, such as assignment of personnel to engagements for clients who are former employers or are employers of certain relatives

The scheduler might have to shift the dates of some engagements in order to provide adequate staffing. Some compromises might have to be made on the personnel assigned.

Obviously, the scheduler must be knowledgeable about the capabilities of all personnel in the firm and must understand what technical expertise is required on an engagement. A record of the personnel assigned to an engagement in prior years — like Exhibit 13-3 — can aid in this effort. At a glance it shows who is experienced on a particular job. This can help the scheduler, especially in a large office, to achieve a balance between continuity of personnel and rotation of personnel (2b).

In smaller firms, the personal relationship between the accountant and the client is more important, and scheduling is set up accordingly. Thus, a record like Exhibit 13-3 would be of little value to a small firm. While rotation of engagement partners is infrequent in small firms, it is required every five years for SEC-regulated clients. Any firm with SEC-regulated clients is advised to specify this rotation in its quality control document.

A summary of individuals' past work assignments can aid the scheduler in achieving rotation objectives. An important part of the individual's professional development is to have varied experience with different types of clients and in different audit areas. Rotation among supervisors is also important. A history of staff assignments like Exhibit 13-4 can be helpful for this task. It contains information on the most important rotation considerations. Since it can require considerable clerical time to maintain this record, it is not worthwhile for smaller firms who have a small number of scheduling alternatives.

Peer Reviewers

External peer reviewers ascertain who is responsible for scheduling. They discuss the assignment process with the scheduler. They try to determine whether scheduling criteria are being followed.

Approval of Scheduling by Engagement Management

Objective 3: PROVIDE FOR APPROVAL OF THE SCHEDULING AND STAFFING OF THE ENGAGEMENT BY THE PERSON WITH FINAL RESPONSIBILITY FOR THE ENGAGEMENT.

The monitoring aspect of assigning personnel is covered by the third objective. Since compromises must routinely be made, the engagement manager — or, better yet, the engagement partner — must approve the schedule. This approval is necessary to assure that adequate technical expertise is available for the job. Close supervision can compensate for less experienced or less technically proficient personnel in some engagement areas, but there are limits to this. For more complex audits, the engagement partner typically is the one to give final approval.

Some firms include methods for resolving disputes over assigning personnel in their quality control document. This seems unnecessary. For one thing, it conveys the impression of a firm with recurring scheduling problems.

The importance responses in Table 13-1, part 3, indicate some resistance to documenting policies and procedures for assigning personnel. The importance scores were only 2.07 and 2.8, respectively, for the "1 to 5" and "6 to 20" groups. The estimated usage scores were low — 1.66 to 2.08 — except for the largest firms (4.01). Thus, assigning personnel is an area where all firms have systems, but procedures apparently are typically unwritten.

Peer Reviewers

In examining sample engagements, peer reviewers check for approval of staff assignments. Generally, partner approval is expected. They judge whether the personnel assigned were adequate to perform the engagement, giving consideration to experience, training, and the extent of supervision.

GENERAL DESIGN

An example of a general design for assigning personnel to engagements is shown in Exhibit 13-6. Engagement managers have responsibility for time budgets and scheduling requests, and partner approval is required. An alternative is to waive partner approval for less complex engagements. Lead time varies by type of engagement. The advantage of this general design is that it is in a concise form for easy discussion by the partners. When approved, it can easily be converted into a quality control document.

A summary of AICPA objectives and sample procedures to implement them is presented in Table 13-3. Each procedure's applicability according to firm size is a generalization based upon current standards. Several characteristics of firms are recognized in the accounting profession's quality control programs as determinants of the appropriate quality control policies and procedures for CPA firms. Therefore, a firm must consider all of its characteristics in designing procedures and assigning responsibilities. Similarly, forms, check lists, and other documentation shown in this book and elsewhere must be modified to fit the individual firm's needs. (Table 13-4 summarizes the documentation for assigning personnel to engagements.)

Exhibit 13-1 Scheduling Request

Client _____ Engagement No. _____ Year End _____

Partner _____ Manager _____ Tax Ptr/Mgr. _____

Personnel requested	Experience level	Interim			Year End			Total Hours
		From	Thru	Hours	From	Thru	Hours	

Estimated total hours:

Partner _____
Manager _____
Staff _____
Total _____

Audited? Yes_____ No_____

SEC? Yes_____ No_____

Industry _____

Can dates be adjusted? Yes_____ No_____ Explain _____

Can personnel be changed? Yes_____ No_____ Explain _____

Comments _____

Requested by _____ Date _____ Scheduled _____ Date _____

Assignment Manager

Exhibit 13-2 Scheduling Master Plan

Scheduling Master Plan

Month of ___July 19X7___

Staff member	Carry forward	Month assign-ments	Nonworking hours							Nonrecurring assignments				Hours for month		
			Vacation	Holiday	Prof. dev.	Comp. time	CPA exam	Admin.	Other	Tax dept.	Review dept.	Other Client no.	Hr.	Total assign	Avail-able	(Over) under
Albert	10	75		7				21		35				148	161	13
Robbins	0	111		7				21		21	28			160	161	1
DeFolio	7	96		7				14				Special	10	162	161	(1)
Evans	20	66	14	7				14				C00200	14	135	161	26
Feldman	30	94.5		7		14		14						159.5	161	1.5
Gomez	7	113		7				21						148	161	13
Harvey	0	98		7				21				L05400	14	140	161	21
Hersh	0	25		7	35			14		70		Special	10	133	161	28
Munsen	0	77	49	7										161	161	—
Cash	35	118		7				14				C0200	(14)	160	161	1
O'Brien	0	131		7				21						159	161	2
Williams	16	117	14	7	7			21		14		L05400	(14)	168	161	(7)
Peters	0	119.5		7				21						161.5	161	(.5)
James	21	53	35	7				14						130	161	31
Jones	10	48	35	7		14		14			42			170	161	(9)
Paul	7	129		7				21						164	161	(3)
Vargan	14	105		7				14		21				161	161	—
Richards	7	73	21	7				21			28			157	161	4
Talbert	14	67		7				14			35			137	161	24
	198	1716	168	133	42	28		315		161	133		20	2914	3059	145

10/77 Rev.

Source: Copyright 1975, 1976, 1977, by the American Institute of Certified Public Accountants, Inc. Reprinted, by permission, from *Management of Accounting Practice Handbook*.

Exhibit 13-3 Client History of Personnel Assigned

CLIENT _____ LOCATION _____

YEAR ENDING _____ AUDITED? Yes___ No___ SEC? Yes___ No___

Fiscal Year	Hours		Enter Names and Chargeable Hours for the Year							
	Interim	Year End	Partner	Manager	Senior	In-Charge	Staff	Staff	Staff	Staff

Exhibit 13-4 History of Staff Assignments

NAME

| CLIENT/LOCATION | DATES | | RESPONSIBILITY LEVEL | TOTAL HOURS | ASSIGNMENT DESCRIPTION | | | |
	INTERIM	YEAR END			INDUSTRY	SEC	AUDIT AREAS PERFORMED	REPORTED TO

Exhibit 13-5 AICPA Quality Control Policies and Procedures for Assigning Personnel to Engagements

1. **Delineate the firm's approach to assigning personnel, including the planning of overall firm and office needs and the measures employed to achieve a balance of engagement manpower requirements, personnel skills, individual development, and utilization.**

   a. Plan the personnel needs of the firm on an overall basis and for individual practice offices.

   b. Identify on a timely basis the staffing requirements of specific engagements.

   c. Prepare time budgets for engagements to determine manpower requirements and to schedule field work.

   d. Consider the following factors in achieving a balance of engagement manpower requirements, personnel skills, individual development, and utilization:
      - (i) Engagement size and complexity.
      - (ii) Personnel availability.
      - (iii) Special expertise required.
      - (iv) Timing of the work to be performed.
      - (v) Continuity and periodic rotation of personnel.
      - (vi) Opportunities for on-the-job training.

2. **Designate an appropriate person or persons to be responsible for assigning personnel to engagements.**

   a. Consider the following in making assignments of individuals:
      - (i) Staffing and timing requirements of the specific engagement.
      - (ii) Evaluations of the qualifications of personnel as to experience, position, background, and special expertise.
      - (iii) The planned supervision and involvement by supervisory personnel.
      - (iv) Projected time availability of individuals assigned.
      - (v) Situations where possible independence problems and conflicts of interest may exist, such as assignment of personnel to engagements for clients who are former employers or are employers of certain kin.

   b. Give appropriate consideration, in assigning personnel, to both continuity and rotation to provide for efficient conduct of the engagement and the perspective of other personnel with different experience and backgrounds.

Source: Copyright © 1976, 1978 by the American Institute of Certified Public Accountants, Inc. Reprinted, by permission, from *Voluntary Quality Control Review Program for CPA Firms.*

Exhibit 13-5 continued

3. **Provide for approval of the scheduling and staffing of the engagement by the person with final responsibility for the engagement.**

   a. Submit, where necessary, for review and approval the names and qualifications of personnel to be assigned to an engagement.

   b. Consider the experience and training of the engagement personnel in relation to the complexity or other requirements of the engagement, and the extent of supervision to be provided.

Exhibit 13-6 Example of General Design for Assigning Personnel to
Engagements

Operational Responsibilities:

The field supervisor prepares time budgets and staffing requests. A minimum of
45 days lead time is required. The lead time is 90 days for engagements with
budgets in excess of 100 hours. Partner C is responsible for assigning personnel 21
days in advance.

Communication:

The accounting and auditing manual contains scheduling procedures. The
personnel manual informs staff members of their responsibilities to plan for
assignments and request time for vacations, professional development, etc.

Monitoring:

The engagement partner approves scheduling and staffing.

Documentation:

1. Accounting and auditing manual states scheduling procedures
2. Personnel manual explains staff responsibilities
3. Scheduling request
4. Engagement time budgets
5. Scheduling master plan
6. Client history of personnel assigned
7. History of staff assignments

NOTE: The profile firm is described in Appendix A.

Table 13-1 Opinions on Assigning Personnel to Engagements Policies and Procedures

Quality Control	Number of Professional Personnel in Firm							
	1 to 5		6 to 20		20 to 80		More than 80	
Policy or Procedure	Mean	CV	Mean	CV	Mean	CV	Mean	CV
(1) The firm periodically prepares written formal projections of staffing requirements.								
Importance	2.93	54%	3.71	29%	4.17	17%	4.73	19%
Usage	2.91	51%	3.13	30%	3.44	35%	4.74	17%
(2) Time budgets must be prepared (written) on a timely basis for:								
a. All audit engagements.								
Importance	3.13	54%	3.35	34%	4.25	15%	4.68	12%
Usage	3.41	47%	2.63	50%	3.65	23%	4.69	13%
b. Selected audit engagements.								
Importance	3.17	55%	3.58	30%	4.50	12%	4.42	23%
Usage	3.54	47%	2.91	46%	4.16	20%	4.14	31%
(3) Policies and procedures for assigning personnel to engagements are documented.								
Importance	2.07	56%	2.80	47%	3.33	30%	4.05	28%
Usage	2.09	49%	1.94	55%	1.66	49%	4.01	32%
Number of respondents	8		21		14		24	

NOTE: The mean responses are based on a five-point scale. They can be interpreted according to where they fall within the following ranges:

Importance	Range	Usage	Range
Unimportant	1.00-1.5	Rare	1.25-1.88
Little importance	1.51-2.5	Occasional	1.89-3.13
Some importance	2.51-3.5	Common	3.14-4.38
Important	3.51-4.5	Almost always	4.39-5.00
Essential	4.51-5.0		

For example, an importance score of 1.81 indicates that the respondents viewed the procedure as being of little importance. CV represents coefficient of variation. The higher the coefficient of variation, the greater the variability in the responses of the CPA firm partners in a particular group. See Appendix C for a description of the study.

Table 13-2 Lead Time for Scheduling Audit Staff

Question	Affirmative Responses Grouped by Number of Professional Personnel in Firm			
	1 to 5	6 to 20	20 to 80	More than 80
How far in advance does your firm generally schedule its audit staff?				
7 days or less	7%	16%	7%	2%
8 to 21 days	39%	31%	27%	0%
22 to 42 days	29%	45%	53%	13%
More than 42 days	18%	7%	7%	85%
No response	7%	0%	6%	0%

Table 13-3 Assigning Personnel to Engagements. Summary Evaluation of Quality Control Policies and Procedures (for inclusion in a firm's quality control document).

AICPA Policy/Procedure	Procedure's Applicability to Firm					Comments
	N	R	LL	SL	SP	
1. Delineate the firm's approach to assigning personnel (state objectives)						
a. Prepare formal projections of staffing requirements on a periodic basis for the firm and individual offices.	H	H	H-M	M-L	L	Projections may be less formal for smaller firms
b. Identify engagement staffing requirements on a timely basis.	H	H	H	H	H	Scheduling requests are helpful
c. Prepare time budgets for engagements.	H	H	H	M	L	
d. Schedule assignments to achieve a balance of engagement staffing requirements, personnel skills, individual development, utilization.	H	H	H	H	NA	The firm should have scheduling criteria
2. Designate the individual(s) responsible for assigning personnel.						
a. Document procedures and criteria for assigning personnel.	H	H	H	H	H	
b. Consider continuity and rotation in making assignments.	H	H	H	H-M	NA	Applies to part-time and per-diem personnel

3. The individual with final responsibility for the engagement approves schedule assignments (state who).

	N	R	LL	SL	SP	
a. The names of assigned personnel are submitted for approval.	H	H	H	H-M	NA	Usually the engagement partner gives approval
b. In making the decision, the experience and training of personnel are considered.	H	H	H	H	NA	Engagement complexity and the extent of supervision are important considerations

Key:

N	=	National or international firm
R	=	Regional firm
LL	=	Large Local firm (possibly two or three offices)
SL	=	Small Local firm (one office)
SP	=	Sole Practitioner, (possibly one part-time staff member)

H	=	High
M	=	Medium
L	=	Low
NA	=	Not Applicable

Table 13-4 Summary of Documentation for Assigning Personnel to Engagements

Documentation — Purpose	AICPA Procedures
Quality control document — informs personnel of procedures	all
Accounting and auditing manual — scheduling procedures	1a, b, c
Personnel manual — staff responsibilities for assignments and making personal requests	1a
Scheduling request — requests personnel	1b
Time budget — engagement staff plan	1c
Scheduling master plan — makes assignments	1a
Client history of personnel assigned — aids in scheduling	2a, b
History of staff assignments — aids in scheduling	2a, b

BIBLIOGRAPHY

Goldberg, Daniel S. "New Light on Staff Scheduling." *Journal of Accountancy*, April 1977, p. 50.

Grimslow, Christopher K. "How to Simplify The Administration of a Public Accounting Firm." *Practical Accountant*, March/April 1975, pp. 53-55.

Chapter 14

Inspection

Inspection entails a periodic self-review for compliance with firm policies and procedures. The AICPA quality control policies and procedures stating the objectives and sample procedures are reprinted in Exhibit 14-2 and summarized with comments in Table 14-2. Recommended inspection documentation is summarized in Table 14-3.

The opinions of CPA firm partners on selected quality control procedures are presented in Table 14-1. These opinions should provide to practitioners some perspective on what other CPAs are thinking and doing with respect to quality control. For the reader's convenience, all tables and exhibits are presented at the end of the chapter.

OVERVIEW

An essential element of a firm's quality assurance system is a self-review program. External peer reviews occur every three years; a periodic check for compliance with policies and procedures can prevent a pattern of deficiencies from developing during this interval. Such a pattern might cause serious concern for external peer reviewers. Annual inspections of engagements and of compliance with quality control policies and procedures will probably become the norm.

A firm's inspection program is normally performed by its own personnel, but outside consultants might be used for some aspects to enhance the objectivity of the review. A major benefit of an inspection program is its educational aspects. It emphasizes the importance of a firm's procedures to the firm's personnel. Deficiencies in engagement working papers and reports are discussed with firm personnel, which is important training. Reviewers can benefit from seeing other people's work. A comprehensive self-review program makes a good impression on external peer reviewers, allowing them to shorten their work program. The result is lower fees for external review. Thus, in planning for an external peer review, a firm is advised to allow enough lead time for its own firm inspection program to operate at least once.

AUTHORITATIVE POLICIES AND PROCEDURES

The AICPA quality control policies and procedures are shown in Exhibit 14-2. Firms should establish policies and procedures to accomplish the three objectives listed. Examples of procedures are identified in Exhibit 14-2 by letters, and in the text by numbers, letters, and Roman numerals (1b(ii), for example). Common procedures and the peer reviewer's approach are discussed below for each objective.

Define the Firm's Program

Objective 1: DEFINE THE SCOPE AND CONTENT OF THE FIRM'S IN-SPECTION PROGRAM.

The first inspection objective calls for a firm to define the scope and content of its program. "Scope" refers to a periodic review of a firm's quality control document and engagements. "Content" refers to the "who, when, and how" of the review.

Procedures Review

Exhibit 14-2 (1a) points out the need to define procedures for periodic inspections of a firm's quality control policies and procedures. A firm's self-review procedures should be guided by the AICPA procedures. The objectives and instructions of a firm's program (1a(i)) should be summarized in the quality control document or in firm materials.

An important procedure would be for a partner to evaluate periodically the firm's quality control document, using the current AICPA or Division for CPA Firms check list. Even if the same check list was used a year earlier for a self-review, this is a useful exercise because it forces the CPA to take another look at the procedures and ask whether they are still appropriate.

To save time and the cost of new check lists, an abbreviated check list like Exhibit 14-1 might be used. This check list focuses on the changes since the last external peer review. For each element, it has room for changes in firm procedures and the profession's quality control standards in parts 3 and 4, respectively.

A firm's program should also include compliance review procedures. The procedures to be followed, such as interviews, review of files, and review of working papers, might be summarized in the quality control document or reference can be made to firm materials.

Engagement Review

A firm's inspection program procedures should indicate how many engagements are reviewed, the basis for their selection, and who does the reviewing. The objective of the engagement review phase is, simply, to test for compliance with the profession's and the firm's standards. One possible procedure is to use the AICPA engagement check lists for this review. These should provide the firm with an approximate idea of what external peer reviewers will see when they use the check lists. With this insight, the firm's ability to prepare for the external review is enhanced.

A disadvantage of using the AICPA check lists is their generalized nature. Since each firm has its own specialized procedures, a customized version of the check list might be better for checking compliance with firm standards. A customized check list makes a good impression on external peer reviewers for several reasons. First, it shows that a serious effort was made to establish a self-review program. Second, the check list evidences the effort to develop firm-wide procedures. A firm's inspection program becomes a method of educating personnel and monitoring compliance with the firm's procedures. Also, a customized firm check list usually has the advantage of being shorter than the AICPA check list.

Although a customized check list seems a burden to prepare, the initial draft can be easily updated as procedures change over time. Preparation time can be decreased by doing some cutting and pasting of the AICPA check list. If a firm is preparing its first accounting and auditing manual, it should be prepared simultaneously with the check list. Since the check list states procedures in question form, the check list can be used as part of the manual. Alternatively, an existing firm manual of working paper procedures can easily be converted by restating the procedures as questions, using the AICPA check list as a guide for format. To save time, firms with accounting and auditing manuals might construct the check list as follows:

1. Use the AICPA check list for:
    a. Functional areas of quality control.
    b. General audit procedures.
    c. Financial statements and reports.
2. For working paper content ask a series of questions. "Were the firm's procedures followed for _____?"

The blanks would include the major areas from the firm's manual, such as cash, accounts receivable, inventories, etc. After each question there should be adequate space to list and discuss deficiencies.

The selection of engagements is normally aimed at covering the work of all firm personnel at the partner, supervisor, and manager levels. This full coverage is desirable, since it minimizes the chance that a pattern of engagement deficiencies will develop within the firm's working papers.

The extent of a firm's self-review of engagements can be expected to affect the number of engagements selected by external peer reviewers. If external reviewers are favorably impressed by a firm's coverage, they are likely to keep their selections close to the 5% minimum of engagement hours to be reviewed. The result is a savings in review fees.

Other Aspects

For multi-office firms, the firm's inspection program must specify the coverage of practice offices, functions, and departments (1a(ii)). Again, the firm's coverage usually affects the external peer reviewer's work program.

Annual self-review will most likely become the norm for the profession. The frequency and timing are considered under procedure 1a(iii). The self-review generally occurs during a time when a firm has the least work to do, but this need not be stated in the quality control document.

Procedure 1a(iv) suggests the need to state procedures for resolving disputes between firm reviewers and engagement management. This procedure can be left unsaid, however, especially in smaller firms. A firm does not want to convey the impression that it expects conflict. If the external peer reviewer is upset by the omission of this statement from the quality control document, the reviewer can ask what would be done.

A committee headed by a partner is the appropriate form for a review team, firm size permitting. The committee can include partners and other engagement management personnel. Some firms have a quality control specialist who continually monitors the firm's quality control policies and procedures and acts as the second reviewer on most engagements. This person is an obvious selection for the review team, and might head the team if he or she is a partner. Other specific requirements for reviewers, such as independence considerations, might be stated (1b(i)).

Reviewers might be selected annually at a partners' meeting, or one person could have selection responsibility (1b(ii)). In a small two-partner firm, the logical procedure would be for the partners to review each other's engagements. A sole proprietor could have an agreement with another firm to do reciprocal reviews.

If a firm has decided to have an external peer review, its inspection program should include external review as a procedure. While most firms schedule these external reviews every three years, some firms have them more frequently.

Views on Inspection

The CPA firm partners' views on inspection are presented in Table 14-1. In part 1, we see the results for the firm review program. For part 1a, the importance scores are high, and practically identical for all but the largest firms, which have an even higher score. These results indicate a considerable receptiveness to self-review. The estimated usage scores were only in the "occasional" range for the medium-sized firms. For the largest firms, the very high estimated usage score is reasonable: the national firms have used self-review programs for many years. For the smallest firms, the estimated usage is in the "common" range. This result is also reasonable, because a less extensive program is needed. A sole proprietor is continually reviewing his procedures; and in a small two or three-person firm, procedures are likely to be discussed periodically.

The results in part 1b of Table 14-1 are very close to those in part 1a. Generally, the scores are slightly higher. The estimated usage scores can be compared to the results of a survey question. The CPAs were asked: "Does your firm have a program for reviewing reports after they are issued?" The "Yes" answers, by group, were as follows:

1 to 5	43%
6 to 20	38%
20 to 80	40%
More than 80	83%

These statistics match up very well with the estimated usage scores.

The views on using outside reviewers are shown in part 2 of Table 14-1. The importance and usage scores are lower than the scores in part 1. Part 2a covers practice reviews. Most state CPA societies have practice review programs. The importance score was low for the smallest firms, with the other groups showing higher scores. The relatively low estimated usage scores are realistic, because participation in practice review programs has not been very extensive. Part 2b also includes working papers. This type of review is called a "technical standards review." The importance and usage scores are not much different from those for practice reviews. The scores are also about the same for part 2c, relating to reviews of compliance with quality control policies and procedures.

Overall, the respondents view self-review to be more important than external peer review.

External Peer Reviewers

External peer reviewers evaluate a firm's inspection program for its adequacy for evaluating compliance with the firm's quality control policies and procedures. Thus, a firm program modeled after the external review program would make a good impression. Reviewers usually check time records for the firm's self-review to see how comprehensive the program is in covering billed accounting and auditing hours. They review the selection of internal reviewers for technical competence and independence. They review the most recent inspection to ascertain whether a firm's procedures were followed and appropriate conclusions were reached. A firm should recognize the implication of this procedure in planning for its initial peer review. It should plan far enough ahead so that the firm's program can be used some time before external peer reviewers visit the firm.

Sole Practitioners

The AICPA sample quality control documents for sole practitioners suggest that the practitioner perform an annual self-review using AICPA check lists. This inspection and any corrective actions taken can be documented by a memo to files.

Report and Monitor Inspection Findings

Objective 2: PROVIDE FOR REPORTING INSPECTION FINDINGS TO THE APPROPRIATE MANAGEMENT LEVELS AND FOR MONITORING ACTIONS TAKEN OR PLANNED.

Since a major objective of a firm's inspection program is to see that procedures are being followed, the findings have to be communicated to the firm's personnel (2a). This is an important educational aspect of a firm's program. Engagement review check lists can be used as the basis for discussion with engagement management personnel. The overall results should generally be summarized in a report to firm management (2b). Since the check lists document the self-review, only a short report is needed. Typically, this would be discussed at a partners' meeting. The minutes could be used to record the results, noting any corrective action. In a small firm, this report could be made orally at a partners' meeting.

There seems to be no reason to copy the report used by external peer reviewers. Instead, a statement on the adequacy of the firm's policies and procedures, the documentation, and the degree of compliance is satisfactory. The report should identify any deficiencies and specify corrective action. If corrective action was recommended in the previous year's report, the report should state whether the underlying problem has been solved. Any difficulties encountered during the inspection process should also be disclosed.

If the inspection report recommends corrective action, follow-up responsibility should be assigned. In a typical case, the report is presented at a partners' meeting. After a corrective action is approved, one partner volunteers to implement the corrective action. Someone else has the responsibility to monitor implementation. For example, the required correction might be a change in the personnel manual. The partner responsible for the manual volunteers to make the change. Monitoring is accomplished by requiring that partner to make a report at the next partners' meeting. The minutes of the partners' meeting would document all of this.

Peer Reviewers

External peer reviewers examine the documentation of a firm's inspection program. They may interview some firm personnel to determine whether the results of engagement reviews were communicated to engagement management personnel. If a written report on the inspection is available, they evaluate the reasonableness of its conclusions. They check the follow-up procedures for recommended corrective actions.

GENERAL DESIGN

An example of a general design for inspection is shown in Exhibit 14-3. The firm's inspection team is changed each year to enhance objectivity and to distribute the educational benefits of being a reviewer among all eligible personnel. There is full coverage of the engagements of all management personnel. All partners participate in the monitoring process.

A summary of AICPA objectives and sample procedures to implement them is presented in Table 14-2. Each procedure's applicability according to firm size is a generalization based upon current standards. Several characteristics of firms are recognized in the accounting profession's quality control programs as determinants of the appropriate quality control policies and procedures for CPA firms. Therefore, a firm must consider all of its characteristics in designing procedures and assigning responsibilities. Similarly, forms, check lists, and other documentation shown in this book and elsewhere must be modified to fit the individual firm's needs. Table 14-3 summarizes inspection documentation.

Exhibit 14-1 Annual Review of Quality Control Document Check List

Instructions: For each of the quality control elements, indicate
all "No" answers that would be appropriate answers
to the AICPA quality control document check list.
Identify check list items by using a number, letter,
and Roman numeral (1a(i), for example).

What AICPA check list is being reviewed?_____
Is this check list still appropriate?_____

INDEPENDENCE
1. "No" answers_____
2. Have any procedures changed since the last external peer review?
   If yes, explain._____
   _____
3. Are there any new areas to be considered?_____
   _____

ASSIGNING PERSONNEL TO ENGAGEMENTS
1. "No" answers_____
2. Have any procedures changed since the last external peer review?
   If yes, explain._____
   _____
3. Are there any new areas to be considered?_____
   _____

CONSULTATION
1. "No" answers_____
2. Have any procedures changed since the last external peer review?
   If yes, explain._____
   _____
3. Are there any new areas to be considered?_____
   _____

SUPERVISION
1. "No" answers_____
2. Have any procedures changed since the last external peer review?
   If yes, explain._____
   _____
3. Are there any new areas to be considered?_____
   _____

HIRING
1. "No" answers_____
2. Have any procedures changed since the last external peer review?
   If yes, explain. _____
   _____
3. Are there any new areas to be considered?_____
   _____

Exhibit 14-1 continued

PROFESSIONAL DEVELOPMENT
   1. "No" answers_____
   2. Have any procedures changed since the last external peer review?
      If yes, explain._____

      _____

   3. Are there any new areas to be considered?_____

      _____

ADVANCEMENT
   1. "No" answers_____
   2. Have any procedures changed since the last external peer review?
      If yes, explain._____

      _____

   3. Are there any new areas to be considered?_____

      _____

ACCEPTANCE AND CONTINUANCE OF CLIENTS
   1. "No" answers_____
   2. Have any procedures changed since the last external peer review?
      If yes, explain._____

      _____

   3. Are there any new areas to be considered?_____

      _____

INSPECTION
   1. "No" answers_____
   2. Have any procedures changed since the last external peer review?
      If yes, explain._____

      _____

   3. Are there any new areas to be considered?_____

      _____

Exhibit 14-2 AICPA Quality Control Policies and Procedures for Inspection

1. Define the scope and content of the firm's inspection program.

a. Determine the inspection procedures necessary to provide reasonable assurance that the firm's other quality control policies and procedures are operating effectively.
   (i) Determine objectives and prepare instructions and review programs for use in conducting inspection activities.
   (ii) Provide guidelines for the extent of work at practice units, functions, or departments, and criteria for selection of engagements for review.
   (iii) Establish the frequency and timing of inspection activities.
   (iv) Establish procedures to resolve disagreements which may arise between reviewers and engagement or management personnel.

b. Establish qualifications for personnel to participate in inspection activities and the method of their selection.
   (i) Determine criteria for selecting reviewers, including levels of responsibility in the firm and requirements for specialized knowledge.
   (ii) Assign responsibility for selecting inspection personnel.

c. Conduct inspection activities at practice units, functions, or departments.
   (i) Review and test compliance with applicable quality control policies and procedures.
   (ii) Review selected engagements for compliance with professional standards, including generally accepted auditing standards, generally accepted accounting principles, and with the firm's quality control policies and procedures.

2. Provide for reporting inspection findings to the appropriate management levels and for monitoring actions taken or planned.

a. Discuss inspection review findings on engagements reviewed with engagement management personnel.

b. Discuss inspection findings of practice units, functions, or departments reviewed with appropriate management personnel.

c. Report inspection findings and recommendations to firm management together with corrective actions taken or planned.

d. Determine that planned corrective actions were taken.

Source: Copyright © 1976, 1978 by the American Institute of Certified Public Accountants, Inc. Reprinted, with permission, from *Voluntary Quality Control Review Program for CPA Firms.*

Exhibit 14-3 Example of General Design for Inspection

Operational Responsibilities:

At the June partners' meeting, a partner is appointed to head an inspection team of three engagement management persons. The team tests the adequacy of quality control policies and procedures and for compliance, and five percent of all engagement hours are reviewed on a selective basis so that every engagement supervisor's work is covered. Partner B is responsible for cooperating with AICPA external peer review teams.

Communication:

Results of engagement reviews are discussed with engagement management personnel. The team head makes an oral and written report at the October partners' meeting.

Monitoring:

The partner taking responsibility for implementing corrective action must report on the progress at monthly partners' meetings.

Documentation:

1. Annual quality control document check lists
2. Annual engagement review check lists
3. Inspection team review report
4. Minutes of partners' meetings

NOTE: The profile firm is described in Appendix A.

Table 14-1 Opinions on Inspection Policies and Procedures

Quality Control Policy or Procedure	Number of Professional Personnel in Firm							
	1 to 5		6 to 20		20 to 80		More than 80	
	Mean	CV	Mean	CV	Mean	CV	Mean	CV
(1) The firm has a program where *firm personnel* periodically review activities to:								
a. Test compliance with applicable quality control policies and procedures.								
Importance	3.65	35%	3.69	25%	3.64	23%	4.88	9%
Usage	3.21	46%	2.05	55%	2.50	43%	4.81	15%
b. Review selected engagements for compliance with professional standards.								
Importance	3.74	28%	4.00	25%	3.93	19%	4.88	9%
Usage	3.51	37%	2.55	49%	2.66	39%	4.76	16%
(2) The firm has a program where *outside reviewers* periodically review:								
a. Selected financial statements and audit reports.								
Importance	2.31	61%	3.21	26%	3.57	29%	3.77	38%
Usage	1.88	53%	1.64	52%	1.84	44%	3.54	48%
b. Audit working papers, reports and financial statements.								
Importance	2.38	59%	3.17	26%	3.64	28%	3.82	35%
Usage	1.95	50%	1.59	35%	1.75	45%	3.40	49%
c. Compliance with quality control policies and procedures.								
Importance	2.44	60%	3.30	30%	3.57	29%	4.04	28%
Usage	2.01	53%	1.49	34%	1.59	46%	3.66	45%
Number of responses	15		26		15		20	

NOTE: The mean responses are based on a five-point scale. They can be interpreted according to where they fall within the following ranges:

Importance	Range	Usage	Range
Unimportant	1.00-1.5	Rare	1.25-1.88
Little importance	1.51-2.5	Occasional	1.89-3.13
Some importance	2.51-3.5	Common	3.14-4.38
Important	3.51-4.5	Almost always	4.39-5.00
Essential	4.51-5.0		

For example, an importance score of 1.81 indicates that the respondents viewed the procedure as being of little importance. CV represents coefficient of variation. The higher the coefficient of variation, the greater the variability in the responses of the CPA firm partners in a particular group. See Appendix C for a description of the study.

Table 14-2 Inspection. Summary Evaluation of Quality Control Policies and Procedures (for inclusion in a firm's quality control document).

AICPA Policy/Procedure	Procedure's Applicability to Firm					Comments
	N	R	LL	SL	SP	
1. Define the scope and content of the firm's inspection program.						
a. Establish procedures to evaluate the firm's quality control policies and procedures for adequacy and compliance.	H	H	H	H	M	
b. Establish qualifications for firm reviewers, and procedures for their selection.	H	H	H	H	H	Partners and other engagement management personnel
c. Conduct inspection of:						
(i) Quality control policies and procedures.	H	H	H	H	H	Annually
(ii) Engagements.	H	H	H	H	H	
2. Report inspection findings and monitor corrective actions.						
a. Discuss engagement reviews with engagement management personnel.	H	H	H	H	NA	
b. Discuss reviews of practice units, functions or departments with appropriate management personnel.	H	H	M	M	NA	

	N	R	LL	SL	SP	
c. Report findings to firm management and corrective actions planned or taken.	H	H	H	H	NA	A partners' meeting might be used as a forum
d. Determine that planned corrective actions were taken.	H	H	H	H	H	SP prepares a memo to files on self-review and corrective actions

Key:

N = National or international firm
R = Regional firm
LL = Large Local firm (possibly two or three offices)
SL = Small Local firm (one office)
SP = Sole Practitioner (possibly one part-time staff member)

Key:

H = High
M = Medium
L = Low
NA = Not Applicable

Table 14-3 Summary of Inspection Documentation

Documentation — Purpose	AICPA Procedures
Quality control document — informs staff of policies and procedures	all
Annual quality control document check list — reviews quality control document	1c(i)
Annual engagement review check lists — document reviews of engagements	1c(ii)
Inspection team review report — reports on inspection findings	2b,c
Minutes of partners' meeting — record the results of inspection and corrective action	2c,d

Chapter 15

A Realistic Perspective

Having discussed the meaning of quality control, as well as firm strategies and procedures for implementing a quality control system, I now want to place these subjects in a realistic perspective. Firms cannot ignore the profession's quality control program. The business environment is changing, and the profession is changing. Since many firms have joined the AICPA Division for CPA Firms, every CPA firm must consider how its competitive position is affected, and must develop a strategy to deal with these new circumstances.

In selecting a strategy, CPA firms must also consider their responsibilities to the accounting profession, to their clients, and to themselves as accounting professionals. These factors are discussed in this chapter. The costs and benefits of quality control systems are also reviewed. The documentation described in the nine element chapters is summarized, and it is classified according to how commonly it will be used by firms of various sizes.

A final section of this chapter — which contains advice on how to ease the process of establishing a quality control system — should be helpful to practitioners. These tips can help reduce the impact and cost of implementing a quality control system or providing for a more effective system.

PROFESSIONAL RESPONSIBILITIES

CPAs are members of a profession with unique responsibilities to the public. The profession's code of ethics emphasizes the CPA's basic responsibility to society to perform the attest function. State boards of accountancy grant CPAs the exclusive right to perform the attest function. This licensing has brought great financial and psychological benefits to CPAs as individuals. The public has placed a great deal of confidence and trust in CPAs. Now the public is concerned about audit failures. CPAs are being asked to revise their quality assurance systems and to open their firms to external peer review. Can CPAs refuse?

Every CPA has a responsibility to the profession to participate in a quality control program. Universal participation by firms with SEC clients would show legislators, regulators, the business community, and the public in general that the profession is capable of meeting its responsibilities through self-regulation. Widespread participation by CPA firms could raise the profession's image to unprecedented heights. It would enable the profession to continue its long-term trend of growth by expanding services to clients.

CPAs must also show the public that their quality control program is effective. Since there will be some skepticism, every effort must be made to convince legislators, regulators, the business community, and clients that external peer review is an effective method of monitoring quality control. Critics' questions should be given serious consideration, and the profession must be willing to change. On the other hand, CPAs are established professionals, and there is no reason for them to be burdened with unnecessary procedures.

In selecting a strategy, CPAs must also consider their responsibilities to clients. The client deserves technically competent and efficient services. Quality assurance systems are designed to meet this need. The client also needs financial statements worthy of the business community's confidence. In time, bankers, investors, and other financial statement users will come to understand the meaning of membership in the Division for CPA Firms. Eventually, many are likely to view the reports of member firms with greater confidence. This greater confidence is important to clients.

CPAs also have a responsibility to themselves. Although a substantial initial investment in a quality control system is required, there are long-term benefits. Improved organization will allow a firm to keep abreast of changes and to upgrade its practice. Thus, an effective quality control system can help a firm enhance its long-term profit potential.

COSTS AND BENEFITS

In addition to their professional responsibilities, CPA firms should consider other benefits of participating in the profession's quality control program. The benefits and costs are explained in Chapter 4, and summarized below. For most firms, the potential benefits are likely to outweigh the costs. An exception might be a small firm with mostly tax clients.

Benefits

Overall, the benefits of a quality control system are higher profits and a high-quality firm image. A firm's ability to expand is enhanced because of its well-defined organizational structure. A serious effort by a firm to improve its quality control system should result in better operating decisions, meaning more efficient and effective auditing. There should be less chance of audit failure. If a firm is threatened by litigation, its legal exposure is reduced if it can show it has a sound quality assurance system. In the long run, it appears that professional liability insurance will be more expensive or unavailable to firms lacking formalized systems and external peer review. A strong system should enhance a firm's ability to attract and retain high-quality personnel, and should provide for faster development of professional personnel.

Costs

A large part of the cost is the initial investment required to design the system and write the quality control document and manuals. There is more paperwork, but this eventually becomes routine. Annual self-review takes time. Many of the forms and checklists are already in wide use, especially in the personnel and auditing areas.

Documentation

Table 15-1 summarizes the documentation described in the element chapters (6-14) of this book. The documentation is commonly included in the firm files indicated in the left-hand column. The probable usage of the forms and manuals is indicated according to firm size. The term "probable usage" is indicated instead of "required usage" or "common usage" because no exact rules exist. The probable usage is stated as "high," "medium," or "low," based on my discussions with practitioners and an evaluation of professional standards.

"High" means that some version of this form (or substitute documentation) should be used unless there are unique circumstances that preclude its use. "Medium" means that the documentation is probably a very useful element of a quality control system, although costs must be weighed against usefulness. "Low" means that the documentation can easily be omitted.

Various versions of the documentation shown in this book are possible. Forms — such as annual evaluation forms and orientation forms — should be modified to fit a firm's unique characteristics. An accounting and auditing manual generally would be small for a local firm.

Other Costs

While the annual participation fees for the Division for CPA Firms are not high, the required liability insurance is costly. However, this cost is irrelevant to a firm that is already covered. A firm not desiring coverage can choose the AICPA voluntary program, which does not require coverage.

The costs of external peer reviews are not really that high. Table 4-2, in Chapter 4, shows that the cost in 1979 for a 12-person firm ranges from $1,660 to $2,650 every three years, which means that annual cost is only about $550 to $900. The net out-of-pocket cost can be reduced substantially if a firm volunteers its own personnel to be reviewers.

Table 15-1 Summary of Documentation and Probable Usage

File	Documentation	Reference	Probable Usage According to Firm Size				
			N	R	LL	SL	SP
A	Quality control document	Ch. 6-14	H	H	H	H	H
A	Personnel manual	E 8-4	H	H	H	H	L
A	Accounting and auditing manual	Various	H	H	H	M	M
A	Firm library	Ch. 12	H	H	H	H	H
A	Minutes of partners' meetings	Various	H	H	H	H	L
	INDEPENDENCE:						
A	Independence check list	E 6-1	H	H	H	M	L
P	Independence compliance letter	E 6-2	H	H	H	H	L
A	Client lists and update memos	Ch. 6	H	H	H	M	L
	ACCEPTANCE AND CONTINUANCE OF CLIENTS:						
C	Check list of factors to be considered in assessing audit risk of clients	E 7-1	H	H	H	M	L
C	New client acceptance form	E 7-2	H	H	H	H	H
C	Client continuance form	E 7-3	H	H	H	H	M
E	Engagement letters	B	H	H	H	H	H
	HIRING:						
P	Professional employment application	E 8-1	H	H	H	H	L
P	Interview evaluation form	E 8-2	H	H	H	M	L
P	Staff orientation check list	E 8-3	H	H	L	M	L
A	Recruiting brochure	Ch. 8	H	H	L	L	L
A	Recruiting program (documented)	Ch. 8	H	H	L	L	NA

ADVANCEMENT:

P	Check list of personnel rating criteria	E 9-1	H	H	M	L	NA
P	Assignment performance evaluation questionnaire	E 9-2	H	M	M	L	NA
P	Knowledge and skill form	E 9-3	H	H	M	L	NA
P	Annual evaluation form	E 9-4	H	H	H	H	NA

PROFESSIONAL DEVELOPMENT:

A	Annual report of CPE hours	E 10-2	H	H	H	H	H
P	History of CPE hours	E 10-3	H	H	M	M	L
A	CPE program participant's evaluation	E 10-4	H	H	M	L	L
A	Check list summary of standards for formal group and self-study program	E 10-5	H	H	M	L	L
A	Routing slip	Ch. 10	H	H	H	M	L

SUPERVISION:

E	Engagement planning check list	E 11-2	H	H	H	H	M
E	Audit pre-planning check list	E 11-3	H	H	H	M	M
E	Working paper review check list	E 11-4	H	H	H	H	M
E	Audit time budget	B	H	H	H	M	L
E	Disclosure check list	B	H	H	H	M	M
E	Reviewer's disclosure check list	B	H	H	H	M	M
E	Report guide sheet	E 11-5,6	H	H	H	M	M
E	Work programs	B	H	H	H	M	M
E	Auditing check lists, etc.	B	H	H	H	H	L
A	Memo to files	Ch. 11	H	H	M	L	L

CONSULTATION:

A	Consultation log	E 12-1	H	M	L	L	NA
A	Subject file memos	Ch. 12	H	M	L	L	L
E	Consultation summaries	Ch. 12	H	H	H	H	H
A	Library log	Ch. 12	H	H	M	L	L

Table 15-1 continued

File	Documentation	Reference	Probable Usage According to Firm Size				
			N	R	LL	SL	SP
	ASSIGNING PERSONNEL TO ENGAGEMENTS:						
E	Scheduling request	E 13-1	H	H	M	L	NA
E	Scheduling master plan	E 13-2	H	H	M	L	L
C	Client history of personnel assigned	E 13-3	H	H	M	L	NA
P	History of staff assignments	E 13-4	H	M	L	L	NA
E	Time budget	Ch. 13	H	H	H	M	L
	INSPECTION:						
A	Annual quality control document check list	E 14-1	H	H	H	H	H
A	Annual engagement review check list	Ch. 14	H	H	H	H	H
A	Inspection team review report	Ch..14	H	H	H	H	H

Key:

Files:

P	= Personnel
C	= Client
E	= Engagement
A	= Administrative

Reference:

E	= Exhibit
Ch	= The chapter describes the documentation.
Various	= The documentation is described in various sections of the book.
B	= The chapter bibliography identifies sources of these forms.

Probable usage:

H	= High
M	= Medium
L	= Low
NA	= Not Applicable

Firm size:

N	= National or international firm
R	= Regional firm
LL	= Large Local firm (possibly two or three offices)
SL	= Small Local firm (one office)
SP	= Sole Practitioner (possibly one part-time staff member)

Since the AICPA Division for CPA Firms requires 120 hours of continuing professional education for *all* professionals, firms face a higher CPE cost. However, if relevant programs are selected, this investment in CPE can pay off.

The possible cost of doing badly in the initial review is minimal under the Private Companies Practice Section rules. If reviewers find a firm inadequately prepared for its initial review, they explain why and allow the firm time to take action. This procedure is necessary because the profession's program is still young. This opportunity to minimize risk is yet another reason for a firm to reject the "wait and see" attitude, and to act now.

HOW TO MAKE IT EASIER

While Chapters 5 through 14 cover detailed aspects of quality control, the following points or tips can be helpful during the design and implementation process. Some were discussed in other chapters, but are worthy of special recognition.

(1) Always keep the reviewer's point of view in mind during the system design phases. Ask the question: What will the reviewer be looking for, and will he find it? The reviewer's point of reference is the AICPA quality control policies and procedures, which are reprinted in the element chapters. The reviewer's check list basically contains items that are restatements of these policies and procedures in question form. The basic review procedures are summarized in the element chapters at the end of each objective. The AICPA's *Peer Review Manual* contains the detailed procedures.

(2) Use available materials to save time. This book contains models of the most common practice management forms needed. Some materials were not included because they are too lengthy. For these, documentation methods were described, or sources of materials (such as auditing check lists) were identified. Use these forms, or modify them to fit your firm's needs, if necessary. Use the AICPA materials listed in Appendix B. Also, the Private Companies Practice Section provides new aid on a continuous basis, including a model accounting and auditing manual.

(3) Always remember that the nature of your firm's practice is an important consideration. There are hundreds of auditing check lists available. Do not use them unless they can be helpful. Some of the quality control procedures are not required for all firms. If a procedure does not seem to be required, do not adopt it. However, take a long-run view in making this judgment. Consider where your firm will be a few years in the future.

(4) Dare to be innovative. For example, one firm recently publicized in *The CPA Journal* that it uses a university professor for audit review.[1] This is a very interesting idea. Consider the use of word processing equipment, microcomputers,

and minicomputers to revise your firm's office system. There have been many new products that can cut costs. Consider extending the quality control document to cover your firm's tax and management advisory services practice. To minimize uncertainty and save billable time, talk to other CPAs or consider working with another firm or hiring a consultant.

(5) Involve all of your firm's partners in the design process. For discussion purposes, use the general design format recommended in Chapter 5 and demonstrated in the element chapters. Your firm's management and staff must be convinced that a quality control system is needed to meet professional standards and to assure your firm's future survival and growth.

(6) In drafting the quality control document, use the same or similar wording as the AICPA sample quality control documents. Every firm should have a customized quality control document. However, in some instances the wording used in the AICPA sample documents can be used with only slight revision.

(7) Use the most effective and efficient documentation available. Some forms can be very inconvenient to use, especially in smaller firms. Reviewers look for some type of documentation. While forms are often best, other methods of documentation may be sufficient. Memos, copies of correspondence, and minutes of meetings are examples of legitimate substitutes for some forms.

(8) Start now while the standards are more flexible. Compliance reviews will be easier to prepare for in the early years of the profession's program because standards are still young and developing. Recommendations for improvement in firm procedures can be made without qualifying the compliance review report.

(9) Several peer review programs are available to firms. While the AICPA Division for CPA Firms is the most common form of peer review, other forms might better serve your firm's needs. Associations of CPA firms have programs. The AICPA voluntary program can be used if a firm does not want to pay the liability insurance required by the Division for CPA Firms.

(10) Pay special attention to the supervision and inspection elements of quality control. Peer reviewers will analyze these elements as soon as possible so that they can modify their standard review programs. Be sure that your firm's quality control policies and procedures are adequate for these elements. If they are strong, the reviewers work program will be shorter. The payoff will be a good first impression on reviewers and lower review costs.

(11) Documentation must be sufficiently extensive to allow reviewers to determine whether a firm's quality control policies and procedures have been followed. Everything does not need to be in writing. Evidence of compliance can be gathered from inquiries. Working papers can evidence firm procedures.

(12) In drafting the quality control document, avoid including procedures that are not used. The problem with doing this is that peer reviewers cannot find evidence of compliance with firm procedures. For example, why mention procedures for using affiliate firms if they are not used. It cannot help you.

(13) Sole practitioners should place their greatest emphasis on the form and content of working papers and financial statements. The AICPA checklists should be used for a self-review of engagements. A reasonable approach for a sole practitioner to take in dealing with "no" answers is to ask the question, "Is there a legitimate and convincing reason for a "no" answer?" If there is no convincing reason, a change in procedures is appropriate. I advise sole practitioners to adopt procedures so that the documentation indicated by "H" entries in Table 15-1 is available to peer reviewers. In my opinion, a quality control document is not necessary for a sole practitioner. Who is going to read it? Just the peer reviewer. Thus, the other documentation is adequate to evidence the sole practitioner's procedures, and the peer reviewer can ask the sole practitioner about procedures. Since some of my colleagues, who will be peer reviewers, disagree with me on this point, my advice to sole practitioners is to not spend much time on a quality control document. Take the AICPA sample quality control document and do a fast editing job on it.

(14) In designing and documenting firm procedures, make a distinction between compilation, review, and audit engagements. In a compilation engagement, the CPA does not express any assurances on the financial statements, which are based solely on information presented by management. The CPA is not required to make any inquiries or perform any other verification procedures. In contrast, review engagements involve the CPA performing certain inquiry and analytical procedures as a reasonable basis for expressing limited assurances. Since review engagements require these procedures, the firm's quality control procedures should be designed to assure that they are done. For example, a firm's supervision procedures are likely to be more extensive for review engagements than for compilation engagements. Similar reasoning holds for audit engagements that require even more procedures.

(15) Find out what is happening. Read the Journal of Accountancy, The CPA Journal and The Practical Accountant. These publications continually report on better ways to manage an accounting practice and more efficient reporting techniques. Go to professional meetings and talk to other CPAs about what they are doing in quality control. Talk to CPAs who have been reviewers. Remember, keep the reviewer's point of view in mind.

NOTES

1. Edward J. Nightengale, "Using a Professor for Audit Review," *The CPA Journal,* April 1979, pp. 93-94.

Appendix A

Profile Firm for General Design Examples

Partner A — Accounting and auditing client responsibilities; nonprofit specialist

Partner B — Accounting and auditing client responsibilities; manufacturing companies specialist

Partner C — Accounting and auditing client responsibilities; management advisory services specialist

Partner D — Some accounting and auditing client responsibilities; tax specialist

Managers — 3

In-charge Accountants — 2

Staff Accountants — 11

Personnel manual — Partner C is responsible for maintenance

Accounting and auditing manual — Partner B is responsible for maintenance

Summary of AICPA
Peer Review Materials

1. Voluntary Quality Control Review Program for CPA Firms (free-*P**)

2. Sample Quality Control Documents for Local CPA Firms (free-*P*)

3. Management of an Accounting Practice Handbook (3 volumes-*B*)

4. Report of Progress, The Institute Acts on Recommendations for Improvements in the Profession (free-*P*)

5. Division for CPA Firms SEC Practice Section, Peer Review Manual ($30-*B*)

6. Division for CPA Firms Private Companies Practice Section, Peer Review Manual ($30-*B*)

7. Sample Quality Control Documents for Sole Practitioner CPA Firms (free-*P*)

---

*P indicates pamphlet and *B* indicates book.

Appendix C

Questionnaire Survey of CPA Firm Partners

In order to obtain information on CPAs' opinions toward quality control and related factual data, I mailed a questionnaire survey in the Fall of 1978. The survey methodology is presented in this appendix. The element chapters contain pertinent survey results in tables.

SURVEY METHODOLOGY

The purpose of the survey was to gather information on CPAs' opinions toward various quality control procedures and quality control systems. Data were sought on the usage of procedures and the receptiveness of CPAs to procedures. The data and analysis of it, I hope, will help the practitioner to decide on the appropriate design for his or her firm's quality control system. For the nonpractitioner, these data provide insight into practitioners' opinions and the current usage of quality control procedures. Questionnaires were sent in the Fall of 1978 to CPAs listed in the AICPA membership directory as partners or proprietors of CPA firms. Of 650 questionnaires, 128 usable responses were received (a usable response rate of about 20%).

The questionnaire was divided into three basic sections.

1. The importance and usage of quality control policies, grouped by element of quality control
2. General questions on the firm's size and its quality control policies and procedures
3. "Agree/disagree" statements on quality control

Exhibit C-1 displays the instructions for the first section and the statements for the element of independence. Since the instructions for the other questions were very simple, they are explained when the data are presented.

Exhibit C-1 Instructions to Respondents for Elements of Quality Control Section of the Questionnaire

ANONYMOUS QUESTIONNAIRE

AICPA committees and/or others have suggested that firms consider adopting the following quality control policies or procedures. The size of a firm is an important consideration. Using the size of your firm as a point of reference, please indicate your opinion of the importance of each of the following procedures, which are categorized according to SAS 4. A procedure's importance should be interpreted on the basis of how effective it is in assuring that professional standards are being followed by firms and their personnel, or assuring that the performance by personnel meets firm standards. The rating scale is as follows:

       1 - Unimportant (useless, not applicable)
       2 - Little importance (very little benefit)
       3 - Some importance (some possible benefit)
       4 - Important (a very helpful procedure, possibly necessary)
       5 - Essential (a firm must use this)

Place a check mark beneath each procedure to indicate your opinion as to the extent of usage of the procedure by firms of a similar size to your firm-- USE YOUR FIRM AS A POINT OF REFERENCE.

Not
important   Important   Independence
1 2 3 4 5   (1) The resolution of important independence questions should
          be documented.
          USAGE: ___rare ___occasional ___common ___almost always

1 2 3 4 5   (2) Independence of mental attitude is emphasized during engagements.
          USAGE: ___rare ___occasional ___common ___almost always

1 2 3 4 5   (3) Client lists are distributed to the staff and updated.
          USAGE: ___rare ___occasional ___common ___almost always

1 2 3 4 5   (4) The firm has training sessions that periodically emphasize
          independence.
          USAGE: ___rare ___occasional ___common ___almost always

1 2 3 4 5   (5) The firm periodically obtains written representations of
          compliance with independence policies and procedures from staff
          personnel.
          USAGE: ___rare ___occasional ___common ___almost always

The initial draft of the questionnaire was six pages long. This presented a problem, since response rate generally declines somewhat proportionally with the length of the questionnaire. In order to shorten the questionnaire to a maximum of four pages, the elements of quality control per questionnaire were reduced to a maximum of six. As a result, three versions of the questionnaire were mailed. All of the questionnaires included the elements of "supervision" and "acceptance and continuance of clients" because I suspected that these were the most controversial areas. The element of "hiring" was contained in the fewest questionnaires, because it seemed the least controversial. The responses per element are indicated when the data are presented in the book. All questionnaires contained the general questions and the "agree/disagree" statements.

Since quality control policies and procedures can be expected to vary by firm size, the data were grouped into four categories based upon the respondent's answer to a question on the number of professional personnel in his or her firm (including partners). A profile of the questionnaire respondents is presented in Table C-1.

Table C-1 Profile of Questionnaire Respondents and Their Firms

Descriptive Statistics	Number of Professional Personnel in the Respondent's Firm			
	1 to 5	6 to 20	20 to 80	More than 80
Number of firms in the category	28	45	15	40
Number of partners per firm:				
Mean	2.1	4.5	8.9	450
Median	2.3	4.0	7.4	401
Low	1	2	4	13
High	5	10	15	1000
Median number of firm personnel	3.8	10	33	4000
Median number of offices	1	1.3	2.4	60
Firms belonging to a regional or local association of CPA firms	32%	40%	33%	30%
Number of years respondent has been a partner:				
Mean	9.5	8.2	12	11.3
Median	6.3	7.6	7.5	10.5

Any survey has some bias. The most common concern is nonresponse bias. In order to increase the response rate, the questionnaires were sent out without identifying marks, and the CPAs were told this. Therefore, nonresponse tests are not feasible. Table C-1 provides some insight into possible bias. It shows that 30 to 40 percent of the respondents' firms belong to regional or local associations of CPA firms. Nationally, this percentage is probably no higher than ten percent. Therefore, these percentages are high. Some of these associations have peer review programs, and most offer their membership the benefit of sharing forms, check lists, and manuals. Consequently, it seems that the respondents' firms are more advanced in quality control systems than most firms. Finally, the number of years the respondent has been a partner shows a considerable amount of professional experience.

Opinions on Quality Control

Respondents were asked to indicate agreement or disagreement with statements relating to quality control. They had a choice of answers on a scale of 1 to 5, as follows:

1 = strongly disagree
2 = disagree
3 = no opinion
4 = agree
5 = strongly agree

The mean response on the 1 to 5 scale is included in the tables to aid the reader's interpretation of the data.

Legislative Regulation

One reason for extensive participation in the profession's quality control reviews is the idea that it will help the profession avert the legislation proposed by certain members of Congress. Table C-2 presents the responses to this idea. Overall, half agreed with the statement, and 39.2 percent disagreed. The analysis by firm size shows that disagreement increases with firm size. Thus, this factor will possibly be a stronger motivation for smaller firms to participate than for larger ones.

Mandatory Reviews

The question of whether peer reviews should be mandatory has been debated for many years. Currently, peer review is voluntary. A firm can choose whether or not to join the AICPA Division for CPA Firms, but firms with SEC-regulated clients are under considerable pressure to join the SEC Practice Section.

Table C-2 Opinions on Legislative Regulation

Statement	Number of Professional Personnel in Firm				
	1 to 5	6 to 20	20 to 80	More than 80	Total
Widespread participation by CPA firms in quality review programs is necessary for the accounting profession to avoid unwanted legislative regulation.					
Strongly agree	11.5	11.1	14.3	15.0	12.8
Agree	46.2	46.7	35.7	15.0	35.2
No opinion	23.1	11.1	7.1	10.0	12.8
Disagree	15.4	26.7	42.9	42.5	31.2
Strongly disagree	3.8	4.4	0.0	17.5	8.0
Mean	3.46	3.33	3.21	2.68	3.14
Number of CPAs responding	28	45	15	40	128

NOTE: All numbers, except means, are stated as a percentage of the column total responding. The means are based on a scale of 1 to 5, where "strongly disagree" is 1 and "strongly agree" is 5.

Table C-3 shows varied attitudes on whether quality control reviews should be mandatory for all firms. As expected, the support for mandatory peer review increases with firm size, since most larger firms had already been reviewed. Of the respondents in the "20 to 80" group, 27 percent belonged to firms who had been reviewed, as compared to 57 percent of the largest firms. Thus it appears that partners of firms who have been reviewed believe it is a worthwhile experience, and that it is good for all. Since the greatest disagreement was among partners of the smallest firms, we might suspect that these CPAs do not believe that peer review is needed for their firms.

There was considerable support for mandatory peer reviews of firms with SEC-regulated clients. The least support ("strongly agree" or "agree") came from CPAs in the "20 to 80" category. However, the appropriate interpretation seems to be that most CPAs expect firms with SEC practices to submit themselves to peer reviews. This is evident from Table C-3 and my many discussions with CPAs.

Procedures or Outcome?

While the profession's recent efforts have focused on quality control policies and procedures, many CPAs feel that the true test is the engagement outcome. If the working papers, financial statements, and audit reports meet standards, then the firm's quality control policies and procedures must be adequate, they argue.

Table C-3 Opinions on Mandatory Peer Review

| | Number of Professional Personnel in Firm | | | | |
Statement	1 to 5	6 to 20	20 to 80	More than 80	Total
Quality control reviews of CPA firms by outside CPAs should be:					
• Mandatory for all firms.					
Strongly agree	3.8	6.7	21.4	12.8	9.7
Agree	26.9	35.6	28.6	38.5	33.9
No opinion	15.4	15.6	21.4	23.1	18.5
Disagree	15.4	24.4	21.4	7.7	16.9
Strongly disagree	38.5	17.8	7.1	17.9	21.0
Mean	2.42	2.89	3.36	3.21	2.94
• Mandatory for firms with SEC-regulated clients only.					
Strongly agree	38.5	27.3	30.8	47.2	36.1
Agree	42.5	36.4	30.8	33.3	36.1
No opinion	3.8	13.6	15.4	2.8	8.4
Disagree	15.4	18.2	7.7	8.3	13.5
Strongly disagree	0.0	4.2	15.4	8.3	5.9
Mean	4.04	3.64	3.54	4.03	3.83
Number of CPAs responding	28	45	15	40	128

NOTE: All numbers, except means, are stated as a percentage of the column total responding. The means are based on a scale of 1 to 5, where "strongly disagree" is 1 and "strongly agree" is 5.

The answer to that argument is that reviewers have a limited ability to make judgments about working papers, given their limited information, and that quality control policies and procedures must be evaluated to compensate for this limitation.

Table C-4 shows substantial support for emphasizing the review of working papers and audit reports. This support was greatest from CPAs in larger firms, which is somewhat unexpected because reviews of larger firms are the most advanced in quality control policies and procedures.

RECEPTIVENESS TO PEER REVIEW

Table C-5 provides data on the receptiveness of respondents to peer review and new quality control policies and procedures. For the first question, the respondents were asked to check just one statement; a few picked more than one. Only two respondents stated that they are not receptive at all (1d in Table C-5). Most were receptive to *necessary* changes (1a) or were willing to do what others do (1b); the

Table C-4 Emphasis of Quality Control Reviews

Statement	1 to 5	6 to 20	20 to 80	More than 80	Total
A quality control review should emphasize inspection of working papers and audit reports rather than firm operating procedures.					
Strongly agree	22.2	28.9	21.4	40.0	30.2
Agree	33.3	35.6	50.0	50.0	41.3
No opinion	11.1	26.7	14.3	2.5	14.3
Disagree	18.5	6.7	14.3	5.0	9.5
Strongly disagree	14.8	2.2	0.0	2.5	4.7
Mean	3.30	3.82	3.79	4.20	3.83
Number of CPAs responding	28	45	15	40	128

Number of Professional Personnel in Firm

NOTE: All numbers, except means, are stated as a percentage of the column total responding. The means are based on a scale of 1 to 5, where "strongly disagree" is 1 and "strongly agree" is 5.

percentage increases with size. This response is encouraging for the profession's quality control program, but remember the possibility of nonresponse bias discussed above.

For question 2, the CPAs were asked to check one or more answers. The responses to 2a, 2b, 2c and 2d seem to correspond with the results for question 1. The responses to questions 2e, 2f, 2g, and 2h show that smaller firms seem to be postponing action. The percentages for question 2c compare favorably with the information available at the time the questionnaire was mailed. The estimates in the Fall of 1978 were that 20-25 percent of the eligible CPA firms had joined the Division for CPA Firms.

Table C-5 Opinions on Quality Control Procedures

	Affirmative Responses Grouped by Number of Professional Personnel in Firm			
Question	1 to 5	6 to 20	20 to 80	More than 80
1. How receptive is your firm to undertaking new quality control procedures?				
a. Very receptive to necessary changes	54	58	60	98
b. Willing to do what others do	4	16	7	0
c. We are still studying the situation	14	13	7	0
d. Not receptive at all, our procedures are adequate	7	0	0	0
e. We are currently reviewing quality control procedures to see what changes are necessary	11	20	40	0
f. Other	4	0	0	3
2. How receptive is your firm to peer review by outsiders?				
a. We have been reviewed already	14	9	27	58
b. We plan to be reviewed in the foreseeable future	11	33	40	33
c. We have joined one of the AICPA practice sections	7	20	27	40
d. We are planning to join one of the AICPA practice sections	0	9	33	0
e. We are still studying the situation	29	16	20	3
f. We are delaying serious consideration until requirements and procedures become clearer	25	24	0	0
g. We are waiting to see what other firms do	7	2	0	3
h. We are waiting until the costs and benefits become clearer	18	7	0	3
i. Other	4	0	0	3
Number of CPAs responding	28	45	15	40

NOTE: All responses are stated as a percentage of the column total responding.

IMPORTANCE AND USAGE ANALYSIS

Survey data on the importance and usage of selected quality control policies and procedures are contained in the chapters on the nine elements of quality control. The data are grouped by the four sizes of firms, measured by the number of professional personnel. For importance, the mean score of the respondents is presented on the basis of the scale of 1 to 5 in the questionnaire. Thus, the means should be interpreted according to the definitions in the questionnaire.

The respondents were asked to indicate their estimated usage of firms similar in size to their own. An alternative was to ask them about usage in their own firm; but from personal experience, it seemed that this would reduce the response rate.

The usage responses were coded on a scale of 1.25 to 5, as follows:

$$1.25 = \text{rare}$$
$$2.50 = \text{occasional}$$
$$3.75 = \text{common}$$
$$5.00 = \text{almost always}$$

This scale should be kept in mind in interpreting the means. A meaningful method of interpretation is to think in terms of ranges, using the midpoints between the above values. For example, the range for "common" is 3.125 to 4.375. A frequency distribution of the responses was not presented, because it would be too much data to comprehend. While a five-point scale was used for both importance and usage, the comparability between importance and usage is limited to their differences by definition.

To measure the variability in the responses, the coefficient of variation is given. The coefficient of variation is measured by dividing the standard deviation by the mean and multiplying by one hundred. The standard deviation is computed by taking the square root of the variance. Both are measures of variability. The standard deviation measures absolute variability. The coefficient of variation has the advantage of showing the relative variation. It shows the standard deviation as a percentage of the mean. The higher the coefficient of variation, the greater the variability in the responses. Thus, the diversity of the respondents in each of the four groups can be compared.

Index

About the Author

Wayne G. Bremser, CPA, Ph.D., is Associate Professor of Accounting at Villanova University. He received B.S. and M.B.A. degrees from Drexel University and a Ph.D. from the Wharton School of the University of Pennsylvania. His business experience includes positions with a local CPA firm and the Bell Telephone Company.

Dr. Bremser's articles on quality control and other accounting topics have appeared in *The CPA Journal, The Accounting Review, Management Accounting,* and several other journals. He is an active member in the American Institute of CPAs, American Accounting Association, National Association of Accountants, and the Pennsylvania Institute of CPAs. He has served on the Committee on Quality Control Review of the Philadelphia Chapter, Pennsylvania Institute of CPAs.